O9-CFT-125

DATE DUE

OC 19 '99			
NO 2 06			

DEMCO 38-296

Spell of the Tiger

❖ ❖ ❖ ❖ ❖ ❖ ❖ ❖ ❖ ❖ ❖ ❖ ❖ ❖

BOOKS BY SY MONTGOMERY

❖ ❖ ❖ ❖ ❖ ❖ ❖ ❖ ❖ ❖ ❖ ❖ ❖ ❖ ❖ ❖ ❖ ❖ ❖

Spell of the Tiger

❖ ❖ ❖ ❖ ❖ ❖ ❖ ❖ ❖ ❖ ❖ ❖ ❖ ❖ ❖

The Man-Eaters of Sundarbans

SY MONTGOMERY

A PETER DAVISON BOOK

Houghton Mifflin Company

BOSTON   NEW YORK   1995

Riverside Community College
Library
4800 Magnolia Avenue
Riverside, California 92506

JAN   '97

GR 307 .S86 M66 1995

Montgomery, Sy.

Spell of the tiger

Copyright © 1995 by Sy Montgomery

All rights reserved

For information about permission to reproduce selections from this
book, write to Permissions, Houghton Mifflin Company,
215 Park Avenue South, New York, New York 10003.

Library of Congress Cataloging-in-Publication Data

Montgomery, Sy.
    Spell of the tiger : the man-eaters of Sundarbans / Sy Montgomery.
        p. cm.
    "A Peter Davison Book."
    Includes bibliographical references.
    ISBN 0-395-64169-1
        1. Tigers — Sundarbans (Bangladesh and India) — Folklore.   2. Tigers —
    Sundarbans (Bangladesh and India)   3. Folklore — Sundarbans
    (Bangladesh and India)   I. Title.
    GR 307.S86M66   1995
    398'.369974428 — dc20   94-23190   CIP

Printed in the United States of America

BP 10 9 8 7 6 5 4 3 2 1

Book design by Anne Chalmers

Map on page xx by Jacques Chazaud

All of the photographs are by Eleanor Briggs

Printed on recycled paper

As always,

FOR DR. A. B. MILLMOSS

Contents

❖ ❖ ❖ ❖ ❖ ❖ ❖ ❖ ❖

Introduction

❖ ❖ ❖ ❖ ❖ ❖ ❖ ❖ ❖ ❖ ❖ ❖

WHEREVER IT IS FOUND, the tiger evokes a reverence, dread, and wonder accorded no other animal.

In Sumatra holy men commune with tigers in order to speak with dead heroes. In South Thailand and peninsular Malaysia, Negrito pygmies tell us the tiger is the avenger of the Supreme Being, Karei, punishing those who break tribal taboos. The Mendriq believe the tiger is the son of the thunder god and the goddess who dwells in the center of the earth — to them the tiger is the connection between the thunderstorm and the underworld. In India gods ride the tiger's back: Jolishmatic, the goddess of miraculous drugs; Aurkah, commander of the thirty-three-year cycle; Shukra, priest of demons; and the avenging Durga, wife of the great god Shiva. All choose the tiger as their *vahana*, or vehicle. In Hindu mythology a vahana does not carry a god in the ordinary sense that a car carries a passenger. Rather, as religious historian Wendy Doniger points out, the mount carries the god "in the way that a breeze 'carries' a perfume." The tiger is permeated, saturated with the god's force and power, imbued with the essence of the god itself.

Everywhere it roams, the tiger is credited with powers beyond those expected of any worldly animal.

Nowhere are those powers more fearful than in Sundarbans, the largest tidal delta in the world. Here, unlike any other place on earth, the tiger regularly hunts people. Hundreds die each year in the tiger's jaws.

Yet there is no eradication campaign directed against the tigers of Sundarbans, as there have been against far less lethal predators in the West. Here the tiger is feared but not hated; here it is worshiped but not loved. For here the tiger is a sacred creature who rules an enchanted land.

Spell of the Tiger is an invitation to visit this land. In Eastern legends vision quests into unknown territories were often made on the back of a tiger. In this book the tiger will carry the reader on a spiritual journey to a land where nature and God are one. But it is a journey we may soon be unable to make, for soon there may be no more tigers to carry us there.

❖

"It is my belief that the end of the tiger is in sight, possibly within ten years." Peter Jackson, chairman of the Cat Specialist Group of the World Conservation Union–IUCN, made this prediction late in 1992. That year an estimated 400 tigers were killed in India, reducing the world's population of tigers to fewer than 7,000.

Events since then have lent his words even greater urgency. In August 1993 a single sting operation — conducted not by government agents but by two unarmed civilians funded by a private organization, TRAFFIC-India — resulted in the seizure of 882 pounds of tiger bones and eight tiger skins from a dealer in Delhi, a stash representing the deaths of perhaps 40 tigers. While this is a victory for conservation, it is chilling to realize that this was the stock of just one dealer at one point in his career in one Indian city. There are dozens more such dealers.

The tiger's future looks so bleak that some people have already given up on it. "I mourn the passing of a beautiful, majestic beast," pronounced Adam Holland, the general editor of *Asiaweek,* in a cover story in that magazine in the summer of 1993, "but the tiger in the wild stands as much chance of survival as an antique building in Hong Kong." In 1994 American and

British networks ran TV specials on the tiger's plight. *Time* put the tiger on its cover with the headline "Doomed."

At the turn of the century, tigers occupied vast areas of Asia, from the Russian Far East to Java. Turkey's Mount Ararat, near the border with Iran, was said to be "infested" with them up to the snow line. Tigers hunted wapiti in the dwarf oak forests west of Mongolia's Gobi desert; gigantic long-furred tigers stalked mountain sheep through Russian blizzards; tigers padded through the steaming rain forests of Bali. An estimated 40,000 Royal Bengal tigers inhabited India's jungles and grasslands — so many that it has been said that in the early decades of this century, two maharajahs could shoot 2,000 tigers between them in their spare time.

Today only five of the original eight subspecies of tigers survive, confined to tiny remnants of their former ranges. The Indo-Chinese tiger, smaller and darker than India's Royal Bengal, may number only 1,000. Only 650 Sumatran tigers, with their reddish coats and exceptionally broad stripes, survive on that island. Researchers estimate that perhaps 150 to 200 Siberians, the biggest tigers, remain in the wild. The South China tiger is nearly gone, with only 30 to 60 individuals. The last Bali tiger was killed in the 1940s; the Caspian tiger went extinct in the 1970s; and the last Javan tiger died less than ten years ago.

India's Royal Bengal is beyond doubt the most numerous tiger subspecies today. But by 1972 only 2,000 of them — the number that two maharajahs could shoot at their leisure — were believed alive.

Today, thanks to twenty-one tiger reserves established under India's ambitious Project Tiger and to tough laws with brave Forest Department staff to enforce them, India has been credited with almost single-handedly saving the tiger from extinction. Authorities believe India's tigers now number around 3,000. But those 3,000 face threats more complex and insidious than the founders of Project Tiger could ever have imagined twenty years ago.

When Project Tiger began, the animals were being slaughtered primarily for their skins. Today tigers are slaughtered for parts previous poachers left behind: the whiskers, sinews, penis, blood, and, especially, bone, all of which are sold to supply a seemingly bottomless market for so-called elixirs. Tiger wines, balms, soups, and pills are believed to ease rheumatism, restore energy, treat fever, cure dysentery. Tiger skins can at least be easily identified. Bone and body parts are far more difficult to track on the way to illegal markets in Hong Kong, China, Taiwan, and Chinatowns in Europe and North America.

These are not the only threats wild tigers face worldwide. Since Project Tiger began, India's human population has risen 50 percent to more than 800 million, and the world human population has swelled to 5.6 billion. Instead of chasing down organized networks of poachers, forest guards have their hands full trying to protect the parks from encroaching villagers and their forest-mowing cattle, sheep, and goats. Even if the slaughter stopped, humans might simply crowd tigers off the planet.

❖

What if tigers vanish from the earth? Do we need tigers in our world? Ancient stories assure us that we do. Anthropologists report that in the past, native people have taken great care in their behavior toward tigers so as not to anger tiger spirits or tiger gods. In their marvelous book *Soul of the Tiger,* anthropologist Jeffrey McNeely and psychologist Paul Spencer Wachel describe the instance of a Burmese man-eater who was shot after it had reportedly killed twenty-four people. Lisu tribespeople gathered reverently around its corpse and offered this prayer to ask the tiger's forgiveness: "We have not been ruthless in killing the tiger. The tiger has killed a number of persons for no reason. May the tiger rest in peace."

In the Annamite mountains of Vietnam, Henry Baudesson, a

surveyor for the French colonial service, described in his journal what happened when a tiger fell into a pit dug to trap deer. "The natives were terrified lest it should die, in which case its spirit would never cease to molest them. So they decided to set it free ... offering humble apologies for having already detained it so long."

In his monograph *The Soul of Ambiguity,* Robert Wessing recounts a story that was widely reported in Indonesian newspapers during the summer of 1979, when one of the last tigresses remaining on Java emerged from the jungle and strolled through the city of Jogjakarta.

She walked through the Gajah Mada University campus and made straight for the chemistry laboratory, where she spent the day breaking equipment. The Indonesian government dispatched sharpshooters with tranquilizer guns, but she eluded them. Finally her mate came to join her. Both were sedated and taken to the zoo. But that evening one of the pair somehow escaped from the locked cage. It was found in a tree near its caged mate.

It was night, and a tiger was loose in the city. Officials decided that it should be killed. The son of Indonesia's President Suharto, Raden Sigit, fired the single shot that killed the tiger. Then the mate inexplicably escaped from its cage and disappeared.

A series of disasters followed the tiger's death. The vice president, Sultan Hamengkubuwana, withdrew. The crown prince and his mother died within one year of each other. A plane carrying Indonesian pilgrims to Mecca crashed, killing 200. Mount Dieng erupted, spewing toxic fumes that killed 160 people, and the neighboring island of Sumatra was subjected to floods and volcanic eruptions. The disasters were widely attributed by the people of Indonesia to the shooting of the tiger and the extinction of the Javan subspecies. Killing tigers, they say, may have terrible consequences.

❖

Skeptical Westerners might dismiss native people's stories about animals as worthless superstition. This would be a grave mistake. Most of us live in cities and suburbs, and we know surprisingly little about animals, for we have distanced ourselves from their lives. As professional scientists begin to pay more attention to events in the natural world, they are confirming that even some of the stories about animal powers that seem most far-fetched turn out to be remarkably accurate and wise.

Some people who live near Florida's swamps, for instance, say the crocodiles there will grab you by your shadow, pull you into the water, and eat you. The story comes from keen observation of the natural world. These crocodiles (who are true crocodiles, not Florida's more gentle alligators) begin to feed at dusk as shadows lengthen. The longer the shadow, the more aggressive the crocodile is likely to be. "As a rule of thumb, if you're close enough for your shadow to touch the water's edge," Florida's state fish and wildlife researcher Alan Woodward recently told a *National Wildlife* writer, "then you're close enough for a crocodile to grab you."

Similarly the Chippewa Indians of the Great Lakes believed that spiders' webs protected their babies by catching the "harm in the air." Often a spider voluntarily wove a web over the infant's cradle; if one did not, a Chippewa parent would carefully collect a web on a hoop and hang it over the baby.

The belief was sound; the practice worked. University of Cincinnati researcher Joe Raver notes that spiders' webs make excellent mosquito netting. In an area besieged with biting insects, the webs protected babies from mosquito-borne encephalitis, allergic reactions to black-fly bites, and other insect-borne "harm in the air."

These are mere facts; the truths that local people tell about animal powers run deeper yet. The people of Indonesia wisely identified the disappearance of the Javan tigers as a cataclysmic event for the earth, and correctly saw that animals exert powerful effects on human beings. Our kind has the capacity to understand the natural world better than many of us do now.

"We need an older, and a wiser, and perhaps a more mystical understanding of animals," wrote Henry Beston in *The Outermost House*. That is why I journeyed to Sundarbans, and that is why I have written this book: in the hopes of presenting an older and a wiser understanding — of people, of tigers, and of tigers' crucial place in the world.

Hancock, New Hampshire
July 1, 1994

A NOTE ON SPELLING AND PRONUNCIATION

❖ ❖

Every effort has been made to spell Bengali words and names correctly, but to little avail: the Bengali alphabet does not correspond to the Roman alphabet. Fortunately for me, Bengalis are used to Westerners' permutations of their words. For instance, the name of one of my chief informants is spelled at least four different ways on books and articles he has written. The cover of one book proclaims its author as Kalyan Chakravarty, while another lists him as Kalyan Chakrabarti. The former is a Hindi-English spelling of the name; the latter a Bengali-English spelling. I have tried to use Bengali-English spellings throughout the text. But there is considerable variation even within Bengali-English spelling. Sajnekhali, site of Sundarbans' tourist lodge and one of its bird sanctuaries, is variously spelled Sajnekhali, Sajnakali, and Sajnakhali on maps and brochures.

The pronunciation of Bengali-English words can also be slippery. Sunderbans is pronounced "Shunderbun." (It is variously spelled and sometimes, especially on maps, is prefaced by "the," although the article is not usually used in conversation.) The name of Sundarbans' tiger god, Daksin Ray, is pronounced "Dawkin Roy." A man whose name frequently appears on these pages is Rathin Banerjee. His first name is pronounced "Row-teen."

How can this be? I asked Rathin how you can get the sound "Row-teen" out of the spelling "Rathin." He answered, "It is spelled wrong on my birth certificate."

Spell of the Tiger

❖ ❖ ❖ ❖ ❖ ❖ ❖ ❖ ❖ ❖ ❖ ❖ ❖ ❖ ❖

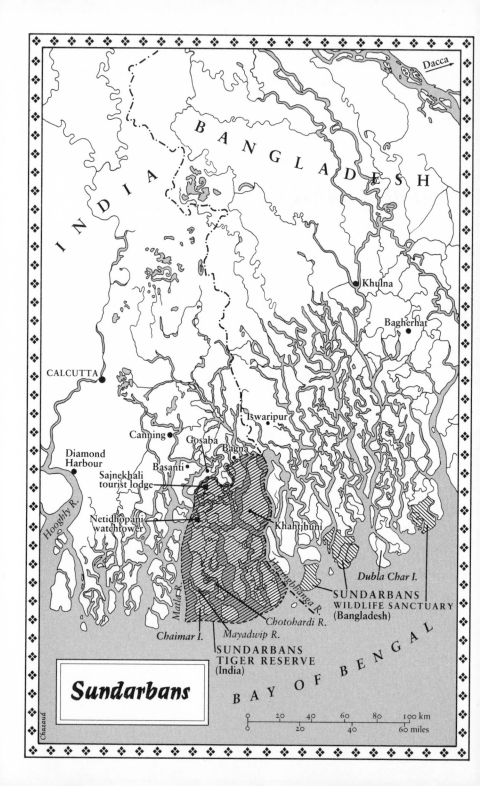

Sundarbans: A First Encounter

❖ ❖

LIKE A ROUSSEAU PAINTING, the journey into Sundarbans, the great mangrove swamp that stretches between India and Bangladesh along the Bay of Bengal, slides you sensually, dreamily, into a time and a place that you almost remember.

As the launch floats farther and farther away from the noisy town docks, the houses and shops on the banks of the river change from brick and tin to mud and thatch, and then disappear entirely. In their place is nothing but trees and mud, water and sky.

Sometimes you might not see an animal for half an hour, not even a bird. Yet the place is palpably alive. Even if you see no movement, you feel it, for all the elements — trees, mud, water, sky — are reaching for one another, yearning, as if in attempted embrace.

Many of the mangroves here grow on stilt roots, their attempt to stabilize themselves on the shifting mud: the trees are reaching for the earth. Others send up pneumatophores, mud-covered "breathing roots" that stretch upward in search of oxygen: the earth reaching for the sky. For half of each day the moon-driven tide stretches toward the land, enveloping its great length with water; during the other half the land stretches toward the water, as the tide recedes like one who falls back from the arms of a lover, satisfied.

Escaping the honk and screech of Calcutta or Dacca, Bengali tourists ostensibly come to Sundarbans to see the tigers. Here, it is said, live more tigers than anywhere else on earth. Seldom do the tourists see one. But here, on the waters surrounded by forest, city folk may find an even more elusive quarry: luxuriant, calm, voluptuous peace.

On the wide rivers you may see Gangetic dolphins rise, smooth as silk, their pink-gray dorsal fins rolling like soft waves along the water's surface. Dreamlike wonders: once, out near the Bay of Bengal, I glimpsed an olive ridley sea turtle as it surfaced for a breath of air. My looking at that spot at that moment seemed as improbable and as blessed as chancing to witness the opening eye of the slumbering Vishnu, the Supreme Hindu Being who, while universes bubble from his pores, sleeps upon a fathomless ocean.

The very name of Sundarbans is a dreamlike blur of meanings: *sundar,* the Bengali word for beautiful; *sundari,* a beautiful, silvery mangrove, once the dominant tree; *samudraban,* forests of ocean. Indeed, here the forest and ocean are often indistinguishable, one bleeding into the other like tints in a watercolor: blue-grays, olive greens, muddy browns. In the morning mists the water joins the sky; in the tides the water dissolves the earth — as the Self, Hindu mystics say, dissolves into the mind of God. The earth itself, fine, silty clay, came here as rain-dissolved fragments of the holy Himalayas, carried by the rivers Brahmaputra and Ganges, themselves considered gods. The soft mud here looks benign, even luscious. You can imagine sinking into it as slowly and softly as you fall asleep.

But this is only one face of Sundarbans. Like the many-headed deities of the Hindu pantheon, it embodies terror as well as peace; but from the safe deck of a big tourist boat, the terrible face of Sundarbans is as invisible as the dark side of the moon.

"If you are going on a big motor launch, it's a different thing," says Kushal Mookherjee, a private wildlife consultant based in Calcutta. "But once you put your foot on the mud bank, you know: this is a strange place. This is a dangerous place. Here you know you are at the mercy of something else."

Once you leave the wide rivers — if you enter the small channels, if you set foot in the forests — you enter a world where the ground sucks you down whole, where the night swallows the stars, and where you know, for the first time, that your body is made of meat.

In Sundarbans you are at the mercy of a world not only unseen but unsuspected. The only constant is change: new land forms so quickly here that on the Bangladeshi side, cartographers must redraw their maps every three years. Nature does not obey the rules: fish climb trees; the animals drink salt water; the roots of trees grow up toward the sky instead of down to the earth; the tide may run in opposite directions simultaneously in the same creek. And here, the tigers do not obey the same rules by which tigers elsewhere govern their lives. They hunt people. They take their prey even in broad daylight. They will even swim out into the Bay of Bengal, where the waves may be more than two feet high. They often swim from India to Bangladesh. The tigers here are bound by neither day nor night, land nor water; these tigers, some say, are creatures of neither heaven nor earth.

With an Open Mouth

❖ ❖ ❖ ❖ ❖ ❖ ❖ ❖ ❖ ❖ ❖ ❖ ❖ ❖ ❖ ❖ ❖ ❖

ON A SOFT MAY NIGHT in West Bengal, when the sweet scent of *khalsi* flowers clung to the wet, warm darkness, when the moon shone round and white, and boatmen's lanterns winked at one another like fireflies up and down the river, death came with an open mouth for Malek Molla.

The day's work was over. Molla and his six companions had collected five kilograms of honey from the fat combs they'd found hanging among the small, curved, downward-pointing leaves of a *genwa* tree. Collecting honey is one of the most dangerous jobs in Sundarbans, yet from April to June hundreds of men leave their mud and thatch houses and their rice fields and fishing nets to follow the bees into the forest.

In little wooden boats they glide down the numberless channels that permeate the sodden land of Sundarbans. Barefoot they wade through the sucking clay mud. Carefully they step around the breathing roots of the mangroves, which spike up from the earth like bayonets. Sometimes they must pass through stands thick with *hental*, the palm from whose leaves the crocodiles build their nests. Its stems are armored with two-inch thorns so sharp that by the time you feel one in your foot, it has already penetrated half an inch and broken off in your flesh.

One man always stands guard for the group. There are many dangers to watch for. Tigers hunt in these forests. Crocodiles lurk in the shallows. Vipers coil in the shade. Even the bees can kill you. They are aggressive, and their sting causes muscle spasms, swelling, and fever. People who have been badly stung say that the pain can last for a year.

The honey itself is said to be an antidote to the bees' poison. Some who have survived attacks by bee swarms say companions saved their lives by smearing the thin, spicy honey over the stings. Sundarbans honey is considered an elixir of sorts. Shamans say eating some each day will ensure a long life. The leaves of the khalsi, whose fragrant, white blossoms supply the pollen from which the earliest honey is made, are curative, too: a paste made from them will stanch the flow of blood.

But no blood had flowed on this day. The group found the first bees' nest easily, eight feet up in a genwa. One man climbed the spindly trunk. With smoke from a kerosene-soaked torch of green hental fronds, he drove the bees from the hive and cut loose the swollen comb with a machete. Another man below caught the comb in a ten-gallon tin that had once held mustard oil. The others waited, armed with clubs, ready in case a tiger appeared; but none did. So they continued their quest through the forest, revisiting the hives they had spotted the day before. That afternoon they emerged from the forest laughing, safe, laden with their riches, the golden honey.

Now, in their low-bodied wooden boat, anchored in the Chamta River, beneath the palm thatch that roofed the cabin, the six tired men relaxed.

Their lantern gleamed. The men talked and laughed and smoked the harsh, leaf-wrapped cigarettes called *bidi*. A pot of curry and India's ubiquitous *dahl* — lentil stew — bubbled on the boat's clay stove. One man offered a song. The notes of the

Bengali melody rose and fell, full and then empty, like the tides that rise to engulf the forest every six and a half hours and then fall back, drained.

❖

No one felt the boat rock. No one heard a scream. But everyone heard the splash when something very heavy hit the water beside the boat.

The men flashed their torches on the water, into the forest, along the shore. And on the far bank of the river the light barely caught the figure of a huge, wet cat slinking into the mangroves, carrying the body of Malek Molla like a fish in its mouth. Molla had been quiet that evening; possibly he had been asleep. The tiger may have killed him without ever waking him up. Without making a sound, without rocking the boat, a predator who may have weighed five hundred pounds and stretched up to nine feet long had launched itself from the water, selected its victim, seized him in its jaws, and killed him instantly.

Molla's body was recovered the following day. The tiger had severed his spinal cord with a single bite to the back of the neck. It had eaten the soft belly first.

❖

In Sundarbans everyone watches for the tiger. But the tiger, they say, always sees you first. Every group of fishermen tells a story like this one:

"Our eyes were toward the higher ground, toward the forest where the trees were thick. We were expecting if danger would come, it would come from the forest."

Montu Halda is twenty-six, a fisherman from the village Hingulgunge. When he was twenty-one, he saw his brother-in-law taken away by a tiger.

There were four in his party that day, he remembers: Halda, his father, his brother, and his brother-in-law. It was late afternoon; the others wanted to return to the village with their catch, but the brother-in-law insisted they stop to collect dry firewood from the forest.

They anchored and waded ashore. They kept their backs to the river and to the boat, their eyes on the darkening forest. They knew this was a dangerous time of day. At low tide the pink-faced monkeys known as rhesus macaques and the little spotted deer called chital come to the edge of the water to pick through the flowers and fruits and leaves the mangroves drop into the water, which the tide then brings to land. Tigers know the tides, and they know the habits of the monkeys and deer. And they know the habits of men.

If a tiger was near, it would know when people were coming. It would hear the oar strokes and the voices. It would know the meaning of a dropped anchor. And it would wait and try to surprise them.

All this Halda and his relatives knew, so they were careful. If there was a tiger, and if it wanted one of them, their only chance would be to see it first. Their eyes never left the forest.

The tiger leaped onto the brother-in-law's back. It knocked him face down in the mud, grabbed him by the back of the neck and, in one fluid motion, bounded into the forest. The tiger had not approached from the forest but from the river, where the men had not bothered to watch.

❖

Agie Bishas, too, saw a tiger take a man away into the forest. Bishas, fifty, from the big village of Gosaba, knows many tiger stories. This attack he had witnessed only three months before he told me about it.

He was on a boat in a group of four or five that were tied together, waiting near the forest for the tide to drop so they could collect wood. No one knew it, but all the while, he said, a tiger was watching them from the opposite bank.

Unseen, the tiger swam across the river until it reached a bush that drooped over the water. With the bush masking its head, and the lower part of its body submerged, it waited, watching. It watched the men for hours, Bishas said. It waited right beside their boat.

In a steady voice, with clarity and precision, Bishas told me, through a translator, what had happened. "The tiger, it had to wait some time," he said, "for it could not climb into the boat because there were so many boats together, and the people were not getting down from the boats because they were waiting for the water to recede. The tiger was getting impatient. As long as the boats were tied together, the tiger was kept waiting."

As the tide went out, the party decided that the man in the head boat, which was tied to a tree on the bank, would collect the wood. The other boats separated to anchor midstream.

"As soon as the tiger saw the boats had separated and that this one was alone now, it swam out from its hiding place," Bishas said. One person was alone at the boat's bow. The tiger surged from the water, its front paws gripping the craft; the boatman fainted from shock. Immediately the tiger leaped into the boat, seized the boatman, and carried him by the back of the neck into the forest.

❖

These stories are told again and again in steady, reasoned voices by people who saw the events take place. The tiger flew from the forest. The tiger launched itself from the water. The tiger lay invisible for hours. The tiger materialized from thin air.

Sometimes a tiger swims after a boat the way a dog chases a car on the road. Kalyan Chakrabarti, a former field director of India's Sundarbans Tiger Reserve, tells the story he heard of a steel-hulled motor launch whose crew of ten tried to rid themselves of a tiger swimming after them. They shot at it five times with a rifle. They threw lumps of coal. They tried to push it away with bamboo poles. The swimming tiger grabbed the poles with its paws and chewed them to shreds. The pilot tried to run over the tiger to drown it; the cook splashed boiling water over the animal's head. But the tiger never tired. In fact, it was gaining on them and even managed to board the dinghy tied to the side of the launch. The crew let the rope out so the tiger could not use the dinghy as a stepping stone to the launch. The terrified crew finally locked themselves in the cabin.

Three hours later the tiger was still there. Only after they entered the rough waters of the river Matla did it depart. The big waves overturned the dinghy, and the tiger swam ashore.

"If a tiger really wants to kill you," Kalyan says, "it can take you. There is nothing you can do. Not even a gun will help you."

According to government figures, thirty or forty people are killed each year on the Indian side of Sundarbans. But these figures are misleading. No one except Forest Department officials are allowed inside Sundarbans Tiger Reserve's 514-square-mile core area, which is set aside for wildlife alone. Ringing the core is a buffer zone of 562 square miles, where people may fish, collect honey, and cut wood, but they must have a permit to do so. If a permit holder is killed inside the buffer zone, the government compensates his family for the loss, and the death is officially tallied. But families of tiger victims who are illegally inside restricted areas are not compensated, so there is no reason for them to inform the authorities; in fact, these families fear they might be prosecuted. In the rare cases when the victim's body can be retrieved, the bereaved cremate it hastily, sometimes at night, before forest officials can find out.

The boatman with whom I travel in Sundarbans, Girindra Nath Mridha, lost three of his four uncles to tigers; one was killed before his eyes. None of those deaths was "official." On a trip in December 1992 I met an older fisherman who showed me a puffer fish he had caught. By the time I returned to Sundarbans in January, the man had been "unofficially" eaten. So many are killed by tigers here that some villages are known as *vidhaba pallis* — tiger widow villages. Arampur, near Gosaba, is one such village; in each of its 125 families is a woman whose husband or brother or son was killed by a tiger.

One hundred years ago it was reported that 4,218 people were eaten by tigers in the Sundarbans over a period of six years. One study estimated that one-third of the tigers here will try to kill and then eat any person they see. Almost invariably the person they see is a man, for in Sundarbans, as in most of India, only men work in the forest, while the women work in the village. Oddly, tigers seldom stray into the villages; when they do, they do not stay long, and they do not hunt people. But in the forest they consider humans suitable prey.

And here they thrive. The number of tigers the area supports is disputed. But no one disagrees that Sundarbans Tiger Reserve is the only park in India with more than one hundred tigers, and the Indian side constitutes only half of the huge mangrove tract. Including both the Indian and Bangladeshi sides, the full 3,861-square-mile area supports more tigers than any other contiguous tract in the world.

No one keeps track of the actual death toll. Forest officials privately admit that the numbers are at least double the official figures. Some experts say the total may be as high as 150 a year on the Indian side and about the same on the Bangladeshi side.

Elsewhere in the world, tigers seldom kill people. David Smith has studied Nepal's tigers at Royal Chitawan National Park since 1977. "Over the years we've had people stumble right on top of tigers and not be bitten," he says. He recalls a story about his colleague Charles McDougal, who has studied tigers intensively at Chitawan at a lodge named Tiger Tops. As McDougal was walking along a knife-edge ridge, he saw a tiger coming toward him. He decided to reverse direction, slowly, and did not look back. The tiger left him alone.

George Schaller relates a similar experience. Taking nighttime photos of wildlife in central India, he needed to adjust some of his equipment. "We stepped away from the blind and walked slowly toward the tigers," he relates. "'Go away, tigers, go away,' I said in a tense voice as I held the cats in the beam of my small flashlight, and Stan clapped his hands several times. The tigers reluctantly retreated."

Smith recalled another instance: a young child, following the path of Smith's airplane flying overhead, crossed illegally into the core area of Chitawan Park and walked right up to a resting tiger. The tiger ignored him. Only when the child pushed the tiger did the animal swipe at him; even so, the boy was not seriously hurt. "Basically," says Smith, "tigers do not attack people."

That one of the largest predators on earth so seldom injures people has given rise to a belief in many parts of tropical Asia that tigers embody the souls of dead heroes. One morning at nine in 1974, a tiger appeared at a school in Jogjakarta, Java. First it sat quietly. Then, like a visiting dignitary, it walked slowly through the classrooms. The newspapers reported that the tiger was a reincarnation of Sukarno, Indonesia's first president. Many tribal people believe that humans and tigers are descended from a common ancestor and that a tiger will not hurt a person who is free from sin.

Even when surprised on a kill, most tigers show commendable restraint. Typically it first gives a warning roar, affording the intruder opportunity to retreat. If he does not, the tiger roars a second time, louder. Finally it may make a mock charge; but if the intruder still does not leave, the tiger may turn and run rather than attack.

When tigers do kill people, it is often by mistake. If a person stumbles on a tiger resting unseen in the tall grass, the animal, alarmed, may strike out with a paw, as if to merely brush the intruder aside; but because of the tiger's great strength, one blow may be sufficient to kill.

Rarely does a tiger instigate an attack. In most of the cases that Western researchers have investigated, the victim has been a child, or a woman bent over washing clothes or cutting grass or squatting to relieve herself. (These tigers perhaps should be more properly called women- and children-eating tigers.) Peter

Jackson of the World Conservation Union–IUCN suggests that because the victim is not standing upright (or, because a child is so short) the tiger probably thinks the person is a monkey.

Even more rarely do tigers knowingly choose people for food. Jim Corbett, one of the world's finest hunters, made a career tracking down man-eaters in India during the first part of this century. While a single man-eater can wreak enormous damage (one tigress Corbett tracked had reportedly killed 200 people in Nepal and 434 people in India before he finally shot her), Corbett stressed that man-eating is not normal tiger behavior. "It is only when tigers have been incapacitated through wounds or old age that, in order to live, they are compelled to take to a diet of human flesh," he reported in *Man-Eaters of Kumaon,* his most famous book.

Colonel Kesri Singh, a hunter and game warden in Rajasthan, offered this portrait of the "classical" man-eater: "an aged, mangy beast with canines — normally huge in a tiger — worn down to stumps, and skeleton thin." His postmortems on slain man-eaters usually uncovered a lead ball embedded somewhere in the tiger's body. Indeed, most *shikaris* who hunted man-eaters in India agreed that the wounds that drive a tiger to man-eating are often inflicted by people.

But in Sundarbans the tigers are utterly different.

❖

"Among these islands, it is in many places dangerous to land," the French explorer François Bernier wrote in 1666, "for it constantly happens that one person or another falls prey to tigers. These ferocious animals are very apt, it is said, to enter the boat itself, while the people are asleep, and to carry away some victim, who, if we are to believe the boatmen of the country, happens to be the stoutest and fattest of the party."

Here healthy tigers have hunted humans for centuries. Genetically these tigers belong to the same race as the others found throughout the Indian subcontinent, the Royal Bengal, the second-largest tiger on earth (the Siberian is largest), with a flame-colored coat. Yet the Sundarbans tigers behave like no other tigers in the world; in fact, no other predator of any species so aggressively seeks out our kind.

"Nowhere else in the world is man so actively hunted out," said one wildlife consultant who has visited Sundarbans many times. "You can feel it: someone is trying to kill you." The idea floats uneasily in the modern mind.

Why do these tigers hunt people? The German biologist Hubert Hendrichs suggested that their ferocity might be linked to the saline water they drink. In 1971 he carried out a three-month study on the Bangladeshi side of Sundarbans. He compared the relative salinity of the water with the locations of known tiger attacks. His data correlated the most frequent attack sites with areas having the saltiest water.

Virtually no fresh water is available in Sundarbans except dug rain-water ponds. The tides of the Bay of Bengal flush through all the rivers; in certain areas the water is 1.5 percent salt. Drinking water so salty may cause liver and kidney damage, Hendrichs suggested, making the tigers irritable. Before he could test this hypothesis, his study was interrupted by Bangladesh's war of independence, and he has never returned. No one since has proved or disproved his idea.

Possibly, some have said, Sundarbans tigers learned to eat human flesh because it was brought to them, like an offering, from the holy river Ganges. Before its tributaries were dammed by the Farakka Barrage, this river nourished Sundarbans, and with its waters came the corpses of the dead who had been incompletely cremated at Calcutta's burning ghats. The tigers could have acquired their taste for our flesh from scavenging.

S. Dillon Ripley, the former secretary of the Smithsonian Institution, theorized that Sundarbans tigers may have learned from fishermen to associate people with food. An ancient fishing method in Sundarbans is to string your net across a narrow creek and wait for the fish to become caught in it as the tide recedes. Perhaps, Ripley suggested, the tigers learned to raid the fishermen's nets, and so learned to seek out the fishermen and their boats. Perhaps the fishy smell also attracts the tigers.

Still others have noted that in the sucking ooze of the swamps tigers might have difficulty catching their normal prey — wild boar, chital, rhesus macaques, monitor lizards, jungle fowl — so they supplement their diet with people.

In Sundarbans a human provides one of the larger food items available to a tiger. An adult male wild boar or a chital doe might weigh a bit over a hundred pounds, and in taking it the tiger faces grave risks. To attack a big animal is not easy when you kill with your open mouth. A fighting boar slashes with sharp tusks, a struggling chital thrashes with antlers and hooves. The average adult male human in Sundarbans might weigh 130 pounds. Relatively large, slow-moving, clumsy, and, without guns virtually harmless, people are easy and abundant prey.

One wonders why Sundarbans tigers do not eat people more often than they do. (One Indian expert calculated that if people comprised a major item of the tigers' diet, then Sundarbans tigers would kill 24,090 people every year.) The wonder is not that tigers eat people in Sundarbans; the wonder is that tigers so infrequently eat them elsewhere.

But this is only one of the mysteries, for tigers are very difficult animals to study. They are secretive, and often difficult to find, even a glimpse. In his long career photographing Indian wildlife, the great naturalist E. P. Gee never got a shot of a wild tiger.

A tiger's range can be enormous: in Nepal Melvin Sunquist found that males established territories of twenty-three to twenty-seven square miles, and females six to eight square miles; in Siberia, where food is scarcer, a tiger's territory may stretch for 1,544 square miles.

Tigers are mostly solitary. They will associate with others of their kind — often at a kill — and a tigress may remain with her one to four cubs for two years. Courting pairs travel together for several days. Still, a scientist usually is able to observe only one tiger at a time rather than the herds or flocks or troops of animals of other species.

Tigers live by stealth. Because they are stalk-and-ambush hunters, it is extraordinarily difficult to see one make a natural kill; you must be as stealthy as a tiger to avoid scaring away the prey, and you must be warier than the prey to see the tiger.

Most of what Western researchers know about these animals derives from two long-term projects. The first was George Schaller's fourteen-month study of deer and their predators at Kanha National Park in central India from 1963 to 1965. He learned to recognize eleven individual adult tigers on sight, and he spent 129 hours watching them. He examined their kills and analyzed their droppings. He listened to their voices. The book presenting his results, *The Deer and the Tiger,* remains a landmark.

A second and larger study, financed by the Smithsonian Institution and the World Wildlife Fund, began in November 1973 at Nepal's Royal Chitawan National Park, and still continues, albeit sporadically. John Seidensticker and K. M. Tamang developed ways to capture and immobilize tigers and outfit them with radio collars to track their movements. Their work allowed scientists for the first time to follow several tigers at once, to monitor their long-term health and growth, and to map their ranges.

But still science knows relatively little about tigers. About tigers in Sundarbans, science knows almost nothing. They are a mystery — the mystery that drew me to Sundarbans and into the spell of the tiger.

The Songs of Rabindranath

❖ ❖

A SHORT MAN wearing pink checkered polyester bell-bottoms was shouting at me in the dark. "You! Helping! *You egg!* ME HELPING EGG! YOU LIKE!"

The outburst followed a discussion in Bengali among the six men clad in *lungis* (a length of cloth wrapped around the waist), who huddled on the terrace of the Sajnekhali Tourist Lodge. Periodically someone would glance at my companion and me with a mixture of irritation, confusion, and disbelief.

Things had been going well only moments before. After our first night at the lodge, the only tourist accommodation in the Indian Sundarbans, my companion, Dianne Taylor Snow, and I had decided that the evening meal of rice and dahl (sometimes supplemented by chicken, strangled loudly in the courtyard shortly after you place your order) was served too late and too cold for us to eat. We had solved this problem by ordering omelettes, which could be prepared quickly and served hot.

We had just ordered our evening omelettes. But tonight we made an additional request: two boiled eggs each, which we planned to eat for breakfast and lunch the next day aboard the boat we had hired from Girindra Nath Mridha, the man in the polyester bell-bottoms.

"*Dui* omelette," I had said to the cook, "*char* egg boil." I held up two fingers and then four fingers to emphasize the number of eggs requested. (This pantomime, I later learned, probably added to the confusion. Bengalis count by pointing the tip of the thumb to the base of the pinkie on the same hand, counting each joint and then the tip of each finger, progressing to the tip of the forefinger — enabling them to count up to sixteen on one hand.)

It was an odd request, badly pronounced, and half in the wrong language. But it seemed to get the idea across.

Unfortunately, Dianne had developed a keen sense of mischief while studying orangutans in Borneo, where we had first met. (She used to enclose little plastic ants in her letters to me, and they would fly out as I unfolded the letter — I never failed to jump.) The temptation was too much for her to resist:

"And don't peel 'em," she added.

With this, the cook was overcome. He recruited five more people — some appeared to be guests — to help decode the unfathomable request. The discussion proceeded in Bengali. (I could only guess what they were saying: Do these people eat nothing but eggs? Do they plan to eat the shells also?)

Girindra, after listening intently, had an idea. Everyone discussed it in Bengali and reached agreement. Girindra flashed a betel-stained smile and explained, "Me. Helping. Me, egg."

But I didn't understand, so Girindra tried to break the language barrier as so many people do when confronted with the ignorance of foreigners: by repeating the same incomprehensible words, only louder. "You!" he shouted. "Helping! *You egg!* ME HELPING EGG! YOU LIKE!"

❖

This was not the kind of conversation I'd had in mind when I started on my first trip to Sundarbans in October. I'd prepared for this trip for a year. I had tried to learn Bengali (or Bangla), though I could find no college or university on the East Coast where the language was still taught. I did manage to purchase some language tapes through Harvard, but to my horror I found they contained no English. I learned to pronounce whole dialogues without knowing what they meant.

I ordered a Bengali-English dictionary. It had to be shipped to Peterborough, New Hampshire, from Dacca, Bangladesh. When it arrived months later, I found that although the English words were spelled out in Roman letters, all the Bengali words were in Sanskritic Bengali script, which of course I couldn't read.

Eventually I was able to match up some of the words on the tapes with those in a *Teach Yourself Bengali* phrase book. I discovered I had learned to converse about the songs of the Bengali poet Rabindranath Tagore ("Would you like to hear the songs of Rabindranath?") and the various instruments that could be played to accompany them ("Will your brother play the sitar?" "No, he will play the behala.") And I had found the most useful phrase: "Ami Bangla boli na" ("I don't speak Bengali").

I had read all I could about Sundarbans' tigers, which wasn't much. At best, the scientist's portrait of a wild tiger is a line drawing, shaping the creature mostly by the map of its travels, as Smithsonian researchers have done at Chitawan. This I could not hope to do in Sundarbans. But there are other ways to understand the tiger, and these I hoped to explore.

The people who live in Sundarbans — the fishermen, woodcutters, and honey collectors who venture into tiger territory each day — understand the tiger in a context vastly different from that of the scientist. "In the land where the tiger roams," wrote Fateh Singh Rathore, who along with colleague Valmik

Thapar has extensively studied tigers at India's Ranthambhore National Park, "he is not a mere animal, but a symbol of the powerful, the fearful, the majestic, the magical and the unknown." In the tangled mangrove forests of Sundarbans, those who live beside the tiger may seldom see him, but his presence and his power are constantly felt. When they do see him, they may glimpse him for only a moment — but that moment is charged with magic and emotion. Their portrait of the tiger is not a scientist's line drawing but a pointillist painting, each encounter a dot of glowing, vivid color.

Who is this tiger? Some would say that only the scientist can provide a valid answer, the only true likeness. But some questions science cannot fully answer: Who is God? Moses asked the burning bush, and God himself replied. Older texts report Yahweh's answer as "I am who I am." But more recent scholarship translates the reply "I am what I do" — a new answer, offering a way to begin to explore even the unknowable God. And, too, the unknowable tiger.

What does the tiger do? At Chitawan researchers could provide a partial answer: the tiger sleeps cool in the shade and hunts in the night, owns land, finds lovers, sires children; the tigress, a loving mother, teaches her children to hunt and to hide, to know the other tigers by scent, and to memorize the schedules of the forest. But this is not the full answer.

What does the tiger do? In Sundarbans the people say the tiger gives life to legends and prayers. The tiger works magic. The tiger materializes from nowhere, flies through the air, lands weightlessly on boats. The tiger disappears in water. "The sea is the womb of the Hindu universe," writes religious scholar Wendy Doniger, "and to return to the womb is to die." But in Hindu mythology water is also the residence of Vishnu, the greatest god. Water symbolizes fluid change, power, and energy. So the amphibious tiger of Sundarbans swims on the surface of divine power, the skin of life and death. He is beauty and cruelty twined tight, worshiped but not loved, feared but not hated. In Sundarbans the tiger is a magical animal.

I had come to Sundarbans to learn the nature of tiger magic. Instead I was arguing over boiled eggs.

❖

Earlier in the journey I had learned that gathering information in Bengal is no straightforward process.

We were traveling on the Bangladeshi side of Sundarbans with Dianne's friend Hasna Moudud. Hasna is a member of the Bangladeshi Parliament, the wife of the former vice president, the daughter of the famous Bengali poet Jassimudin. Beautiful and genteel, in her high, light voice she drapes conversation with words as gracefully as she drapes her rounded body with a sari. Dianne, who works with the International Primate Protection League, had met Hasna at the 1992 Earth Summit in Río, where Hasna was honored as one of the "Global 500" who had contributed importantly to preserving the environment; when Dianne told Hasna about my project, Hasna kindly invited both of us to visit her and see her country's side of Sundarbans.

Because our time there was short and Hasna's agenda busy, I was able to conduct only one formal interview in Sundarbans itself. In the fishing village of Alorchole, on the island of Dubla Char, villagers told us a man had been carried off and eaten by a tiger just the year before; two years earlier, a man had been attacked by a tiger but survived. I asked to speak with the survivor. A handsome mustached man in his thirties came forward, giving his name as Nironjan.

A huge scar swept his right shoulder, and below it his arm hung limp. With his slender legs folded into his lungi as neatly as bat wings, he sat proudly in the hot sun surrounded by more than one hundred villagers. He spoke with me through Hasna and our local Chamber of Commerce guide, Sharfuzzaman Topy.

I asked, "Please tell us the story of the day the tiger attacked you."

A stream of Bengali words followed.

"He was looking for the corpse of a man who was taken by the tiger, so he could be properly cremated," began Sharfuzzaman.

Another stream of Bengali words.

"He was traveling with one other man at the time," translated Hasna.

More Bengali.

"Two armed forest service guards were with him," Sharfuzzaman translated. "The tiger attacked his friend and then came at him from the front, pulled his hair, and bit him in the head."

Bengali.

"The tiger jumped on him from the back and tore his arm," said Hasna.

The interview proceeded in this manner for perhaps twenty minutes.

Although I tried to confirm the details of the story, no one — neither Nironjan nor Sharfuzzaman nor Hasna — seemed at all perturbed by the inconsistencies. In fact, they all seemed either bored or annoyed with my insistence on reviewing the details. As the interview continued, the responses Hasna and Sharfuzzaman reported from Nironjan strayed farther and farther from the point of my questions. Hasna, whose English is far better than Sharfuzzaman's, was increasingly distracted by queries from the other villagers, who were eager to talk with such a celebrity. Finally I closed the interview as any dutiful journalist would:

"How do you spell your name?"

Sharfuzzaman didn't even bother to ask. Nironjan's name, of course, if it was written anywhere, was not recorded in the alphabet I knew but in the balletic strokes of Bengali script. But most people here can't write anyway. They sign their names with a fingerprint.

How should I spell this name? Sharfuzzaman answered, "Any way you like."

Bengalis, it seems, do not place a Western premium on precise, factual information. They love to talk; they are masterful storytellers. Bengali poetry — that of Rabindranath Tagore, Jassimudin — is among the most moving and lyrical in the world. But the exchange of fact, the quarry of journalist and scientist, is not the heart of Bengali discourse. "I always modify what I'm told are facts," the first secretary for development at the Canadian High Commission in Bangladesh, Sara Camblin Breault, told me. This, she explained, is not because people want to lie to you; it is simply that facts, per se, are not what Bengalis consider most important to convey.

Bengali sentences convey less information than English sentences but perhaps carry more meaning. Once I asked a Bengali from Chittagong, a man of numbers employed by a shipping company, to tell me about the disastrous cyclone of April 29, 1991. He had been educated, he told me, in Texas; I expected him to cite the wind speed and air temperature. Instead he said, "The wind, it was as if it had fire in it."

Bengalis do not generally use their language as an envelope for bartered facts. It is a vehicle for metaphor, miracle, and magic. Nowhere was this more evident than at the Mosque of Sixty Domes.

The mosque is located on the edge of the town of Bagherhat — "Tiger Market" — which is considered the entryway to the Bangladeshi Sundarbans, three hours' drive from the capital city of Dacca. The Mosque of Sixty Domes is one of the most famous monuments in the country. Its terra cotta bulk hunches on twenty-taka notes, on stamps and postcards and travel posters. It has been here for centuries, yet it is said that the number of its domes can't really be counted.

Hasna read and translated the sign in front of the mosque:

"The Mosque of Sixty Domes," she read in her light, musical voice, "really has seventy-nine domes.

"No," she corrected herself as she continued reading, "it has seventy-four . . . Actually, it has eighty-one domes, if you count the domes outside . . . It says here that no one can actually count them all."

She continued reading: "Behold, the Mosque of Sixty Domes is built with solid stone." In fact the outer walls are terra cotta, but large stone pillars support the inner domes. But because this is a country that makes everything from earth — it is said there are no stones in Bangladesh, only mud — the stone pillars are believed to be miraculous.

We met the muezzin, who calls people to prayer at the mosque. He explained that the stone from which the pillars were constructed came floating down the river fifteen centuries ago.

Floating stones? "So the mosque is beyond our perceptions," the muezzin told us. "The stones are a miracle."

❖

The people of Sundarbans have witnessed many miracles. Near the Mosque of Sixty Domes is the majestic terra cotta tomb of the Muslim saint Rahmatullah Elahi, a leader in the effort to spread Islam through Bengal. Among his many miracles, he could change the troublesome evil spirits called *jinn* into crocodiles, who then would obey his commands. It is believed that these same crocodiles, who would now be more than five hundred years old, still live in the big pool near the tomb of their master. Worshipers come today to offer live chickens to the crocodiles, who emerge, sudden and monstrous, from the brown water, to seize the offerings in their tongueless, toothy mouths. It is widely believed that the crocodiles grant children to the childless.

Not only Muslim saints worked the miracles from which the fabric of Sundarbans' past is woven. At the now-demolished city of Ishwaripur, along the Jamuna River, the avenging black goddess Kali presided and predicted the future. Appearing in the form of a bright light emerging from the sea, Kali visited the sixteenth-century Bengali chieftain Pratapaditya. For three days Pratapaditya prayed and fasted until Kali agreed to dwell in his city. He constructed for her a great temple, and the city honored her with its name: Ishwaripur means "City of the Goddess."

The people prospered under her protection. Then one day the goddess came to Pratapaditya, disguised as his own daughter, with a message for him. But the chief did not listen to her; he sent her away, angry at the girl for immodestly appearing in public. The next day the stone image of Kali, which had faced south, as all such images do, so that the gods can enjoy the soft southerly breeze, was found facing east. The chief still paid no heed. Shortly thereafter the Muslim conquerers invaded — from the east, as Kali had foretold. They overthrew Pratapaditya and converted the temple to a mosque.

The religions of conquering invaders have swept over Bengal like tidal waves. On both sides of Sundarbans, Hindus and Muslims worship together at shrines, praying for protection from the tiger, the crocodile, the shark, the cyclone. For these people, steeped in a mystic tradition of animistic belief, nourished by a land both impossibly fertile and impossibly hostile, miracles are as real as the rain — and as necessary.

For here land and sea are laced with treachery: the water itself seems to conceal and connive. Many of the main streams have double currents. "Even to skillful swimmers, this treacherous current is most dangerous," a nineteenth-century explorer, John Rudd Rainey, observed, "for one falling accidentally and suddenly into a stream naturally sinks at first below the surface, when the undercurrent drags him in one direction, while the upper current flowing in a contrary direction prevents his rising to the surface and he soon gets asphyxiated or drowned, and the body is sometimes never found." There is a spot off the coast, in the Bay of Bengal, called "The Swatch of No Ground," where the depth suddenly changes from 65 feet to more than 1,600. It is said that there the sea has no bottom.

For centuries sea pirates have taken refuge in Sundarbans' innumerable channels. In *Travels in the Mogul Empire,* François Bernier wrote that at the close of the seventeenth century these pirates "surprised and carried away whole towns, assemblies, markets feasts and weddings of the Gentiles and others of that country, making women slaves great and small, with strange cruelty and burning all they could not carry away." An issue of the *East India Chronicle* described how pirates kidnapped 1,800 men, women, and children from South Bengal in 1717. Most of them, the *Chronicle* reported, were taken to Burma and sold as slaves for twenty rupees each — less than a dollar in today's money.

Pirates, known as dacoits, still ply the waters of Sundarbans. Their boats look unremarkable, but they are equipped with powerful motors to speed toward their victims and outdistance police. One bright day as we steamed along in the spacious tourist boat Hasna had secured for us, a small craft with a red sail sped out of a small channel, heading straight for us. Our accompanying forest service guards emerged from below deck holding Russian-made rifles. Instantly the little boat U-turned and vanished back into the channel.

Apparently this encounter was not unusual. The visitors' book on board our vessel recorded this comment from a party of five who had visited a few months before: "We'd suggest . . . that the armed guards ensure that all passengers are *behind* the gun before they fire on suspected dacoits (one of us has a temporary hearing loss now.)" Yet, the party wrote, they considered their cruise "very relaxing." In spite of pirate attack and deafening gunfire, they had fallen under Sundarbans' hypnotic spell, and were mesmerized, lulled by the mantra of its tides.

❖

Because Sundarbans is a border area in two countries, foreigners are required to obtain permits before entering. Hasna had seen to these formalities for us in Bangladesh. In India we were on our own.

For months I corresponded with officials who had assured me our permits could be negotiated in advance; for months I mailed photocopies of our passports and visas to various Indian agencies along with self-addressed return envelopes in which I hoped our permits would be enclosed. But to no avail: we would have to apply for permits in person.

We had been forewarned. "The British invented red tape," my friend, Jenny Das, a Brit who married a Bengali, told me, "but the Indians embroider with it." One reason the Smithsonian chose Nepal's Royal Chitawan Park as the site of its tiger study, rather than taking the more logical course of building upon George Schaller's work at Kanha, was to avoid India's infamous red tape.

We arrived by taxi at the huge yellow Victorian complex in Calcutta known as the Writer's Building, where permits of many kinds are issued. When we attempted to walk though the first door we found, we were told to go to Door One. At Door One, which is actually an archway, we stood in line to sign a guest book. We stood in a second line to fill out a two-inch by one-inch slip of paper with our names and addresses, the bureau we wanted to visit, and the reason. We stood in a third line to hand the slip to a ticket taker in a booth. He stared at it, signed it, and handed it back. This we handed to a guard at the door. Only then were we allowed to enter the building.

We were told that the Forest Department was on the second floor. Avoiding the huge line for the elevator (which, as it turned out, was out of order) we found a flight of stairs. Up we climbed, past piles of crumpled paper and orange peels, along staircases guttered with stains of urine and betel nut. At the second floor, precisely as we had been told, we found the Finance

Department. But where was the Forest Department? We were pointed through a maze of cubbyhole offices with saloon-type doors, through big rooms where dozens of people in suits and saris stood reading newspapers or sat at desks beside fat stacks of folders that smelled like rotting leaves. We passed the offices of innumerable Senguptas and Chatterjees, Muhkerjees and Banerjees. We passed basins overflowing with water. We passed a closed door stenciled "Secret Room." We climbed more stairs. On one floor we passed a white-clad *sadhu,* a holy man with matted hair, his face painted with the trident of Shiva. His business here we could not imagine.

At last we reached the top floor, where we were directed to a thin woman in a blue sari with scars at the corners of her mouth. She handed us a form to fill out. When we were finished, the woman copied the information from this form onto another one. I counted twenty seconds while she formed the letter O with her pen. Finally, finished with her task, she took the paperwork away and returned to her desk. We sat and waited.

Around us the population of the room fluctuated between nine and twenty-five. All were government employees. We were the only ones waiting for a permit.

An hour passed. We scanned the room. On one desk I noted a file dated 1988; a large cobweb tethered its edge to the ceiling. The cobweb itself was covered with dust. Another file, marked "Plywood Concessions for Calcutta Plywood Co.," contained a dark blue sweater.

Another hour passed. Some workers sat behind desks layered with cardboard folders thick with dog-eared, yellowing correspondence, staring at the contents. Some chatted pleasantly in Bengali with coworkers. Others leaned back in their chairs and read the day's *Statesman,* opening the newspaper wide, like a yawn.

A third hour of waiting began. No fan stirred the air. Few people moved. Half of the fluorescent light bulbs were missing or burned out. Those that remained pulsed with a flickering glow, the way the edge of one's vision wrinkles before a migraine.

More than three hours after we had filled out our applications, we were handed our permits.

The next day we were to present them to Mr. P. Sengupta, the field director for Sundarbans Tiger Reserve, at his office in Canning, a few hours' drive south of Calcutta.

For months I had corresponded with Kalyan Chakrabarti, the former field director, whose articles on Sundarbans and its tigers outnumbered any other author's. He had graciously agreed to guide Dianne and me through the area. He would secure a government launch and a speedboat for our transport and act as our translator. Unfortunately, on the day we arrived in India, Kalyan informed us he had just been promoted and could not leave his new job to accompany us. But he had spoken with the Sundarbans field office, and everything, he promised — a government launch, a speedboat, a translator — had been arranged. Our launch would be leaving Canning at ten.

We arrived at the field director's office, a room on the second floor of a dirty yellow concrete building, at nine. No one was there.

Sengupta arrived at ten-thirty. A thin man with a pencil mustache, dressed in a blue business suit, the field director greeted us, stared at our business cards, and showed absolutely no sign of ever having heard of us. He chatted with us briefly, exhausting his English. He rang a little bell, ordered some tea from his orderly, and then, while Dianne and I sat facing his desk, he opened the *Statesman* and, behind its newsprint curtain, began to read.

We continued to sit there for about half an hour, thoroughly unsure of what to do, when Rathin Banerjee swept dramatically into the office. The tiger reserve's assistant field director, Rathin is a compact, forceful man in his early forties, with dazzling white teeth set off by a cropped black mustache. He snapped his fingers at his subordinates and barked orders in Bengali. He was dressed in field clothes — camouflage vest, T-shirt, and green pants. His beige faux-suede cap was pulled down over his eyes so far he had to lift his chin to see, giving him a look of defiance.

An orderly announced that we were invited into Rathin's office. Rathin listened, hyperalert, like a mongoose, as I explained what we were doing there. Yes, he said, he would ferry us to Sundarbans. He had to take the government launch, a 140-foot vessel named *Monorama,* out on patrol anyway. He could tell us about the land and the people along the way. Besides, he was glad of a chance to exercise his English; mainly, he said, he used the language only to fight with his wife. "You say 'you dirty rat' in Bangla," he told me, "and it sounds like you are saying something adorable. But in English it is much better."

❖

As we sailed away from Canning, Rathin told us of many wonders: packs of dog sharks that cordon off schools of small fish and take turns swimming through them to feast. Once he watched them hunt like this for ten minutes. Occasionally he would see a shark fly out of the water with a fish in its mouth, as if jumping for joy.

Tigers? Oh, yes, he had seen tigers. Just recently he had investigated the death of a forest guard who, with his finger on the trigger of his shotgun, had been killed by a tiger. Rathin said he could imagine how that man felt. "You feel a four hundred fifty volt leave you," he said. "My eyes are simply locked on the creature! Thick saliva comes out of the mouth. It takes a very strong person to pull the bolt of the gun."

Fortunately, Rathin said, he had never had to fire on a tiger.

And unlike many other areas of India, where tigers are killed for their pelts and their bones, in Sundarbans the poachers are few. The forest is too thick, the tigers too dangerous. But dacoits — they are another matter. Often the Forest Department must contend with smugglers and pirates shipping illegal timber, ferrying contraband from Bangladesh. The pirates are so bold they will fire upon Forest Department boats, Rathin said, and he told us about the times he had exchanged rounds with them, gunfire flashing red and green in the night.

We entered Sundarbans at evening, when everything was in half-shadow.

❖

That night we traveled south down the river Matla — no longer a river, since the Farakka Barrage diverted the Ganges, but only a trough filled and emptied daily by the tides. In the morning we continued south to the sand island of Chaimar, at the tip of the core area between the Mayadwip River and the Bay of Bengal.

Monorama dropped anchor and we boarded the little jet boat that was tethered to her stern, so that we might more closely approach Chaimar's jettyless shore. Within a few minutes our bare feet sank into the soft gray-brown mud. Rathin warned us to be careful of hental thorns. There's only one way to remove them, he said: you take a hollow skeleton key and, by pushing it deep into the wound, you can expose the tip of the thorn and grab it and pull it out with tweezers. He'd figured this out after he'd gotten his soles full of thorns while collecting eggs for a crocodile breeding project. "But oh! It is so painful!" he said, drawing his face up tight.

Soon we were on sandier ground. Bright orange fiddler crabs scuttled sideways in great rafts, moving oddly in unison, with the jerky motion of a child's remote-control toy car. There is always one lead crab, Rathin told us, who decides when the group is in danger and leads everyone to the water, where they bury themselves instantly in the sand.

It was low tide. About a hundred yards from the water grew a small patch of *Saccharum* grass, a green smudge on the bald landscape between the mangroves and the sea. Here the beach was crisscrossed with hoofprints of chital. And there, between the mangroves and the grass, Rathin pointed to the footprints of a tigress.

She had walked leisurely, slowly, her back feet stopping short of the prints left by her forefeet. And here, Rathin showed us, she had lain down behind the grass to watch the deer. Later we walked along the fringe of the forest and saw her pugmarks joined by those of her cub. Two days ago, Rathin told us, he had read a story in the sand of how she and her cub had played with a live monitor lizard, killed it, and eaten it.

That afternoon, after routinely checking the fishing permits of passing boats, Rathin interpreted while I interviewed two fishermen concerning their beliefs about tigers.

Does the tiger have supernatural powers? I asked.

"The tiger victim's body shrinks in half in the mouth of the tiger," Rathin translated. "But" — he said in an aside — "there is a biological reason for this. Because the tiger seizes its prey by the neck and holds its prey by the axis . . . our nerve system, when it gets squeezed there, the body folds up and gets the shape of a prawn. It twists into a comma shape, and, shorter and smaller, it cuts a smaller silhouette. When the tiger lifts this thing up, it's found that only the toes — only the biggest digit in the feet" — and here Rathin paused, hitting the first English snag since we'd met. "This," he asked, pointing to his big toe, "is the toe?"

"Yes."

"They are *all* called toes?"

"All five are toes."

"And what do you call the biggest digit?"

"The big toe."

He considered this information for a moment, as if it were some treasure to be carefully stored in his brain. I later learned that in Bengali each toe has a distinct name, as has each finger. He was amazed that this is not the case in English.

"Acha," Rathin continued — the Bengali equivalent of "okay." "Big toe. Only the big toe touches the ground. So the tiger has no difficulty in carrying the victim away. So the body does become smaller."

Also, the fishermen told me through Rathin, the tiger can fly through the air. Rathin offered a biological explanation for this, too: "The tiger is capable of leaping up to twenty feet with a human kill, so leaping twenty feet with a human kill is symbolic of flying," he said.

So, I asked, how can a person protect himself from such a being?

"Their main form of protection," Rathin said, "is to call upon the forest goddess, Bonobibi." They honor her by offering sweets. Before they get off the boat, before their feet touch the sacred mud of the forest, they place the sweets on a large leaf and float it on the water, he said.

Do you pray to Bonobibi? I asked through Rathin.

"They do not say prayers, but the persons who know the prayers, the local shamans, do," Rathin interpreted. "But so many shamans themselves have been taken away by the tiger, they say they are running short of shamans nowadays."

When the interview concluded, Rathin pulled me aside with a nudge. "These primitive people!" he said, chuckling. "They really believe these funny things!"

Rathin was raised as a Christian, but he doesn't believe much in Christianity either. Later, though, he offered to read our palms. From the lines on her hands he correctly assessed that Dianne's life had recently been threatened by a serious illness (she had spent the past year recovering from malnutrition and various ailments picked up working with orangutans in Borneo). He saw that I had been quite sick when I was very young (I had mononucleosis before I was two) and that I had always been a very serious student. His own palm, Rathin told us, predicted that he would never lose in court; the one time he had been legally challenged, true to his palm, he had won. "Do you agree," he asked us, "that palmistry is a science?"

❖

The next night Rathin deposited us at Sajnekhali Tourist Lodge, a concrete and wood complex of thirty tiny, two-bed rooms. He promised to come back later in the week to help us.

As it turned out, Rathin was unable to return. He was suddenly sent to Dehra Dun for a training course at the Wildlife Institute of India. The day after he left, Hindu fundamentalists destroyed a Muslim mosque at Ayodhya, which they said was rightfully the site of a Hindu temple, and the entire Indian subcontinent erupted in violence. On Dianne's shortwave radio each night we heard the BBC announce the death toll: in Uttar Pradesh, the state in which the mosque was burned, 362 people were killed in riots; in one of the eastern states angry mobs pulled 200 people from a train and knifed them to death. By the sixth day of the siege, 1,100 Indians were dead, 5,000 injured. Violent protests also erupted in Bangladesh and Pakistan, which closed their borders. In India's cities people traveling in groups larger than four were arrested. All the major cities were cordoned off by the military, so no one could enter or leave.

We did not fear that the violence would reach Sundarbans, where Hindus and Muslims worship side by side. But even if he could have abandoned his new duties, Kalyan Chakrabarti could not leave Calcutta. Rathin could not leave Dehra Dun. We could not return to Calcutta to hire a translator, nor could we hope that tourist boats would bring English-speaking Bengalis from Calcutta.

What I was to learn about Sundarbans would come from mute observation and from Girindra, a man who did not speak my language and whose language I did not understand.

The Tiger Is Watching

❖ ❖ ❖ ❖ ❖ ❖ ❖ ❖ ❖ ❖ ❖ ❖ ❖ ❖ ❖ ❖ ❖ ❖ ❖

BEFORE DIANNE AND I left Calcutta, we sought out local wildlife experts familiar with Sundarbans, hoping they could tell us what to expect.

No one presumed to predict what might happen to us in Sundarbans. Instead, people offered their own experiences, from which we began to assemble a partial, preliminary picture, a gap-toothed mosaic of science, mystery, fantasy, and contradiction.

We traveled to Buxa Tiger Reserve in northern West Bengal to talk with Pranabesh Sanyal, a former field director at Sundarbans; we went to Kanha National Park, where George Schaller had worked; we talked with Kalyan Chakrabarti at the Tollygunge Club, where we stayed in Calcutta. I'd chosen to stay at the Tolly because Anne Wright, a tiger expert and member of the World Conservation Union–IUCN Cat Specialist Group, lives there. (Her husband, Bob, also an ardent conservationist, manages the club.) Anne generously introduced us to other tiger experts.

One of them was Bonani Kakkar. Bonani is unusual for a middle-aged Indian woman: instead of the traditional draped sari, she wears Western pants and shirts; she does not decorate her forehead with a *bindi,* which most Indian women place between and above the brows; she keeps her dark, wavy hair cropped short rather than coiled into a bun on the back of the head. Both alone and with her tall, green-eyed husband, she has traveled all over India as well as to Africa, Europe, and America, working for the World Wildlife Fund, the United Nations' Environmental Program, and the World Bank.

Bonani has met tigers on foot. Little frightens her. She is a tough woman, whose aura of sternness disappears only when she looses her waterfall-like laugh. We first met her at Kanha, and later she came to visit us at the Tolly. There she told us the story of how a tiger she never saw changed forever the way she thought of Sundarbans.

❖

Bonani wasn't studying tigers when she went to Sundarbans in February of 1986, she explained. A private wildlife consultant, she was searching for traces of a rare river terrapin, *Batagur baska.* Once common, the pointy-nosed terrapin was thought to be extinct over most of the Indian subcontinent, but it was rumored that some might have survived undetected in Sundarbans. Perhaps, she thought, the *Batagur* might share the same nesting beaches as the olive ridley sea turtles, who come ashore from the Bay of Bengal each winter to lay their eggs in pits they dig above the high-tide line. With a small team of other researchers, she planned to search for the *Batagur*'s tracks, nests, and egg fragments on the island of Mechua.

The night before the expedition was to depart, Bonani got a phone call from Pranabesh Sanyal, who was then field director of the reserve. She remembers his exact words: "Mrs. Kakkar, just be a little careful when you go to this island, because I forgot to tell you that the tiger there is an aggressive man-eater."

"What do you mean 'aggressive man-eater'?" Bonani tossed

back. She thought he was joking. "I thought all man-eaters were aggressive!"

But Pranabesh was serious. "No, there are categories of man-eaters," he told her. "This one is very aggressive. And we know he is found in that general area." The island of Mechua is located on Sundarbans' eastern sea face among a block of islands collectively known as Baghmara, which means "tiger-killed."

Bonani is not easily frightened, so the field director's words did not deter her. Besides, she said, it was too late to cancel the trip.

❖

That was not Bonani's first trip to Sundarbans, she told us. In 1983 Pranabesh had invited her to witness the results of a new field experiment.

He had commissioned a local clay artist, who normally made idols for Hindu festivals, to create several life-size dummies of villagers engaged in their work in the forest: a woodcutter, a fisherman, a honey collector. They were positioned in lifelike poses: the woodcutter swinging an axe, the fisherman sitting in a boat, the honey collector holding a basket beneath a tree. They were dressed in used garments redolent of human skin and sweat. And their expressions were heartbreakingly real: black-rimmed eyes wide with terror, red lips pursed — painted faces mesmerized with fear.

Around their necks Pranabesh circled galvanized wire. Each dummy was hooked up to a car battery hidden some yards away under a bush. In an effort to deter tigers from attacking people, the field director was marshaling the wisdom of Pavlov, teaching the tigers to associate attacking people with a painful electric shock. But first he had to see if the tigers would attack the dummies.

He placed several in the forest, and one day word reached

him at his home in Calcutta that one of the models, a fisherman, had been struck.

Bonani, along with two forest guards, went with Pranabesh
to see the results. They found the clay dummy face down in the
mud. The tiger had ripped into the model as if it were flesh.
Claw marks stretched from shoulder to waist. An arm was torn
off. Fresh pugmarks showed that the attack had occurred early
that morning.

The experiment — this phase at least — was a success. Both
of them were excited, Bonani said, but then they felt something
else. Pugmarks led away from the model into the creek. "Two
or three of us walking back and forth with him, looking at these
pugmarks," she told us. "And then suddenly — it was a very
narrow creek, and the other side was all fresh pugmarks — we
realized the tiger could have been lurking just in the bush."

Pranabesh, a lithesome man in his early forties, exudes an extraordinary Buddhalike confidence and cheer; Bonani considers
him completely fearless. But he said to her, "Let's go back."

"You see," said Bonani, "you really can't walk on foot in
Sundarbans and feel safe for even a minute."

The dummies were the latest in a series of efforts to reduce
what the Forest Department euphemistically calls "man-animal
conflict." These measures, which include a supplement to the
insurance paid to families of tiger victims, comprise the single
largest item in the reserve's modest budget year after year.

The department's efforts reflect successive field directors' diverse ideas about why the tigers kill and eat people. In earlier
programs the Forest Department bred wild pigs and released
them into the reserve's buffer zone to provide tigers with more
prey — like placing offerings before an altar. The department
dug freshwater ponds in the core area, hoping this resource
would entice the tigers to stay there, where people were not
supposed to go. Staff members say that the tigers do drink from
these ponds, but they drink salt water also.

Other efforts attempted to fortify forest workers. Some were outright bizarre. In 1981 an experimental Tiger Guard Head Gear was fashioned from bulletproof fiberglass, which you were supposed to wear over your head and neck in heat that reaches 100 degrees; another model, equally bulky and uncomfortable, featured long spikes poking macelike out of the nape. Of course no one wore it.

In 1986 a new approach was tried, an elegant type of deception. Arum Ram, a member of a science club in Calcutta, noted that the tigers almost never attacked from the front; they always sprang from behind, biting the back of the victim's neck. His idea: plastic face masks worn on the back of the head. They were cheap, they were light, and they worked.

The first year the masks were used in quantity, none of the 2,500 villagers who wore them were attacked. Some men reported that tigers would still follow them, sometimes for hours. Often the person would hear the tiger growling, as if it were frustrated that the Janus-man had somehow cheated it, yet it seemed unable to perpetrate a similar breach.

The tigers' unwillingness to attack men head on is well embedded in Sundarbans lore. Muslims explain it this way: on each man's forehead Allah has written that man is king of all animals; this so irritates the tiger that he cannot bear to look upon it. Tigers adhere to this code of etiquette so strongly that they have been known to abandon human prey if the corpse, as they drag it off, becomes wedged by roots or logs in such a way that the animal must look into the victim's face.

The masks worked as long as the tigers believed in them. Which was not for long. "After five or six months, they were finding out that this was not the front of the human being," Kalyan Chakrabarti told me when he visited us at the Tollygunge Club.

Kalyan is an intense and fervent man in his fifties, possessed of a dense energy, as if all his intuitions and theories and stories and plans were physically compacted into his short, stout body. He is adamant on this point: "They know what a human being looks like," he insists. "They know there is a back and a front. Then they are finding out that one is not a good front." The masks, he said, were "a little gimmick that worked for a particular period."

(Today, although some officials still consider the masks effective, almost no one seems to use them. Of all the villagers I met in Sundarbans, I found only one fishing group carrying the masks on their boat.)

Other measures have met with varying degrees of success. The pig-release project was discontinued years ago. Five or six electric dummies still occupy the forest, standing like sentries at timber-cutting and pond-digging projects. Each year the Forest Department strings more electric fencing around the reserve's boundaries to allay people's fears that tigers will stray into their villages. And in much the same way that developers erect street lights to discourage parking-lot vandalism, the Forest Department has installed more than a dozen solar-powered lights along a twenty-eight-mile stretch of shore. The villagers find the solar lights very convenient, whether they deter tigers or not.

But the man-eating has not stopped. Nothing — neither laws nor permits nor patrols — stops men from illegally crossing into the reserve's forest core; and nothing — neither offerings nor armor nor trickery — stops the tigers who come to meet them.

❖

"We arrived at Mechua at high tide," Bonani remembered. "It was about two P.M." The Forest Department had loaned the team searching for terrapin five guards, a double-barreled shotgun, a .315 rifle, and a ten-foot motorboat as well as a large launch and its crew. The pilot anchored the launch in a creek, and the research team took the motorboat up a channel from which they could wade to the sandy beach.

For four hours they searched the tall *Saccharum* grass and the white sand for traces of turtle tracks or eggshell fragments. Always a guard watched the creek for an approaching tiger. Another guard watched the forest, where a tiger might also await them.

Finding no traces of terrapins, the researchers gathered samples of the area's plants and soils until the sky began to darken. Then they turned back.

Where the sandy beach ended, they moved into mud along the creek. Here they came across their own footprints. But now, superimposed on them, and moving in the opposite direction — the direction the team was now heading — were the pugmarks of a tiger.

❖

Walking toward a dangerous animal you cannot see is one of the deepest human fears. Even people who spend their lives looking for tigers never get over the feeling of shock when they find one. And so Kalyan Chakrabarti was shocked — horrified — when, following the pugmarks of a tigress over a little ridge one day, he came face to face with a tigress and her cub. He told us about the encounter while we shared tea at the Tollygunge Club.

"She was looking at me as I was approaching, though I was not making great sound," Kalyan said, leaning forward. "Her look was of curiosity at first, then aggression. She was thinking of her cub." The pair, perhaps twenty yards away, was a potentially lethal combination. In other areas tigresses who normally ignore human beings will sometimes attack if they think their cubs are threatened; in Sundarbans tigresses teach their cubs to hunt people, just as tigresses elsewhere teach their cubs to hunt animal prey.

Kalyan's mind raced: "If the tigress jumps, what will I do?" He had no weapon, not even a stick.

His first instinct was to run, but he knew that would have the same effect as pulling a string of yarn along the floor in front of a house cat. And he could not outrun a tigress.

His only hope, he realized, was to remain still.

For thirty minutes the tigress and the man watched each other. Kalyan remained motionless. A hermit crab crawled up inside his pant leg; still he didn't move.

"Then," Kalyan told me, "she made a judgment: this man is not my destroyer, this is my friend."

Finally the tigress leaped to her feet, and the cub followed her into the forest.

❖

"We were very worried," recalls Kushal Mookherjee. Thirty-five and athletically slim, Kushal, like Bonani, is a private wildlife consultant. He lives with his gracious young wife in a large walkup apartment with a balcony they have filled with flowers, where we visited them. Bonani describes Kushal as "a careful, cautious person," but not a fearful one. Otherwise he would never have gone on the terrapin expedition to Sundarbans with her. But at the point he was now describing, he wished he hadn't.

By the time they spotted the tiger's tracks atop their own, it was already getting dark. "The sun had set — it would be totally dark in forty-five minutes," Kushal told us. "And then suddenly we saw that something was lying on the vast stretch of mud flat ahead of us. It was our boat."

The tide had receded a few hundred meters and left their motorboat stranded on the mud.

For a precious fifteen minutes of lingering light, they pushed and heaved and shoved at the boat, trying to get it to the water. In the process one of their photographer's cameras fell into the muddy salt water. And while trying to help the scientists retrieve it, the guard dropped the cartridges for his gun into the water too.

The guard picked up the cartridges, wiped them on his hand, and replaced them in his belt. Bonani asked if they would still fire. No, he answered matter-of-factly, "but they have been issued to me," he told her, "and I must have the right number when my superior asks me."

Even when they all heaved against the boat, the craft didn't budge. Only the tide could lift it. The Forest Department guards refused to abandon their vessel. "We are government servants," they told the team. "We have to stay here with the boat. It is already stuck. Now it may drown. Even if we die here, we have to save the boat."

So two of the guards stayed with the boat. They kept the rifle. The other guard took the double-barreled shotgun, with its sodden and useless cartridges, and started walking with the researchers in the direction of the launch, several kilometers away — walking toward the tiger.

❖

Kalyan firmly believes that a tiger will not attack a person who it thinks means no harm. "In this way, I think that they have some sixth sense, to find out who is a protector of the forest and who is a destroyer.

"So this animal," he asserted, "must have got full control and wisdom about him and the area and human behavior; so regarding the reduction of human casualty, it is my thinking that if we can show that we are all protectors of the forest, respectful of the forest, and not destroyers, then there could be no question of a person being killed by a tiger."

For this reason, he claims, forest guards are seldom killed by tigers; the animals have learned to recognize the khaki Forest Department uniforms and identify these people as "forest protectors."

A forest guard, however, had been killed just that March. But, Kalyan told me, the guard was not in uniform at the time;

he was wearing the traditional Bengali lungi. "Then the tiger's system of discrimination between a protector and a destroyer failed," he said. "A careful, watchful, respectful person is never killed by the tiger in Sundarbans."

Later, on board *Monorama,* I asked Rathin about the incident. He had personally investigated the forest guard's death. According to his report the guard, who was with three companions, had seen that the tiger was coming for him. He turned, and knelt to better aim his gun, but the gun wouldn't fire. Two of his companions stood helpless, mesmerized as the tiger leaped on him. A third, who held an axe, fainted with fear; but before he passed out, he managed to strike the tiger, who ran away without taking the guard's body.

As part of his investigation, Rathin had to view the corpse. Kalyan was wrong, he told me. The guard was wearing full uniform.

❖

"The forest was gradually moving towards us — the water and the forest is converging — and it is very difficult to move," Kushal remembered. As they struggled to reach the launch, the researchers were nearly exhausted. Mud devoured their limbs. Carrying backpacks laden with photographic equipment and plant and soil samples, they sank up to their knees in the mud. The muscles in their legs shook and cramped. Finally one man fell and could not get up.

Unable to do anything else, they rested. Around them loomed the forest, clotted with the gnarled and stunted genwa mangroves. At last they were able to pull their companion from the mud. His legs shook so badly he still could not stand, much less walk. They contemplated climbing a tree, but the tallest was only fifteen feet. Local people, if marooned overnight in the forest, will sometimes climb a tall tree to sleep. It is generally believed that tigers, unlike leopards, do not climb trees; this is not true. In the state of Rajasthan, Colonel Kesri Singh shot a tiger who had climbed a banyan tree overlooking a water trough in order to ambush the cattle who watered there. Two hunters, F. W. Champion and Oliver Smythies, reported oddly identical experiences: each watched a wounded tiger swarm up a tree wherein his wife waited, horrified, as the tiger shook the treetop violently with both front paws. Kenneth Anderson was clawed in the backside when the man-eater he was hunting climbed fifteen feet up the tree in which he was hiding.

Tigers everywhere enjoy clawing trees, which they may do to mark them, to sharpen their claws, or to avail themselves of some medicinal value; at least one favored tree, the biga, exudes an astringent, blood-red gum that may act as a disinfectant. But in the forests where these trees grow, the people say the tiger likes to see blood running down the trunk.

Rathin later told me of a case his staff investigated one June. Three villagers had gone to cut wood illegally at Khatuajhuri Compartment, a government-owned block of forest harvested periodically by Forest Department contractors. Since their village was far away, they stayed overnight in the forest, leaving their boat anchored as each man slept in a different tree.

That night a storm raged for several hours. During the lightning and thunder the men could not hear each other's low whistles, the means by which they kept in touch.

At dawn, when the storm stopped, two of the men descended their trees and looked for the third. His tree was empty. Perhaps, they thought, he had climbed down earlier. They went to look for him in the boat, but he wasn't there, either. Frightened, they went to the Forest Department camp close by.

Forest Department officers climbed the tree where the man had been sitting on a bough sixteen feet from the ground. There they found claw marks and blood and bits of flesh.

Pugmarks at the base of the tree would have confirmed that a tiger had climbed it, but now it was high tide, and the forest floor was immersed in water. Any footprints were obliterated.

Local people believe that tigers do not climb trees; they derive a different conclusion from such an attack, Rathin said. This death was the work of a *bagho bhuth,* a tiger ghost, and bagho bhuth don't leave any footprints.

❖

The research team, carrying their injured companion, trudged on through the mud. Finally, through their binoculars, they could see the outline of the launch, but no one was out on deck.

"Now we were in a big dilemma," recalled Kushal. "Because if we called out, they might hear us and bring the launch to us, and we would go into the water and climb aboard — but it will also make the tiger aware of us."

Although the launch was still far away, they decided to shout. The water carried their voices. Still, no one came out on deck.

"We figured, now the tiger knows where we are," Kushal said. "We have started calling, we should go on calling. Like hell we shouted!" And then they heard the launch's engine roar. "The most beautiful sound I ever heard!" Kushal said, and laughed.

By the time the launch picked them up, it was seven P.M. — pitch black, new moon. The launch pilot then navigated the narrow channel back to the tiny motorboat, where the guards waited with their old .315 rifle. The launch crew turned on a strong searchlight and finally spotted the little boat, still stuck in the black mud. Then they saw the guards:

"They were sitting about fifty feet from the mangrove forest," Kushal said, still in awe. "They were in a boat hardly bigger than a sofa. They wouldn't shout because this would attract the tiger. And that Mechua tiger, we heard later, had killed thirty or forty people in the past five or ten years. Those two people — I don't know how they got the courage."

High tide retrieved the motorboat around nine or nine-thirty, and the researchers heard the guards start the motor. "Until then we were really afraid the tiger would get them," Bonani remembered. "But the tiger was on the other bank. He was waiting and watching us."

In the darkness chital barked an alarm — a high yip like a terrier's. The tiger, the people thought, must be moving nearby.

❖

Where is the tiger? The question surely pulses in the minds of the deer as they bend their slender necks to sniff and nibble at leaf litter. From a watchtower in Bangladesh I had seen a chital doe approach a freshwater pond, her staccato walk on mud-caked hooves occasionally punctuated with nervous stamps, her funneled ears swiveling to sounds we could not hear. Only six times in five minutes did she dare bend her neck to the ground, revealing the parallel rows of white spots on either side of her spine. On the beaches of Sundarbans, away from the forest soils that digest death so quickly, you can sometimes find the vertebrae of these deer, porous with age and bleached beyond white.

In daylight the deer often keep company with rhesus monkeys. Beneath the trees where the monkeys sit, showing pendulous pink testicles and orange rumps, the deer wait for a shower of food, bits of the olive-shaped, berrylike *keora* fruit and leaves. It is said that the deer follow the monkeys because from their treetop position the macaques can spot a tiger from far away. Each species knows the other's calls, and at the monkeys' chattery screams or the deer's barked warning, both groups will scatter in an explosion of hooves and hands. But even with so many eyes watching, so many ears cocked, the tiger is often too quiet, too lithe, too cunning to give away its presence.

The tiger oozes through the forest, quiet as the mud, invisible as the wind. *What is the tiger doing?*

The tiger is watching.

"As we are studying them," Kalyan assured Dianne and me, "they are also studying us. They also study human beings: their nature, their movement, their posture, their walking system; all these things are coming to the brain of the tiger. They are all the time monitoring our behavior, as we are monitoring their behavior."

Two decades of research, he said, support his assertion. Kalyan's data, collected between 1962 and 1982, reported at international symposiums and published in some of India's most prestigious scientific journals, show that well over half of the tiger attacks on humans occur between seven and nine A.M. and between three and five P.M., precisely those times when people are most likely to be entering or leaving the forest — times, Kalyan says, when people are least alert to danger.

Tigers are acutely aware of the schedules of their prey: this has been well documented at Chitawan and Kanha, where observers chronicled the activity periods of three species of deer — chital, hog deer, and sambar — and how these varied from the cool season to the hot season, from cloudy days to sunny days. They found, not surprisingly, that the tigers adjusted their hunting hours to the times when their prey was most active and thus easiest to spot. (The structure of their retina makes it difficult for cats to detect motionless prey.) Observations of American mountain lions and of Asiatic lions at the Gir Forest in India confirm that they too adjust their daily rhythms to those of their prey. At Chitawan, where tigers have been known to kill leopards at baits set out to attract cats, leopards altered their schedules to avoid tigers.

So it is no wonder that Sundarbans tigers know when people enter and leave the forest and when they go to sleep. Most nighttime attacks happen around eleven P.M., when people are fast asleep on their boats. The tigers know when the honey collectors come to the forest: the honey season begins in April, and that is the month when the most people are killed. The areas in which honey collection is permitted change from time to time according to Forest Department rules, and this the tigers know too. When eight of the fifteen forest blocks in the park were closed to human entry in 1974, tigers migrated to the new honey collection areas.

With A. B. Chaudhuri, the former director of the Forest Survey of India, Kalyan analyzed the factors surrounding human kills by tigers: time of day, time of year, habitat type, location of kill, profession of the person attacked. "These factors also prove high degree of intelligence and diabolical understanding of human behavior by the tiger of the area," they wrote in a paper presented at the International Symposium on Tiger held in Delhi in 1979.

"The tiger understands the human mind," Pranabesh Sanyal wrote in the park's management plan in 1987, "and all their plans of attack are designed on human movement."

❖

With everyone safe and accounted for, the terrapin team was at last on the big boat. They washed the mud off their feet and legs and unpacked the plant collections while the crew prepared tea.

Then they heard a loud *thump*. The boat jerked. "It felt as if someone had just pulled down the back of the launch," said Kushal. "The front came up and then — *bang* — it came down."

For a moment everyone froze, silent. Something had landed on the ledge outside the lower deck, on the planks where the boatmen walk back and forth with their long bamboo poles to free the boat when it gets stuck in the mud. Someone hurriedly shut all the windows to the lower deck.

And then the crew of the boat began to chant: "Ma-ma-ma-ma." *Ma-ma* is Bengali for mother's brother. "Ma-ma-ma-ma." *Ma*, Bengali for mother, is also the term used to call on the powers of a goddess.

Bonani remembered then that earlier in the trip she had asked one of the boatmen if he had ever seen a *bagh,* the Bengali word for tiger.

"And this man was so angry with me," Bonani remembers. "He said you never use the word *bagh* in Sundarbans. You must call him *Ma-ma.* You don't call him bagh. It's disrespectful. It's inviting danger to call him just a bagh."

For ten minutes no one moved. Bonani said it felt like ten hours. Kushal's face was ashen. Then they heard a splash, and the boat rocked slightly.

❖

"Strange things happen in Sundarbans, and people are reluctant to talk about them," a forestry official told me. So reluctant, in fact, that before he would tell me this story, he made me promise never to reveal who told it.

Once he was traveling on a government launch just outside the core area of the tiger reserve. It was about eleven at night, but a mild breeze was stirring, which tempted him to stay awake and sit up on deck through the night.

He watched the forest idly. At a bend in the creek he noticed that the mixture of vegetation differed markedly on the two banks. To his right a pure stand of keora trees leaned like willows over the water; on the bank to his left was an association of mangroves: *dhundul* with melon-sized green fruits; *gorjon,* standing as if on tiptoe atop masses of stilt roots; the short genwa with downward-pointing, curled leaves.

Just then, quite suddenly, the breeze gathered itself into a strong wind that heaved and sighed and moaned. It blew so hard that the big keoras on the right bank swayed and bent. But that was not the remarkable thing about the wind that night. What was odd, even eerie, was this: on the mangroves along the left bank, 300 feet across the water, not a leaf stirred.

"It was so unbelievably strange," the man told me, "that I called up Mourali, my orderly, who was sleeping on the bunk on the deck, to be a witness to this strange phenomenon and to explain it if he could." Mourali had worked in the Forest Department for thirty years. He had been born and raised in Sundarbans, and he knew many things.

"He looked me straight in the eye," the official recalled, "and with a mild smile asked me not to take notice of it at all. But he insisted we go down to the cabin, that we should not remain on deck any more."

The officer had been trained at university to ask questions of the natural world, to find explanations for what he saw. "I said, 'This is very strange, yet you appear as if you have experienced this before.' Mourali took it very casually. 'But,' I asked, 'how is this possible? The left bank was absolutely calm.' Mourali kept on smiling — as if he knew what was happening, but that I would not believe him if he told me."

Mourali said that he had on occasion experienced strange things in Sundarbans. The officer continued to press him for information. Finally, still smiling, Mourali replied, "Spirits of the dead often raise up sudden whirlwinds; however, it doesn't harm anyone." But still he suggested they retire below.

This convinced the officer. "I left immediately without waiting to know how long this continued," he said. "I was scared."

The *sareng* piloting the craft later told him the wind continued like that for twenty minutes, affecting only one side of the river, until the vessel reached an area called Chogazi, when it abruptly stopped.

"They say that these are the spirits of people killed by tigers," the man said, "and because the spirits are restless, they shake the trees."

"Do you believe this?" I asked.

"If you had been with me through that," he said, "you would believe almost anything."

❖

As scientists, both Bonani and Kushal say they still don't know for sure what moved the boat that night. "It was certainly something powerful, something very heavy, to either push up the front or pull down the back of that boat — a huge shark, maybe, or a crocodile," Kushal said. The splash? Some mangroves grow large fruits called *gol,* said Bonani, that fall into the water with a loud *plop.* But the crew had no doubt: it was a tiger.

Before that trip Bonani had heard a sad story from her mother's maid, who had moved away from Sundarbans after her husband's death. One day, after a visit to her family, she returned to Calcutta in tears. Her son, who was a fisherman, had been fishing in one of the creeks, she said, and a tiger had come out of the water, grabbed him in its jaws, jumped overboard, and swum away. There was nothing anybody could do.

At the time, Bonani thought, "Well, maybe he fell overboard. But did the tiger really come and take him off the boat?" Surely it could not be true.

But now she has changed her mind. "After this incident," she said, "I think all of us who were in the boat that day, if we go to Sundarbans again, we'll listen, now, to what the local people say."

Yesterday

❖ ❖ ❖ ❖ ❖ ❖ ❖ ❖ ❖ ❖

IN *MABISAKA,* the fifty-foot hand-hewn wooden boat Girindra had named after his mother, we chugged up the river, following the incoming tide.

So we began each day. From the single, pewlike white bench on the foredeck, Dianne and I watched Sundarbans in the act of recreating itself: the tide filling the forest with slow, deep, sensuous regularity, the way a person breathes during sleep. Little eddies formed in the water, gathering the gifts of the night: silt from the Himalayas, swirls of dropped leaves and flowers and fruits, the live-born young of the mangroves, whose seeds sprout while still on the branch, fish scales and guts thrown overboard by fishermen, the ashen remains of the cremated dead — a garland of bloom and decay. With this the Sundarbans feeds its mouths, sculpts its own shape. The slopes of the mud banks sprawled expectantly before the water, awaiting its embrace.

On this day we were headed to Netidhopani watchtower, to which *Mabisaka*'s ten-horsepower engine, actually an all-purpose generator, would take us in about three hours. The dug freshwater pool there, Rathin had told me, was often frequented by a tigress with two cubs. So we had set out at dawn as the sun rose round and red like a vermilion bindi on the clear forehead of the morning. We headed south on the Biddyatori River.

Smoke curled from the mud and thatch kitchens of the village houses, carrying the scent of chapatis, the pliant Indian flat-bread. Along the shores women in saris dragged fishing nets behind them, wading chest-deep in water the color of crocodiles.

But soon we were far from the villages. Black-capped king-fishers dropped from trees, red bills gleaming translucent in the sun. A wading pond heron opened wings the color of mud, then flew on wings the color of sky. At the sound of *Mabisaka*'s generator, S-shaped egrets rose and transformed themselves into clouds. Mist rose like breath above the water as the river turned itself into sky.

Now the banks we passed belonged to the wild creatures alone. No people are allowed to walk here, for the area is a sanctuary. But planted in one mud bank we saw a slender pole topped with a knotted, faded cloth, like a flag. What was it doing there?

"Ekhane" — Bengali for "here" — I said to Girindra, who had joined us on the bench, while his teenage son, Sonaton, operated the rudder. "Keno?" — "Why?"

"Yesterday," he told me in phrase-book English, "tiger accident this channel."

Yesterday! A tiger had killed someone here only yesterday, and the survivors had hastily marked the spot with this pole! Dianne and I grabbed each other's hands. "Tini ke?" I demanded — "Who is that?" (I hadn't learned to use the past tense), hoping to find out if the victim had been a fisherman, woodcutter, forest ranger, or poacher.

I then remembered that the only job titles I knew in Bengali were "poet" and "author."

What had happened? Who had been killed? Who else was in the party? What were they doing? At what time of day did the attack occur? Did the tiger eat the body? Had the people prayed first to the tiger god? Or had this death been punishment for a sin of omission? Had the tiger come from the forest? From the water? Was the victim wearing a mask?

All these questions I tried to ask. I interspersed English with Bangla. I mimed. I changed the order of the words. For simplicity I excised all the articles. Still I was unintelligible.

My few words were merely parlor tricks. The gracious Bengalis appreciate being greeted in their own language and enjoy the novelty of conversing with a foreigner in Bangla: "How-are-you, where-are-you-from, I-am-an-author, we-live-in-America, your-country-is-very-beautiful, the-food-is-very-good." But for the sorts of questions I needed to ask, and the answers I needed to understand, my Bangla was useless. I would have to rely on Girindra's English — for despite my four years of university education and access to the libraries of Harvard, Girindra's foreign language skills, learned thirty years earlier in a grade school made of mud, were far better than my own.

"Please, can you tell me what happened with this tiger accident?" I asked in English.

Girindra looked at me as if trying to pry the sense of my words from my eyes. He drew hard on his bidi, perhaps to inhale coherence.

"No idea," he said.

I rubbed my head. Dianne rolled her blue eyes upward. "Never," she said, "have I seen anyone work so hard and prepare so carefully to achieve so little."

Girindra, a hospitable host, hated to see his guests disappointed. As if to cheer us up, he offered, "My uncle, tiger accident."

"Your uncle, tiger accident?" I asked, almost in disbelief.

"*Three* uncle, tiger accident."

Rather than ask questions I simply listened.

"Little uncle, I," he said. "I luke. Wood collection, two man, uncle, I." Warming to his story, Girindra began to gesture: he showed how they had dropped anchor and waded ashore and chopped the wood with their axes. The team had to hurry, he explained, for they did not have permits. The veins stood out on the insides of his strong arms as he mimed, straining with the exertion of gathering the wood again. Then he straightened up and, sucking air into his slender chest, boomed: "Tiger come!" Then softly, with a wave of his wrist, "Uncle go."

My God, what a story, we whispered.

When, I asked Girindra, had this happened?

"Yesterday."

❖

We arrived at Netidhopani watchtower about nine. A shallow rainwater pond, fringed with palms, lies about two hundred yards from the wooden tower. Beyond the pond looms a temple ruin, an oversized anthill of tumbledown red bricks overgrown with trees and stumps. A billboard erected by the Forest Department perches atop the bricks, reminding me oddly of a Howard Johnson's. "Netidhopani Temple" announces the sign, depicting a white, domed, pillared building by a blue sea. A cobra rears in the foreground, and a white-robed priest sits on a canopied float on the sea.

Here people once came to worship Manasa, the four-armed goddess of snakes. The serpent is the Hindu symbol of water, the life force of a region reliant on monsoon rains. The snakes bring the rains, many Hindus believe: although you can see snakes at any time, they appear in greater numbers right before and during the monsoon. Many kinds, including the cobra, hatch just before the rainy season, and the monsoons drive snakes from their holes.

In India snakes kill thousands of people each year, yet the reptiles are honored and loved. Vishnu, slumbering on the fathomless ocean, reclines on Annata, the serpent, whose body is endless; sometimes a seven-headed cobra is pictured, its seven hoods spread to canopy Vishnu's sleeping face. Snakes are considered a manifestation of the god Shiva, whose symbol — the life-giving phallic lingam — they resemble. (According to the American herpetologist Sherman Minton, in the nineteenth century along India's Malabar Coast, women tried to get cobras to enter their vaginas as a way of welcoming and worshiping Shiva.)

The goddess Manasa looks after these deadly, life-bringing creatures and also protects people from their poison. It is said that worship of Manasa was implemented by a merchant named Chand Saudagar. At first he refused to worship her, so she ordered snakes to kill six of his sons. Only one son, the handsome Lakindor, remained, and on the night of Lakindor's wedding, Manasa sent a snake to kill him too. Behula, Lakindor's bride, refused to cremate her husband's body. Instead she took the body with her on a river raft to heaven, where she delighted the gods with a spectacular dance. Her grace won her a boon. She begged Manasa to bring her husband and brothers-in-law back to life, which the goddess did. Thereafter Chand Saudagar, his family restored, worshiped Manasa daily with offerings of milk and sweets.

The worshipers have abandoned Netidhopani Temple, leaving its bricks to the snakes. But in Sundarbans, as throughout India, people still worship Manasa and believe deeply in her powers. That is why those who die of snakebite are not cremated. The bodies are sent downriver on a raft — where, perhaps, Manasa may grant them, too, resurrection.

Ruins scattered through the region testify that Sundarbans once sustained many grand temples, evidence of vanished wealth. When the European traveler Ralph Fitch journeyed to Sundarbans in 1586 he found "fertile land, lofty houses, to withstand storms and tidal waves." The remains of a walled city covering two and a half square miles, perhaps dating from the fourth century, were recently discovered at a site to the north called Chandraketugarth. There Indian archaeologists have unearthed the sites of temples and monasteries, found elaborate pottery, and discovered gold, silver, and copper coins. They believe this now-desolate tract was once a flourishing international port.

Today the freshwater rivers that nourished that city have dried up, as has much of Sundarbans. Once the mangrove forests stretched nearly from the outskirts of today's Dacca to modern Calcutta. Even as recently as 1895, surveyors reported the undivided Sundarbans stretching for 7,722 square miles, twice its present-day size.

Over the last six centuries the land has dried, shrunk, and tilted, cut off from its freshwater rivers by siltation, settlement, and the slow, restless heavings of the earth. The geological structures underlying the Bengal Basin are sinking, tilting the Gangetic delta from west to east. The holy Ganges, in her rush to join Vishnu's ocean in the Bay of Bengal, has shifted progressively eastward since the seventeenth century. Two decades ago the Farakka Barrage, constructed 155 miles north of Calcutta to improve the Hooghly River's flow through the city, severed what remained of India's direct connection between the Ganges and Sundarbans; today in the Indian Sundarbans only the river Thakuran regularly receives fresh water from the Hooghly upstream; the Harinbhanga River receives fresh water from Bangladesh in the east. In Bangladesh only the river Baleswar brings the Ganges' fresh water to Sundarbans. And as the region's human population has exploded — Calcutta alone supports 9 million people — cultivation and construction have further clogged those rivers with more silt. Sundarbans grows ever saltier.

The process was well under way by the time François Bernier visited this area at the close of the seventeenth century. Silt already clogged the channels, and fields formerly nourished with fresh water succumbed to ocean-drowned forest. "At present, there are seen in the north of Ganges so many fine sites quite deserted," Bernier wrote, "which were formerly well-peopled, and where no other inhabitants are found but wild beasts and specially tigers."

Until midafternoon, we watched and waited at Netidhopani tower. Never did the tigress or her cubs appear, though we could see, through our binoculars, her footprints in the mud.

When had she come here last? Where were her cubs? Had she lapped the water in the light of the half moon, under the sparkling stars? Had she come to refresh herself from noon's heavy glare? Or had she been hunting the other creatures who came to the waterhole — the chital, the wild boar, the jungle fowl? Had people seen her?

The pugmarks by the water, like the bricks of the crumbling temple, testified unintelligibly to a creator, vanished.

❖

We often had the feeling we had just missed seeing something. A flash of movement, and we would turn our heads and see only a hole in the mud, down which a hermit crab had just scuttled, or perhaps a mudskipper, a little fish that sometimes climbs trees. Both creatures are exactly the color of the mud.

When we visited the shrine to Bonobibi, the forest goddess, right next to Sajnekhali Tourist Lodge, it looked as if we had just missed a *puja*, an act of worship. The Forest Department had built the shrine at the Mangrove Interpretation Center, right next to the captive python exhibit. Beneath its thatched roof a crechelike circle of clay beings posed, frozen in a moment of a wordless play: a small, blindfolded boy rode a crocodile's back; two honey collectors reached up to a fat comb in a tree; a mustached warrior in pointed shoes raised his club. Daksin Ray, the tiger god, was depicted as a handsome, bare-chested man with bloodshot eyes, riding on a tiger. At center stage, in a pink sari trimmed with silver lace, beautiful Bonobibi sat on her throne, her right hand upraised in the gesture of granting a boon. At her feet sticks of incense had recently smoldered; freshly plucked red hibiscus lay wilting in the sun. Earlier in the day someone had prayed here, begging protection from the tiger.

We saw the footprints of tigers everywhere. At the entrance to the Sudhanyakhali watchtower, only a ten-minute boat ride from the tourist lodge, pugmarks ringed the chain-link-fenced walkway. Here a tiger had patrolled, inhaling human scent. What had he thought of us? He knew so much more of us than we knew of him. Perhaps he had watched us as we stared blindly at the forest with our binoculars. Surely he knew who had come and gone here, and when. Perhaps he recognized the boats that regularly passed by the sounds of their motors (as dogs and owls recognize the neighborhood cars in American suburbs). From our scent the tiger probably knew we were foreign and female; he may have known something of our ages, perhaps even the phase of our reproductive cycles. Sifting scent through chemical sensors in the roof of the mouth exposed in the grimacing, sneerlike gesture known as *flehmen,* a tiger knows these things about his neighboring tigers and tigresses. But about the tiger we knew nothing.

Often we saw where a tiger had crossed a river: footprints leading out of the forest into the water and then, across the channel, tracks leading out of the water into the forest. Once we spotted the tracks of three tigers who had all come out of the forest at once. They had swum about five hundred feet across the river and then, claws extended, hauled their wet bodies from the water. We could see where the water had sheeted off their fur, rendering the mud more sodden. Their pugmarks, four inches deep, were perhaps ten minutes old.

"Bagh kothai?" I would ask Girindra daily, almost as a running joke: "Tiger, where?"

"You luke, tiger no come," he answered playfully. "You no luke, tiger come."

He was right, of course. The reason we were seeing no tigers is that tigers do not want to be seen. So they make themselves invisible. Once I asked a shaman how he knew the tiger was a supernatural animal, and he replied with an observation many scientists have reported: everyone knows the tiger is magical, he said, because it can disappear behind a blade of grass and materialize from nowhere. The tiger expert Charles McDougal reported such an experience, a moment that gave his fine book, *The Face of the Tiger,* its name. Sitting in a clearing atop a small plateau in the Indian state of Orissa, he was keeping vigil in the moonlight next to a buffalo he thought had been slain by a leopard. He was hoping the leopard would return to the kill, but it had not, and he was considering leaving. Then "I suddenly registered a great head appear over the top of the bushes to my right at the edge of the clearing. It stood so tall that for a second or two it made no sense, seeming almost like something supernatural." At first, even though the night was clear, the creature nearby, and McDougal then a professional hunter, *he did not know what it was.* "Then," he wrote, "the head resolved itself into that of a very big tiger."

From nothingness, a head; from a head, the face of a tiger. The Sanskrit word for "it is" also means "it becomes"; the word for "world" is a modification of the word "to move." That the world is transitory is well known in India.

Nowhere is this more obvious than in Sundarbans: whatever you are now looking at was, just moments ago, something else. A log becomes a crocodile. A lump of mud becomes a crab and climbs a tree. Kingfishers and bee-eaters come to life from leaves: from the drab olive foliage they burst blue, turquoise, orange, red, black. The transformation is like time-lapse photography of a New England autumn. Summer leaves, though they appear green, hold a rainbow of colors — autumn's golds and oranges are carotenes always present, but in summer they are masked by green chlorophyll.

But what is the *real* color of the leaves? As a child I was once told that our blood is really blue, like the blue veins of our wrists; we only *think* blood is red because it turns color during a chemical reaction with the air. At the time I wondered how to test if this were true; I could think of no way to examine blood without exposing it to air. Unless blood is exposed to air, I thought then, we can't see it at all.

Perhaps this is what happens to the birds here: perhaps it is the act of joining the air that calls forth their colors; perhaps the rest of the time the birds are really all green, and the leaves, though disguised by chlorophyll, are really the color of plumage.

❖

After only a few days in Sundarbans, you can feel its eerie magic stalking you. The water follows you onto land: at night, in the tourist lodge, you still feel the waves beneath you, the way the touch of your beloved lingers, even in his absence, on your skin. The day follows you into night: you wake repeatedly, surfacing like a turtle, as if on waves of sleep. And the night follows you into dawn. When you wake, your dreams cling like spider webs — translucent, gossamer, spun from the body of a many-legged creature, an alien who shares the same planet. Each morning, although I could still feel my dreams, could remember their shape and sound, I could not remember the words or their meaning. It was as if I were dreaming in a language I could not understand.

Often, it is said, we hear the voices of gods in our dreams. (I asked a shaman why gods choose to speak to us through dreams. "It is more graceful," he told me.) In sleep, perhaps, gods may reveal to us that which, awake, we cannot face.

But as gods reveal, so do they conceal. The great Indologist Heinrich Zimmer pointed out in his writings that along with creation, destruction, maintenance, and granting of favors, the Hindus honor concealment as one of the "five activities of eternal energy." Because so much is concealed, our world is masked; it is an illusion, a trick, a display. The Hindu mystics call this phenomenon *Maya*. The Maya of the gods is their power to assume diverse shapes, displaying various aspects of their essence. Maya is why Hinduism needs so many gods to depict the divine, eternal energy. (A forest guard at Buxa Tiger Reserve used this example to try to explain Hinduism's pantheon. "It is like the color white," he told me: "all our gods are one god, like white holds all colors at once.") The gods themselves are productions of the greater Maya that makes the universe.

Maya, then, is Hinduism's holy mystery. The Bengali saint Ramakrishna used the following parable to illustrate the nature of Maya. An ascetic, Naranda, won the grace of Vishnu and was invited to ask of the god a boon. He asked to see Vishnu's Maya. God and man walked together for a while, and when the god became thirsty he asked Naranda to fetch him a drink of water. Naranda went to a house to ask for water. A beautiful woman opened the door. He looked into her eyes and immediately forgot what he had come for. He fell deeply in love.

Naranda felt immediately at home at the young woman's house, and when he asked her parents for her hand in marriage, they cheerfully agreed. The couple lived happily in the home of the parents for twelve years; three children were born. When Naranda's father-in-law died, he took over as head of the household, farming the paddy and tending the cattle. But one year the monsoon was exceptionally violent. Floods threatened to carry away the straw huts, the cattle, the people; everyone in the hamlet fled. Naranda took his wife by the hand, guided his two children with the other, and bore his youngest child on his shoulder as they set out to seek shelter from the storm. But the swirling flood waters were too strong: he stumbled, and his youngest child fell from his shoulder. He let go of his other children to catch the smallest, but to no avail; all three were carried away by the current. And then the torrent tore his wife's hand from his, and Naranda himself was swept beneath the waves.

He was washed up on a shore, and when he opened his eyes, there, still waiting for his drink of water, was Vishnu. Asked the god, "Do you now comprehend the nature of my Maya?"

Like Naranda, the visitor to Sundarbans loses track of time and unknowingly crosses the boundaries between the real and unreal, the natural and supernatural. Dreaming and waking, on land and on water, I wandered, lost, in a landscape peopled with gods and animals unseen, a character in a story told in a language I could not understand.

❖

We spent our days wandering, offering our presence to whatever might choose to show itself to us. Some days we had a destination in mind, a place Rathin or Bonani or Kalyan had mentioned. Other times we asked Girindra to choose. He would think, and then announce: "My decision, always follow!"

One day he took us to visit Gosaba. Worlds removed from the forest, the village is orderly and smooth, with spreading rain trees and palms laden with coconuts. Curly-tailed yellow dogs sleep in courtyards, chickens scuttle, and women nurse their babies and carry earthen jugs curved into their hips and waists as they pad on red-painted soles through their golden rice paddies. The littlest children are often naked but seldom unadorned: the smallest girls' ears and nostrils are pierced with jewelry, and their eyes are often outlined with black *kohl,* which is said to keep them cool. The little boys wear metal amulets tied around their waists with string. When Girindra wore his lungi, I could see he also wore an amulet on a string tied around his waist, and I asked him what was in it. He said he didn't know; "My mother know," he said.

We met his strong, toothless mother, in whose honor he had named his beloved boat. One day Girindra took us to his immaculate mud house in Jamespur, the village across the river from the tourist lodge. We met his beautiful wife, Namita, a graceful, round woman with a lovely shy smile. Until their youngest was born four years ago, she had borne a child every two years for the past sixteen.

We visited the shrine to Bonobibi in his village too. Here, as at the shrine near the tourist lodge, someone had only recently burned fresh incense, both at the goddess's feet and at the clawed feet of Daksin Ray. When Girindra stood in front of the shrine, he pressed his palms together, raised them to his forehead, and quietly muttered, "Ma."

We saw wonders everywhere we went: troops of pink-faced macaques materialized from trees; dainty chital tiptoed around the spiked pneumatophores; a twenty-foot-long crocodile heaved her armored bulk from a mud bank and, like a soul leaving a body, slid into watery weightlessness; nighttime fogs dissolved the moon.

Each evening, as we returned from the forest, Girindra would sit between Dianne and me on *Mabisaka*'s white bench and sing — less to us, I felt, than to the night itself, a night so black sometimes that it seemed to swallow even the stars. The song swelled like a wave, subsided, then swelled again. I didn't understand the words, of course, but I recognized their shape, for I had felt them in my dreams: pleading, calling, searching. He cast each note into the night as a fisherman casts his net into muddy water, the voice of longing, of loneliness laid bare, in the face of Mystery.

❖

One day we traveled two hours north to Bagna, an area Rathin had told us was particularly "infested" with tigers. Once we got there Girindra refused to take the *Mabisaka* down the narrow channels without an armed Forest Department guard. "Yesterday, big tiger accident here," he told us.

But no guard would accompany us; because of public anger over the destruction of the mosque at Ayodhya, a national strike day had been declared, and no one was working. We decided to cruise the larger river, combing the banks with our binoculars.

Along one mud bank, at a distance of perhaps a thousand yards, we saw a huddled mass of white and brown. We approached, straining to see through our field glasses. What was it? A heap of fishing net? A pile of sticks? The remains of a crumpled sail?

By ten in the morning the glare on the water was so severe it took on weight, like fog. Even with our binoculars it was difficult to make out details, for along with the image they magnified also the blurring vibrations of *Mabisaka*'s motor.

At five hundred yards we could see a white swatch stretched over a third of the mass, draped like a sari. Other than this, the object was mostly brown. Now we could make out its size and shape. It was fairly large: about as big as a person on his side, folded up for sleep. At one end was a bloated purple oval about the size of a human head.

And then we could see, in areas not covered by the white swatch, gleaming bright against the surrounding brown skin, ribs.

We braced ourselves to see the face.

The boat reeled to approach the body, closer and closer. Still we couldn't see. The flesh was crawling with flies. We peered down at the corpse. Only when we were close enough to scare away the flies could we see it clearly.

It was a cow. The white swatch was a sheet of mesentery, the purple oval its rumen.

❖

In Sundarbans, what seems benign often turns out to be sinister; what first appears sinister turns out to be benign.

As we were leaving Bangladesh for India, our friend Hasna had arranged for a car to take us to Zia Airport. Near dusk a driver and his companion (there always seem to be two men in every cab; one to drive, the other to fix it) picked us up at our room. As the sky grew darker, along a lonely stretch of highway, where no gas station or shop or tea stand could be found, the driver inexplicably pulled off the road. "This is the part where we get robbed and murdered," Dianne noted beneath her breath. She began fishing around in her purse for her Mace. At the driver's signal, his companion opened the glove compartment. What he pulled out we couldn't see. Then the driver opened the door, and the two men got out.

It was a prayer mat. They had pulled over to say evening prayers.

And so it was with Girindra. At first we didn't trust him. In Calcutta we had heard that Sundarbans boatmen try to cheat you: they tell you a day out on their boat costs three hundred rupees (about eleven dollars), but by the end of the day they've jacked up the price to a thousand, including extra petrol and the rice and dahl they cooked for your lunch, they claim. So at first, at the end of each day, when we paid our three hundred rupees, we asked Girindra to sign a paper attesting that he had been paid. Even after his honesty was obvious, we still had him walk us to our little room at the tourist lodge, where he would happily smoke one of Dianne's India Kings, chat a bit, and then sign the paper — a ritual display of his achievement, for he did not sign with a thumbprint but would write "G. Mridha" in Roman cursive.

He had learned some English in grade school. To better communicate with us, each night after he dropped us off and went home, he would study a paperback phrase book by lantern light. (Once he brought it with him and showed it to us. I looked up "Animals" and found, listed among the tiny handful of mammals whose English names the authors felt its readers should know, the zebra and hippo — animals found nowhere in India, but creatures, the book's authors imagined, that English-speaking foreigners might bring up in conversation.)

Still, we had relatively few words in common, so Girindra used each one variously, like a Swiss army knife. "Big" meant "rich," "older," and "many" as well as "large." "Luke" meant "look," as in "search for," and also "watch" and "see." "Black" meant "angry," but it also meant "illegal" — people who cut wood or fished without permits were engaged in "black collection." Another word he often used, "his-story," did not mean history at all, as we use it in the West, but rather expressed a more Eastern view: "My his-story" meant "*My* version of the story is . . ." When he asked, "You his-story?" he was asking for your opinion on the same matter.

And so I slowly came to realize that "yesterday" — when Girindra's younger uncle was killed, when the pole was planted in the bank, when the accident occurred at Bagna — was a word equally elastic. It meant "sometime in the past."

"Yesterday," Girindra revealed, his parents came from Khulna district, in what is now the Bangladeshi Sundarbans, to the Indian side, and here, about forty years ago (he was never very specific on his age), Girindra was born. "Yesterday" — shortly after his father died, when Girindra was still a child — he began to help his mother earn money to support the family. He had worked as a fisherman, a woodcutter, a honey collector, a boatman.

"Yesterday" he married his beautiful Namita, built their home, started a family. "Yesterday" they lived between the house Namita's parents had built and the house shared by Girindra's four uncles. And "yesterday" all but one of those uncles had died in the jaws of the tiger.

The tiger had nearly got Girindra too. He had been standing quite near his youngest uncle when the tiger leaped out of the forest and took the young man away in its jaws. Another yesterday Girindra had docked *Mabisaka* in order to run back to his house briefly; when he returned to his boat he found a tiger waiting for him on the bank. He turned and fled.

Once, as Girindra was fishing with two companions, he chanced to look up and saw a tiger flying toward him through the air. But the tiger miscalculated; Girindra leaped overboard and escaped.

Why, I asked him, was he so lucky?

"Goddess," he said, bowing his head and touching his right hand to his forehead. "Goddess always, I luke."

❖

One afternoon our explorations brought us down a little channel. We had been down so many others, which at first looked just like this one: mud banks and hental palm, dhundul, genwa . . .

But this channel felt different. It was low tide, and the banks loomed two meters over our heads; that night would be the full moon. The holes made by scuttling little hermit crabs gaped like craters. The pneumatophores, earlier such metaphors of desire, now seemed menacing and daggerlike, suggesting tombstones, upraised spears. The boat's sputtering motor, once comforting, now suggested a heart about to stop.

The tiger would know well the map of this creek, would know exactly where to meet our boat, if he chose. The sound of the motor would be calling him.

Other than the motor there was no sound. We saw not one animal or bird. Even the water, it seemed, had run away. For the first time I was frightened. I looked at Dianne and knew that she was too. In his blue checkered lungi, Girindra sat cross-legged in the front of the boat, back erect, brave.

The channel narrowed to about the width of *Mabisaka*. Suddenly Girindra shared our fear. "This very risk," he announced. "This way not go." Sonaton tried to turn the boat around. But as he tried to turn, *Mabisaka* became stuck in the mud bank.

Girindra and Sonaton pushed at the banks with bamboo poles. They tried repositioning the boat by pulling on overhanging branches of a *posur* tree. But first Girindra handed me the machete and Dianne an axe. We stood back to back on the deck — emulating the effect of the face masks that forest workers wore on the back of their heads.

It took three minutes to push free.

We never saw the tiger. But we were sure it was watching us.

We were never that frightened again. We were not worried when we traveled in country boats, the low-riding, motorless wood and reed crafts the fishermen paddle down the channels. Girindra was not eager to let us ride in one, for a tiger can easily outswim a country boat with only one man rowing, and leap aboard. But Girindra was careful, and in the country boat we stuck to the larger waterways, far from the forests.

On *Mabisaka*, he said, we would be safe so long as we did not get stuck in a mud bank again. So on another day we ventured again into a small creek. This time we felt confident. We did not bother to look behind us, only ahead. At the end of the short creek, we had no trouble turning around.

When we did, we were astonished. Almost immediately we saw fresh pugmarks along one bank. They had not been there five minutes before.

Here the tiger had emerged from the water. We had just missed seeing it. We looked for the pugmarks on the opposite bank, where we assumed it had begun its swim across. But we saw none.

We retraced our route. We had first come down a larger channel before turning to explore the little creek. Back up the larger channel we went, looking carefully for fresh footprints.

And here, a few dozen yards from where we had turned to enter the creek, we saw them. Here, shortly after our boat had passed, a tiger had come out of the forest and melted into the water. Here it had swum down the channel and turned down the creek, as we had.

Less than five minutes before, a tiger had swum after our boat.

The Sacred Breath of God

❖ ❖ ❖ ❖ ❖ ❖ ❖ ❖ ❖ ❖ ❖ ❖ ❖ ❖ ❖ ❖ ❖ ❖ ❖ ❖

HUNTED BY A TIGER.

So seldom do we Westerners think of our own flesh as meat. So seldom do we consider ourselves another being's food. So seldom do we dare think that a clawed predator could stalk us, kill us with its face, chew our meat from our bones.

Surely the idea surfaces periodically from the sea of our unconscious, the way a sea turtle surfaces to breathe — but when it does, we are not looking. Like the turtles unseen beneath the sea, like the crocodile submerged in the tea-colored water, like the tiger invisible behind a blade of grass, the fear lurks large though hidden, so frightful we dare not even utter its name.

Early in his career my friend Dr. Richard Estes (who is now a world-renowned expert on antelopes) worked on a wildlife survey in Burma. For two nights he was forced to camp in an area where a man-eating tiger was known to range. The first night, as Dick was hunting the big sambar deer for dinner, the back of his neck prickled; he felt that he was being hunted too. The next night he woke at three A.M. to find the flames of his fire, the only guard at his thin tent, had gone out. He rebuilt it and slept, but at daylight, when he woke, he saw that his tent was encircled with the footprints of a tiger. Dick, then in his twenties, does not remember feeling terror so much as indignity. A tiger had considered eating him, and he recalls thinking, "Doesn't this tiger know *who I am?*"

But of course the tiger knows exactly who we are.

At the Sajnekhali Mangrove Interpretation Center, a photo in one of the small wooden buildings is captioned "tiger accident victim." The photo shows a small brown man lying on the mud, coiled like a prawn. His belly and back are ripped open; his intestines boil out through his lower back. (Rathin once examined the corpse of a man similarly injured: "The intestines came out through the wound like bulbs, like sacs full of pain," he said.) When Dianne and I first arrived, we looked at that photo and thought: not me, not me.

We live in a land where our ancestors felled the forests and eradicated the predators so that we could pretend we are not made of meat.

But the tiger knows this is not true. For beneath our professions and our words, beneath our culture and our clothing — beneath our very skin — we are still, we are always, as we have been since the creation of our kind, prey in the mind and the jaws of the tiger.

It is a truth we remember in our childhood dreams of monsters lurking in the dark. The ancestors of the tigers, the leopards, stalked our progenitors from the Pliocene through the Pleistocene; their fearsome cousins, the saber-toothed tigers, with curved, stabbing canine teeth as long as a woman's forearm, hunted us for eons. This fact, like our instinctive fear of falling — legacy of our tree-dwelling ancestors — we cannot even now completely forget. Though we may work in steel-boned skyscrapers, though we can conceive children in test tubes, though our scientists have invented chemical substitutes for human blood — still, in our darkest dreams, monstrous predators hunt us in the night.

Perhaps the tiger who followed our boat was merely curious.

Perhaps it just happened to choose the same route as we. Or perhaps the tiger was hunting us. We can't know. What we do know is that if the tiger had chosen us, our entrails, too, would have been pulled from our bellies, and our bones would have yielded up their marrow. Opening our bodies with its teeth, the tiger exposes the truth that we in the West try to ignore: we are all — chital and boar, frog and fish, astronaut and beggar — made of meat.

The people of Sundarbans, though, understand. But they understand as well that beneath our meat lies the sacred breath of God.

❖

With the help of young Sonaton and two forest guards, Girindra began to build a tiny shrine beneath a *piara baen* tree at the edge of the water hole at Sudhanyakhali watchtower.

We had come many times to this watchtower. Each visit was a sort of pilgrimage. With Dianne beside me in the crumbling wood and cement structure, perched above the water hole, I had spent many hours silently staring, sweating, waiting. Sometimes we watched wild boar trotting out of the forest: sturdy little army tanks wearing ballerina slippers. We saw delicate chital mince over the pneumatophores; we watched monitor lizards writhe from the water, the tracks of their tails and clawed feet following them. Still we watched and still we waited. I grew increasingly desperate.

For what? For an interpreter to fall from the sky? For Rathin to come bounding out of the forest? For a tree limb to fall on my head, after which I would suddenly understand Bangla?

No less. Wordlessly watching the mangroves, day after day, I awaited a miracle: for Sundarbans to reveal itself to me.

This was part of the reason we had asked Girindra if we might prepare a puja, a worship service, for Sundarbans' forest gods. We wanted, of course, to show our respect for Girindra and his beliefs. We wanted to see how the forest gods are worshiped. But also, although Dianne is agnostic and I am Christian, we both hoped, secretly, in the back of our minds, that Girindra's gods could coax a miracle from the forest.

For many mornings we had climbed up the slippery jetty of wrist-thick *goran* saplings to walk the brick path leading to the watchtower's cement steps. To protect tourists and staff, a chain-link fence encloses the watchtower and its walkways, separating people from the water hole and the tigers who come here to drink. A metal gate stands at the threshold between these two worlds. Now, with Girindra and Sonaton and the three unarmed forest guards, we went out through that gate, stepping over old tiger tracks at the fence's perimeter.

Earlier that morning, at a thatch-covered stall of woven bamboo in Jamespur, we had bought some of the sacred items for the puja. From a five-gallon screw-top jar crawling with ants, Girindra had selected *batasha,* flat, circular white sweets. These, he said, were the favorite sweets of the forest goddess, Bonobibi. He had bought a length of red yarn and two red and gold cellophane necklaces, like cheap Hawaiian leis. Red, the color of our blood, is holy to the Hindus, Girindra explained, and it is a color that very much pleases Daksin Ray, the tiger god.

Girindra also purchased sticks of incense and two small paper wands, each about the size of a bidi, tipped in pink and purple paper and fringed with white string. These Girindra called *latu.* He said they were for Sha Jungli, Bonobibi's brother.

Other than these few items we brought nothing. To build the little shrine, the altar, and the images of the gods, Girindra and his friends relied upon the forest. With a machete one of the guards cut several three-foot stakes from a nearby bush. These would become the beams of the small shrine. A frond from a nearby coconut served as the roof for the structure, lashed to the beams with more coconut leaves. The finished shrine would stand about as tall as a squatting child. Girindra gathered mud from the edge of the water hole for the floor. The men went about their work quietly and smoothly. Although the motions were vastly different, their gentle efficiency reminded me of a mother braiding her child's hair.

About ten minutes after the men began building the shrine, a big male macaque strode out of the forest. Dianne and I remembered the first time we had seen him. After a silent morning waiting on the backless bench in the watchtower with our binoculars plastered to our faces, our vigil had been interrupted by Bengali voices below. We had been horrified to see three forest guards, dressed in lungis, carrying plastic bags, open the gate to the water hole. Through it they strode right to the edge of the water — and there, noisily chatting, they had unpacked shampoo, detergent, and dirty laundry and proceeded, to our astonishment, to wash their hair and their lungis.

"Well," Dianne had said, "we have just spent four hours motionless in the heat in order to observe three Bengalis do their laundry."

We almost left right then, so sure were we that the men had irreparably soiled the motionless silence we had so carefully offered the wildlife we hoped to entice. But just as the men finished their washing and passed through the gate, the big male macaque had appeared hesitantly at the edge of the forest. He entered, oddly enough, from the side of the forest closest to where the men had been washing.

At first the pink-faced male approached the water cautiously. He sipped its surface. Then, at some signal we could not detect, the other macaques appeared: smaller males, one with a missing tail tip; females with long nipples, their babies clinging to the light fur of their bellies; scampering youngsters. We counted thirteen monkeys in all.

They drank; the youngsters chased and chatted; two females climbed a tree and plucked tangerine-sized, hairy fruits, biting off chunks of pale yellow flesh and dropping much of it. The

We often watched for wildlife from the Sudhanyakhali watchtower, which overlooks a dug rainwater pond. To protect tourists and staff, a chain-link fence encloses the watchtower and its walkways, separating people from the water hole and the tigers who come to the pond to hunt and drink.

When we traveled aboard the large government launch *Monorama*, we often woke to misty dawns as the river turned to sky.

On the sand beaches of the Bay of Bengal, you can often see the footprints of a tiger.

When we removed the dead chital from the river, blood was still oozing from the holes a tiger had bitten in her neck. Eleanor felt nearly blinded by the beauty of the doe's body floating on the skin of life and death, the eyes reflecting the blue sky and white clouds.

Above: Aboard *Monorama* Rathin (wearing cap) pores over the map of Sundarbans as he debates the route with Girindra Nath Mridha, at right, and Forest Department staff.

Right: Phoni Guyan, a powerful gunin, bears scars from a tiger attack in 1984. He survived, but the tiger killed another man in the party and carried the body into the forest.

Aboard his hand-hewn boat, *Mabisaka*, Girindra skillfully opens a green coconut without spilling a drop of the sweet liquid.

Girindra illustrated his stories in Bangla with gestures to help me understand.

I could barely speak with Girindra's beautiful wife, Namita, but often we simply held hands. Here she stands with her younger sister, Sobita, at right, and some village children.

Girindra's fourteen-year-old son, Sonaton, offers a puja, or worship service, for *Mabisaka* to ensure the boat's good fortune and offer thanks for its service.

Left: At the Mridhas' mud and thatch compound in Jamespur, relatives gather to repair fishing nets. In the foreground sits four-year-old Mudhushudon, nicknamed Nantu, the youngest of Girindra and Namita's children.

Below: Clay images of honey gatherers adorn the diorama at the puja for Bonobibi, the forest goddess. Gathering honey is the most dangerous job in Sundarbans, but the faithful believe that prayers will induce the tiger god to spare their lives.

As "Lord of the South," the richly ornamented tiger god, Daksin Ray, was said to own all the wealth of Sundarbans; to command armies of crocodiles, demons, and ghosts; and to be able to enter the body of a tiger at will. Now Daksin Ray shares his land and wealth with Bonobibi, and Hindus and Muslims gather at joint shrines to worship both deities.

At Sajnekhali, Bonobibi is adored with offerings of prayer, song, incense, candles, sweets, rice, fruits, and money. At left is part of a diorama depicting the story of the goddess's forest birth: her father, Ibrahim, is about to abandon her mother, Gulalbibi, who sleeps by a tree in the jungle.

Left: Mabisaka ferries Daksin Ray to the puja at Khahtjhuni. Musicians protect the idol on the journey with the sounds of the sacred drum and the cymbal-like *kanshi*. Amarendra Nath Mondal, who translated for me during the puja, is sitting on the white bench; the Brahmin priest who officiated at the puja is seated above him, in white; Girindra stands atop the boat at left.

Below: At the shrine at Khahtjhuni, preparations begin for the Daksin Ray puja. The man at right is painting the double trident of Shiva in vermilion on a clay pot. Daksin Ray will be offered every honor and comfort, including carefully prepared fruits, sweet-smelling incense, welcoming music, pleasing words, and even a refreshing bath.

first tree the monkeys chose to climb stood only five yards from where the men had just left, even though there were other fruiting trees of the same species nearby, and in fact the monkeys later moved on to feed in these.

Why had they come on the very heels of the guards' noisy visit? Dianne immediately understood. The clumsy men — four hundred pounds of meat among the three of them — would have provided an easier target and a bigger meal for a tiger than would the small and agile macaques. From the forest the monkeys had been watching *to see if the men attracted a tiger.* No tiger had appeared to take the easy bait, so the monkeys knew it was safe.

For forty-five minutes the macaques played and fed and chattered all around us, sometimes so close we could see the straw-colored lashes of their pale eyelids. Then they simply dematerialized, dissolving into the forest like salt in the ocean.

Now, as we stood in this clearing by the edge of a tiger forest, we were very glad to see the big male macaque again. Soon he was followed by the rest of the troop. Their appearance showed us that in the opinion of their leader, no tiger was nearby. Had a tiger been lurking, it would have attacked us by now.

The monkeys drank peacefully at the water's edge, less than fifty yards away, even as Girindra and the other men continued to construct the shrine. All of us — monkeys and people — felt safe.

On the shrine's floor of mud, Girindra constructed three mud platforms. On each of these he placed a round ball the size of a baby doll's head. Each mound was then topped with a leaf, like a hat.

The men then washed in the pond and ceremonially purified Dianne and me by sprinkling its water on our heads. A guard lit two sticks of incense and placed them before the two front "pillars" of the shrine.

Girindra laid a shallow carpet of shiny green piara baen

leaves in front of the three mounds. A guard strung the two stubby pieces of latu onto the red string we had bought at Jamespur, then hung it inside the roof of the shrine, the latu dangling like two lanterns. The red and gold lei was placed, carefully and with great reverence, to encircle the three mud balls. On each leaf-topped mound a white sweet was placed, with two for the center one. The bag of remaining sweets was placed inside the shrine.

Everything was prepared: the shrine was ready for its occupants. Girindra spoke softly in Bangla, invoking the gods to enter the balls of mud. Glare poured from the sun like milk from a pitcher.

In much of Western tradition, it is said that Yahweh conjured us from the dust, but here in Sundarbans the relationship is more mutual. Ordinary men conjure gods from the mud.

Hands flat on the ground, Girindra bowed before his gods.

❖

As they wander a magical landscape, even the saints can become confused.

Hindu mythology relates the story of Markandeya, an ancient sage. For thousands of years the sturdy old man happily roams the ideal world inside the body of the sleeping Vishnu. But Vishnu is sleeping with his lips slightly parted; Markandeya unwittingly slips out of the mouth of the god and plunges into the sea upon which the god floats.

Markandeya is horrified to find himself drowning in the dark waters of the cosmic ocean. Hindu teachings tell us the water, too, is Vishnu, as is Annata, the endless serpent upon whom the floating god reclines. Yet to Markandeya the sea seems not the fullness on which a god rests, but nothingness. The world as he has known it is gone. Did it ever exist at all?

But then the forlorn saint spies the giant glowing form of the sleeping god, floating in the waters. Just as Markandeya is about to ask where he is, Vishnu seizes him and swallows him.

The saint finds himself again inside the body of the god — as easily and mysteriously as dreams enter our sleep, as food enters our mouths, as breath enters our lungs.

The universe, the mystics tell us, is more permeable than it seems. The boundaries between man and animal, ghosts and gods are only an illusion, an artifact of the Maya-spell masking the identity of opposites.

All breath sings of the miracle of the permeable world. With each inspiration, it is said, we make the sound "ham"; our exhalations speak "sa." "Ham-sa," we breathe, pronouncing the word for gander — a bird that swims on the surface of the water yet also flies through the air — the mount of Brahma, the four-faced creator-god who springs from the lotus growing from Vishnu's navel. Spoken separately, "ham" means I; "sa" means "this." "Sa-ham," we breathe, proclaiming "This am I." With every breath — as we gather the oxygen that reddens our blood — we speak the name of God alongside our own. With every breath, we draw inside our bodies the inseparable spirit of the Absolute; "the divine essence," writes Heinrich Zimmer, "abides with the individual like the gander gliding on the water."

Here in Sundarbans, where the sea penetrates and enfolds the land and the land penetrates and enfolds the sea, boundaries dissolve easily, like mud in water. Here fish pulled from water dry to the color of sunrise; here the tips of trees put forth birds as well as buds; and so here easily do men made of meat call gods to enter balls of mud.

❖

Into our presence Girindra called three gods: Daksin Ray, the tiger god of the jungle; Sha Jungli, the club-wielding warrior, protector of men; and Bonobibi herself, the forest goddess.

Each of us bowed before them, one after the other. Girindra

spoke softly in Bengali. Kneeling, he touched his right hand to
the forehead, the heart, the top of the head — a sign of
reverence we then imitated. Then, from the carpet of leaves
in front of the gods, each man chose a leaf and selected two
sweets from the bag. Each leaf, with a cargo of sweets, was
floated like a raft on the water at the drinking hole. These were
retrieved, and the now-moist batasha crumbled over each
person's head. Then we ate the rest of the sweets, for they
had become holy. We swallowed them as easily as Vishnu swallowed Markandeya.

Girindra and Sonaton went back to *Mabisaka,* and Dianne
and I returned to the watchtower to collect our things.

At the shop that morning Girindra had bought two cellophane necklaces, but had used only one in the puja. I wondered
what he would do with the other. When Dianne and I returned
to *Mabisaka,* we found it garlanded about her bow. Six batasha
were laid out in a line like buttons along her red bowsprit, and
we could see the remains of a stick of incense wedged into a
seam in the wood.

❖

"Bonobibi, Daksin Ray, Sha Jungli — have they come to you
ever?" I asked Girindra later.

"Yesterday, Bonobibi come," he told me. "Sleep-time, Bonobibi, I luke."

Girindra has seen many things in his dreams: gods in the
form of tigers, tigers in the form of ghosts, ghosts in the form of
animals. In his dreams he has been chased by fantastic creatures
that are not found in real jungles or even in mythology. He has
traveled to parts of the jungle he has never seen. Some of his
dreams, he realizes, are merely sleep-plays, without significant
meaning; others, he is convinced, are visions. And some have
been dark and frightening.

Girindra could not tell me then about these visions. The only
dream simple enough to accommodate our shared language was

this: in the forest Bonobibi came to him, glowing like the moon, and took him in her arms like a mother.

✦

After the puja Girindra seemed visibly bolder. The very next day he decided to take us again to Bagna, the "tiger-infested" area he'd previously feared to explore.

"Bagh kothai?" I joked on our way. "Tiger, where?"

"Shekane bagh ache" — "The tiger is there," he assured. But, he continued in English, "You no luke!"

When we arrived at Bagna, we met with forest ranger M. S. Hazra, who produced an armed guard to accompany us into the small channels of Jhingakhali Block ("Very tiger-infested area," he promised).

As if on a razor's edge, we cruised the waterways, hoping to see a tiger. But in the entire two-hour trip, for the first time since we had journeyed to Sundarbans, we saw no mammals at all.

The guard clung to his ancient Russian-made rifle all afternoon, as if a tiger might leap at us any minute. Dianne and I stared into the forest, trying to make our eyes into x-rays. Bagna's shores are thick with thorny fronds of hental. In these areas the scrub grows so dense the deer are said to get caught in the thickets. The patterns etched by the black voids between the palm leaves look exactly like the stripes of a tiger.

How can a four-hundred-pound tiger hide behind a hole? How can a forest so green camouflage the tiger's blazing orange? These forests form a dark hall of mirrors, each reflecting its opposite, where spaces hide bulk and orange mirrors green, where violence appears unexpectedly beautiful, and beauty turns violent and strange.

All afternoon we saw nothing, yet we returned with deeply unsettled souls.

✦

Listen for the voice of the Absolute: "This am I," sighs the moon-driven surge of the sea; "This am I," promises the white egret in flight; "This am I," says the sun's gold mirrored on the water.

Like Markandeya wandering the ideal world inside Vishnu, you may see peace and power perfected in the ebb and flow of Sundarbans. The mangroves give up their dead leaves to the water with careless cheer. They do not flutter and struggle in the wind like the autumn leaves of northern forests, but detach of their own volition and plunge directly into the water, as if the water, not the branches, were their home. And in the water the leaves indeed enter new incarnations, for here they are transformed, recycled like the souls of men and animals in the great wheel of rebirth.

Even in the mud you may see the glory of the greatest gods. Or you may instead see an orgy of breeding and feeding, in the twine and tangle of the stilt roots, in the mud that greedily devours your skin the way a gourmand sucks a duck bone. And in the boat, with the roll of the water rising beneath you like desire, the sea seems an open mouth, forever licking the land, forever lusting, forever hungry.

In this spirit-drenched tiger forest, the gods are as close as breath, as alien as dreams; what seems at first obscenely obvious may, the next moment, sink from sight or transform itself to its opposite. Looking into these forests is like glancing absently at your own hand and finding in its place a claw.

One morning, as we were heading to Jamespur to buy coconuts, we heard the thud and tap of drums and the nasal call of a flute. On the spine of the mud embankment separating the river from the village, we saw a crowd gathering in festive clothes. Girindra told us it was a wedding. We stopped to watch the couple exchange vows.

Everyone seemed to be watching a beautiful woman wearing a red veil. Draped in a red and gold sari, her tall, sinuous body writhed seductively to the notes of the flute. The men around her grinned broadly. As we approached, we looked at her more closely: she was wearing pink pancake makeup, her eyes outlined in kohl; the long black hair was a wig, and her little round breasts were false. She was a man dressed as a woman. Later, back in Calcutta, Kushal told me the dancer was probably a eunuch. Eunuchs, he said, are also often called upon to bless that other great public celebration of sex, the birth of a first child.

As the dancer twirled to the music, most people were ignoring the three-foot by four-foot palanquin sitting on the dirt, although it had been carefully decorated with crepe paper flowers, colored newsprint, and paper and foil butterflies. We looked inside, and found there, like the prize in a box of Cracker Jack, the bride. You could tell she had been crying for a very long time. Now there were no sobs left, only tears. She looked to be about twelve years old.

She was not a pretty girl; she had a severe overbite and a boxy body that her billowing pink wedding dress did not hide; her red and gold bangles only accentuated the thickness of her wrists. But, to the merry assembly her beauty was in her dark eyes glazed with tears — the height of feminine modesty.

It is considered respectable for the Bengali bride to cry: she is about to leave her home and her village and all she knows and loves, to live with a man she almost certainly did not choose and may never have even seen before. Here, as in most of India, marriages are arranged by the parents of bride and groom. The depth of her sorrow reflects respect for her parents' wishes. "Tomorrow I am going to a new country, where my relatives cannot come," goes one Bengali bride's song, translated by Katy Gardner in *Songs at the River's Edge.* "They will carry me off in my death casket, and I will wear a shroud for my gown."

The groom never looked at the girl he was taking as his wife. The thin young man, just old enough to sprout the soft shadow of a moustache, seemed as terrified as she. Standing stiffly in a neat, white Nehru-collared shirt and cream-colored pants, he was dwarfed beneath a tall, pointed hat, which appeared to be encrusted with ivory carvings. (Later, at a little shop in James-pur, we saw the unadorned wedding hat for sale; it was made of newspaper.)

The bride got out of her palanquin and stood beside him; they joined pinkie fingers and stared at the mud at their feet while words were said over them in Bengali. Then they entered the palanquin and, lifted on the shoulders of their bearers, rid-ing on the good wishes of the gathered crowd, were carried to the wedding boat. Little boys shot off firecracker rockets, drum-beats swelled and the notes of the flute twirled, the boat's motor putted to life, and the couple and the wedding party floated off upon the waters like a sweet batasha on a floating leaf. The bride, still crying, waved to Dianne and me. We wondered later if perhaps she thought we were visiting dignitaries who might somehow save her.

❖

Dianne later discovered that someone in the crowd had unbut-toned a snap on her vest pocket. Had the pickpocket chosen to unzip her money belt, he could have stolen hundreds of rupees, some American dollars, a priceless American passport; instead he had gotten Dianne's little spray can of Mace. We imagined the thief's initial disappointment. Then we imagined his alarm if he tried out the stolen item to discover whether it was, as he probably assumed, perfume — or breath spray. We laughed at this small imagined act of violence; this was storybook justice.

It is the violence of innocents that takes your breath away, for it is always unexpected; one day we watched it unfold at our feet. When Girindra was taking us home from a day in the for-est, he stopped two boatmen and bought crabs from them in ex-change for two of Dianne's cigarettes. From the shallow alu-minum pot in the dark hold of the little country boat, the older of the two men, his head wrapped in a *gamcha,* his feet wrinkled and callused like an elephant's, selected two fat, greenish crabs from the mass of windmilling pincers. He set them on the deck of *Mabisaka.* "Lady and gentleman crab," Girindra announced; he knew because he had once worked as a crab fisherman.

Immediately the male grabbed the female by the eyestalk and pulled off her eye. With his other claw he crushed through the shell of her head. At the same moment, with pincers like pliers, she ripped his right claw from its socket, her eyestalk still clutched in his chitinous grip. Then gentle Girindra, seeing our afternoon snack about to self-destruct, grabbed the crabs, snapped off all their claws and legs, and dumped them, still living, into the water bucket.

Listen for the voice of the Absolute: This am I.

❖

We were returning to Sajnekhali, waiting for the sunset to spill across the sky, when we saw the tiger.

We had spent the whole day on *Mabisaka,* exploring the channels. We had seen a particularly big crocodile, perhaps twenty-one feet long. We had seen pigs and deer. We had passed several poles marking tiger accidents, and again Girindra had tried to tell me what had happened there; again we had concluded our frustrating conversation by apologizing to one another:

"I very sorry not full English have."

"I very sorry I not full Bangla have."

"I very sad."

"I very sad, too."

Dianne had spent much of the day trying to photograph kingfishers. They endlessly play tag with boats; one will burst from its perch, zoom down the river, an arrow of turquoise and white; it alights on a branch overhanging the river, waits for the boat to catch up to it, then flies off again. "I'll get that little bastard yet!" Dianne would vow, letting loose a laugh like a pirate. And then she would squint through her lens and fold up her legs and elbows on the deck — and the shutter would click just as the bird again left its perch.

Girindra cooked us some curried fish for lunch that day. For a later snack, on his clay stove we boiled up a packet of freeze-dried Maritime Pasta Supreme, a treat I had brought from America. Sonaton didn't like it, but once Girindra added green chilies, he pronounced the dish "very nice."

Normally, Girindra ate with his hand, an act of mundane yet alarming grace, a ballet of the fingers and palm. I remembered the first time I had watched our friend Hasna eat this way: with her index finger she would pick up a pad of salt, then with finger bent inward, dab the curry; and then, with thumb and all fingers pressing the food into her palm, she would knead the fish, rice, and dahl until her whole hand, even her gold rings, shone with grease. Eating with the hand adds to the sensory experience of food, Hasna explained. "A Bengali would never dream of eating a traditional dish with knife and fork," she told us; "it wouldn't taste the same." Girindra must have followed this reasoning about Maritime Pasta Supreme; to more fully experience this, his first taste of "American" food, he ate with the spoon he used to stir the dahl.

After lunch we relaxed. Dianne packed away her big lens, Girindra did the dishes. Dianne and I sat on the white bench on *Mabisaka*'s foredeck watching the afternoon light fade, waiting for the sun to melt on the water. We rounded a bend in the river.

Sonaton saw the tiger first. His arm shot forward as he pointed, and he shouted its name as vehemently as a person in a flaming house would yell "FIRE!" "BAGH!" he cried, and then, for our benefit, "TIGER!"

For a second it looked like a rock: a roundish, shadowed object in the middle of the 130-foot-wide river, a rim of white water foaming at its edge. But the rock was moving. The rock was a head — the face of a tiger — and the tiger was swimming across the river, at a right angle to the path of the *Mabisaka*.

The tiger's body was so wet it looked black in the water. But the head was dry, and impossibly colored with flame and coal and cloud. How can any creature look like this? It seemed impossibly big, impossibly powerful; it seemed at least ten feet long. The tiger didn't look at us. To the tiger we were nothing; all that mattered was crossing the river, reaching whatever was drawing it to the other side.

We could see the white spots on the back of the ears. Within ten seconds of our first sighting it, the tiger reached the bank. It climbed out onto the mud, water sheeting off its fur, off its long, curved tail, and slipped into the forest.

Every day I had watched and waited for this moment, for this miracle, waited for Sundarbans to appear, like a god in a vision, in the form of a tiger.

But the tiger's magic was as impenetrable as the forest itself. It took the animal less than two seconds to climb from the water and disappear. Seamlessly it melted into the tangled mangroves — without shaking its coat, without rustling a leaf, without bending a branch. Weightless and bulkless, invisible as breath, the tiger evaporated into the forest.

Tiger Tracer

❖ ❖ ❖ ❖ ❖ ❖ ❖ ❖ ❖ ❖ ❖ ❖

MANY RESEARCHERS, including some who know tigers well, would say that the tigers of Sundarbans are not real.

Of course, no one denies there are tigers here, with so many pugmarks stamped everywhere in the sand and the mud. But tigers who swim after boats to prey on people? Tigers who fly through the air? Tigers who before men's eyes grow to twice their normal size? Tiger gods who must be propitiated with prayers and incense? These are the tigers that the people of Sundarbans know, and Western science says that such beings cannot exist: they are impossible. How can a swimming tiger rocket out of deep water onto the deck of a boat? How can a big mammal survive drinking nothing but salt water? How can an animal weighing up to five hundred pounds leap aboard a ten-foot wooden boat without rousing the entire crew? It's as impossible as materializing from thin air.

But even impeccable sources report that the tigers of Sundarbans do not behave like the tigers at well-studied research sites.

George Schaller's studies at Kanha and the Smithsonian project at Chitawan confirm that tigers typically hunt at night. That tigers evolved as night-hunters is mirrored in the *tapetum lucidum,* the light-gathering crystals of the retina, which cause their golden eyes to glow green in the moonlight, red in the beam of a torch. By daylight a tiger's vision is considered to be about as sharp as a person's, but at night, when the deer are most active, the tiger's eyes are stronger than ours by sixfold.

During the glare and heat of the day, tigers typically prefer to rest, especially if the night's hunt was productive. Often they "lie up" under cover next to the night's gnawed-over kill. Chitawan researchers found that during the hot season (March to May), if they were able to locate a tiger by midmorning, they would find it in the same place one to six hours later, 82 percent of the time. Even in the cool season, when tigers are most active, the researchers could count on finding the tiger in the same spot one to six hours later well over half the time.

But Sundarbans tigers, by all accounts, hunt at least as often by day as by night. In fact, they seem to prefer to hunt people by day. When Kalyan Chakrabarti analyzed estimated times of death of people killed by tigers in Sundarbans, 80 percent of the reported casualties occurred during daylight hours, he claimed.

Fishermen, guides, and forest guards say that time of day matters little to the creatures of Sundarbans; water is what matters. Low tide spreads the water's offerings like a banquet on the mud, drawing the chital, the monkeys, the wild boar, the jungle fowl, even the monitor lizards to investigate. This is the best time to see animals in Sundarbans, and no one knows this better than the tigers. So they hunt by the tides, careless of day or night.

Tigers everywhere can swim, and they enjoy water; in the hot season tropical tigers often rest in a cool stream. But in Sundarbans the tigers are as at home in water as on land. They are considered *completely amphibious* — the term appears again and again in the scant scientific literature about them.

Many normally land-bound creatures swim here. Monitor lizards, relatives of Komodo dragons, are excellent swimmers — at first sight they can be mistaken for crocodiles. The deer swim. The pigs swim. Even the monkeys swim. It is often said that monkeys and apes cannot swim — not even orangutans, our orange-coated cousins, who often wade in Indonesian swamps — but on one of our first days out with Girindra, we saw a rhesus macaque dog-paddling across a channel, a sight so strange Dianne and I could not even imagine that it was a monkey until the boat was almost on top of the animal.

Sundarbans tigers are strong, swift swimmers. Rathin told me he'd once clocked a tiger who swam 1,800 feet, against the current, in seven minutes, eighteen seconds. Rathin, lying on his belly on the bow of the boat, with his face and camera overhanging the swimming tiger, had ordered the launch to circle the animal; the tiger, he said, reared up out of the water, a full six inches higher than its swimming position, to snarl and hiss at him. Rathin says that the tail of the Sundarbans tiger is more muscular and consistently thicker at the base than that of other tigers; he says they use it as a limb for swimming, in the sinuous, sweeping, side-to-side manner of the crocodile.

Sundarbans tigers may even hunt in the water. No one knows, for no one has recorded seeing a Sundarbans tiger kill anything but a member of the observer's own party. These tigers do love fish, though, and their scats sometimes glitter with silvery scales. But they could also hunt fish from the shoreline, as do Sundarbans' little-known fishing cats, who bat fish from the water with their odd, nonretractable claws.

Sundarbans tigers may also differ from tigers elsewhere in the way they feel about territory. Both Schaller and the Smithsonian's Mel Sunquist found that the tigers they studied literally owned property: in the scientists' words, they maintained "a land tenure system based on prior right." All the tigers in their studies observed this rule: occupancy confers rights to an area, and these rights are respected by all for several years, if not for the life of the resident. At the study sites the range of each tiger or tigress is not shared by any other adults of the same sex, although a tiger's territory may overlap those of three to six tigresses. Female offspring may inherit their mother's range.

Resident tigers do not defend or patrol their land per se, the Kanha and Chitawan studies showed. Instead, residents spend a great deal of time and effort advertising their presence: they etch their claw marks deep into the bark of trees. They leave neat piles of dung in prominent spots — often on a road. With tail held high, they spray urine backward onto tree trunks and tall tufts of grass. David Smith likens the scent to that of buttered popcorn. Schaller learned to detect the smell even three months after it was first sprayed, though resident tigers are careful to refresh their scent every few weeks.

If a territory is unused for a month, other tigers consider it vacant and may move in. For this reason, a resident will visit most parts of its range every few days to every two weeks. These travels, Sunquist stressed, are not always hunting expeditions: the tigers include in their ranges "nonproductive" areas, like *sal* forest, where they are unlikely to find meat. Tigers use these areas as buffer zones between their own and other residents' land, and as access corridors to other parts of their territory.

Similar land tenure systems have been documented in mountain lions, jaguars, leopards, bobcat, and lynx — all of whom, like tigers, although acutely aware of one another's identities and activities, spend most of their time alone.

But Sundarbans tigers' territories, if they exist at all, may be completely different. About half of the area is under water. Can an amphibious cat own water as well as land? If so, how would one declare ownership? About this we know nothing.

Some of Sundarbans Tiger Reserve's experts feel strongly that these tigers do not maintain territories at all. Pranabesh Sanyal points out that in vast portions of the lands they roam, the scent and scats tigers use to tag their territories would be washed away daily by the tides. Others, like Kalyan, say that Sundarbans tigers *are* territorial. He says they carefully scent-mark only those areas they know will not be inundated by high tide. Still others suggest that these tigers may be hyperterritorial. The constant washing away of their scent-marking, in fact, could account for their extraordinary aggression toward intruders.

"The Sundarbans is a peculiar place, very unlikely tiger habitat," notes Peter Jackson, the World Conservation Union–IUCN cat specialist. He visited Sundarbans in 1986 to make a film with the BBC. He saw only one tiger there — it came to drink at a watchtower water hole at dusk — but, he says, these animals do seem different from the many dozens of tigers he has observed elsewhere in India and other parts of Asia. "Obviously these tigers must have been cut off from tigers in other habitats by the destruction of local forests for many, many years." Evolving in isolation, this group may have established — or preserved — a system of behavior, a culture, different from that of all other tigers on earth.

But no one knows. No formal long-term studies have ever been attempted here. No one knows how far the tigers range. No one knows how long they live. No one even knows how many there are. For the methods that have served science so well at Kanha and Chitawan simply do not apply in Sundarbans.

❖

When I was planning my first trip to Sundarbans, I asked George Schaller what he thought of the place. As part of a brief comparative study to complement his Kanha data, he had visited Sundarbans for three days. He had immediately rejected it as a study site, he said; it was too densely forested to spot tigers, much less follow them. "Don't go there," he told me, wrinkling his nose and frowning. "You won't see any tigers in Sundarbans. If you want to see tigers, go to Kanha."

This I did. Shortly after arriving in Calcutta, and before our trip to the Indian side of Sundarbans, Dianne and I traveled to the site of Schaller's landmark study: a great green and gold expanse of sal and bamboo forests, tall grasslands, deep ravines, and low hills in central India. This is the idyllic, wild India we most often see in nature films; Belinda Wright filmed most of her Emmy Award–winning *Land of the Tiger* here. Chital gather in herds of several dozen; rutting seven-hundred-pound sambar stags garland their antlers with sal leaves; and the electric green, lyrically named blossom-headed parakeets streak through the sky.

Walking through Kanha's meadows and along its forest roads or watching from his Land Rover, Schaller was sometimes able to observe tigers for half an hour — longer if the tiger was on a kill. A kill provided a social occasion for the usually solitary cats, and several times Schaller observed two families — two tigresses and their cubs — share a meal. Sometimes he staked out a live animal as bait while he waited in a blind. One evening he watched a tigress teaching her cubs to kill a tethered buffalo.

Baits no longer are used to lure tigers for observation in India. But today it is easy to see a tiger at Kanha. Protected by national decree and conditioned by decades of tourism, Kanha's tigers are far less wary of people than they were in Schaller's day. Early each morning park staff on specially trained elephants locate tigers and then return midmorning to meet the tourists waiting at the information center. In two days Dianne and I saw a tigress and her year-old cub, and a tiger lying up with his kill.

The elephants, despite their great bulk, seem to float through the forest like clouds. (Hindu mythology in fact holds that elephants were once winged and, like clouds, roamed freely in the sky; white elephants are thought to be able to produce clouds.) Because of the structure of the bones of their feet, elephants walk on tiptoe; their footprints may be shallower than a tiger's.

With their careful, shallow steps, the elephants inspire their passengers to silence and reverence. The morning we visited the tiger on his kill — a chital doe whose shoulder he had already eaten — twenty-two carloads of tourists were packed in silently on the backs of elephants. Tapping instructions with his bare heels against her head, the mahout asked the elephant to move this way and that for various camera angles. Shutters clicked furiously, but no one spoke. The tiger looked up at us with golden eyes, serene and dispassionate as a statue.

For centuries, Rajput, Mogul, and then British shikaris hunted tigers from elephant back, enjoying both relative safety and a fine vantage point from which to search for game. Elephants have proved equally practical for research. Smithsonian researchers used trained elephants to drive tigers off their kills and toward trees where men waited with dart guns. After darting the tiger, they weighed and measured the animal, examined it for injuries, collected its ticks. They measured the canines and removed an incisor — sectioning it can determine the animal's age. Five to seven hours later the tiger would awake with a tattoo and a radio collar. Thereafter, on elephant back, from a Land Rover, from a plane, or on foot, researchers can follow that individual and map its movements. With a hand antenna, listening for the kissing sound of the radio signal in the earphones, the researcher notes the direction of the loudest sound. From another point a second direction is noted, and where the lines cross the researchers locate the tiger.

But such work is not possible in Sundarbans. Elephants can't be used. (For one thing, there is no way to transport them in, and no wild elephants are known to have existed here, though there once were rhinos.) Neither can you use Land Rovers, since there are no roads. Radiotelemetry won't function here: it works only on fairly open ground, like the meadows at Kanha or the tall-grass *terai* of Chitawan. Trees blot out the signal.

The one standard tool available to Sundarbans' researchers is the dart gun. But even darting tigers does not seem to work here as well as it does at other study sites.

In his first year as Sundarbans field director, Pranabesh Sanyal was called to tranquilize a tigress who had entered a villager's cattle shed. When Dianne and I visited him at Buxa Tiger Reserve, a planted teak and sal forest where he is now field director, we shared tea on the porch of one of the bungalows while he told us the story by lantern light:

"By local inquiry we found that the previous morning, when the cowherd was about to let out the cattles, the boy had found this tigress was there. Immediately the boy came out and locked the door! So the villagers were dispatched to call us from Gosaba, which has a telephone to the trunk line at Canning."

Pranabesh got the call at six P. M.; by ten he had reached the village of Uttarbanga and slogged his way through half a kilometer of mud in the dark. There was the tigress, still in the cattle shed.

"That night we found a very peculiar thing," Pranabesh said. "Normally, to tranquilize a tiger you use five milliliters of Ketaset. But we used our first dose, and no reaction. Then we used another five milliliters. It had no effect. We were scared. There were about one thousand spectators there, and the tigress was trying to come out of the cattle shed! Then, of course, we tried ten milliliters — twenty milliliters in all. But there was still no effect."

No one seemed to know what to do. Then the field director's boatman stepped forward. His name was Ben Behari — Jungle Walker. "At that time, as the tigress was trying to come out," said Pranabesh, "he took a small bamboo stick, long but slender, and tapped her on the nose three times." At this the tigress lay down.

I asked him how Ben Behari knew to do that. Did he know why it had worked? Was Ben Behari some sort of shaman? Pranabesh bobbled his head from side to side in that Eastern not-quite-nod, not-quite-headshake, neither yes nor no that so confuses Westerners. "I don't know how he got that in mind," Pranabesh said, "but it worked."

Then, by hand, Ben Behari put a five-milligram Valium tablet in the tigress's mouth. He brushed her eyelids closed. The men loaded her into a cage, and she was taken to the Calcutta zoo, where she still lives and where she is called Sundari.

❖

How can you study an animal you cannot see? How can you manage an unseen population?

Most of the time in Sundarbans you cannot see the tiger. Neither can you see the gods or the wind, but you can see what they have touched. And this is what the West Bengal Forest Department relies upon: in attempting to trace the outlines of the tiger's mystery, the men look for impressions in the mud.

The tiger census, which is conducted about once every two years at each of India's twenty-one tiger reserves, is based on the premise that every tiger's footprint is as individual as a human fingerprint. Shikaris used this method to track individual man-eaters. Expanding on the idea, India's tiger experts have developed a way to trace pugmarks onto paper and, by comparing them, to identify and therefore count each individual. From these tracks Indian officials, like palmists, have tried to trace the fates of the country's tigers since the creation of the network of tiger reserves in 1972.

Almost all of the 130 people on the staff of India's Sundarbans Tiger Reserve — officers, forest guards, cooks, orderlies — are involved in the census. They travel in hundred-foot launches like *Monorama,* with its powerful forty-horsepower engine and tall, whiplike radio antenna and porcelain sink; they take smaller boats with names like *J'ai Guru,* powered by ten-horsepower all-purpose generators; they use dinghies and motorboats; even the Forest Department's eighteen houseboats, on which the patrolling staff live in squalid good humor, set sail.

There is an air of gaiety as the enumerators and their support staff leave for the thirty-seven field recording camps where they will work for the next six days. One hundred or so volunteers are recruited to help count the tigers; extra boatmen are hired from Sundarbans villages to ferry the 250 enumerators to their work sites. Aboard the boats each night there will be long lamp-lit card games, country liquor, and laughter.

Each team of five or six enumerators leaves the boat at ebb tide, when the widest swath of land is exposed. Each is equipped with a set of two rectangular clear glass plates, 20 by 25 centimeters, held together by screws in the corners; a felt-tip pen; a one-meter steel tape; paper; and two rubber bands. This is the Tiger Tracer, with which they will attempt to identify every unseen tiger in the tiger reserve's 998 square miles.

Seven months after the December 1992 census was conducted, the Forest Department released the figures to the state minister for environment and forests. It reported 251 tigers in the Indian Sundarbans. In the 613 paw-print tracings collected, they counted 92 individual tigers, 132 tigresses, and 27 cubs.

These census figures are popularly credited with such precision that even small changes are scrutinized. Compared with the figures released two years before, the 1992 census reported a decrease of 18 animals. "Only 250 tigers left in the Sundarbans" headlined the *Calcutta Telegraph*. (The article also reported that 295 tigers had been counted in 1988, and only 196 in 1990 — a decrease that should have been far greater cause for alarm. The Forest Department's figures were actually 265 in 1988 and 269 in 1990.) But Rathin, a sixteen-year veteran of government service, was ready for that. The report he prepared for the ministry assured them that the decrease was merely an artifact of previous, less precise estimates. "However, this estimate," he wrote, "has a definite aura of authenticity."

In the dry dust along a dirt road you can learn in a few hours to tell the sex of a tiger who has recently passed by: the print of the male's hind foot is squarer than that of the female; his four toes are also shorter and blunter. At parks like Kanha and Ranthambhore fresh pugmarks are etched into the dust along the roads with the precision a detective would wish for in dusting for fingerprints. (Tigers seem to like traveling on roads.) Often there are other characteristics that help distinguish one individual's pugmarks from another's. At Chitawan one tigress's distinctive prints earned her the name Chuchchi, or "pointed toes." The shape of the three lobes of the paw pad, too, may be unique. Where the lobes join, two conically tapering valleys in the pad leave ridges in the dirt. A good, clear print in light dust will show very well defined tips of these ridges in the bottom line of the pugmark.

Raghu Chundawat, an instructor with the prestigious Wildlife Institute of India, teaches the Tiger Tracer technique to park staffers around the country. On my second trip to India I met Raghu at Ranthambhore, Rajasthan's spectacular tiger reserve, gathered around the remains of a thousand-year-old fort and necklaced with lakes. Here the young, mustached teacher was instructing park research officers in the fine points of identifying individual tracks.

"You must pick your pugmarks carefully," he advised as he leaned over a four-toed impression in the dust. "Only a perfect print will do." He stressed how you must place the glass Tiger Tracer right on top of the print. You must position your eyes and your pen directly over the portion you are tracing — otherwise parallax error will grossly distort the outline. You must be wary of glare and shadow. You must pay particular attention when tracing the flat edge of the top of the pad, the pad's lobes, the tips of the toes.

There are, in fact, more than a dozen "parameters" considered "diagnostic" of an individual print, but any of them can be distorted by the slightest glitch. A piece of gravel underfoot can

cause a pugmark to twist or splay. Wet ground will grossly en-
large a print; claw marks, as the cat tries to gain purchase on
slippery ground, further distort it. "For instance," he continued, "this pugmark here" — it was decidedly smaller than the
prints headed in the opposite direction along the road, which
we had identified as belonging to an adult tiger. "Is this a female
or a cub?" Raghu asked. The heel impression indicated the animal had a problem with its feet, causing it to place more weight
on the outside of the heel — but as we followed the track we
saw that this was not consistent.

"These kinds of individuals create confusion," he said, tracing the footprint onto paper. So, I asked, how do you resolve
the confusion? How can you identify this individual if the pugmarks aren't consistent? "This," he answered, "is the art."

Even under ideal conditions, reading the subtleties of the
tiger's paw is difficult. At a normal walking pace on hard
ground, a tiger places its hind paw exactly where the front paw
of the same side has just trod, creating a double print. Tracking tigers at Ranthambhore, Harsh Vardan and T. K. Bapna
claimed that a tiger "may leave pugmarks of differing size and
style as he or she may walk in a different mood, to chase a prey
or to hide itself."

Is the Tiger Tracer's art reliable enough to produce an accurate count of individuals? The Smithsonian research team tried
it at Chitawan and didn't think so. In a research report the authors concluded that "it was not usually possible to relate
tracks to specific individuals except in cases [such as Chuchchi's] where the animal had an unusual track pattern." They
also said, "A census based only on tracks would tend to under-
estimate the number of tigers using an area." Often they would
find no tracks from a tiger that their radio collar told them was
in fact quite nearby.

At many of India's tiger parks, officials use the Tiger Tracer
method to supplement visual counts of tigers made at dry-

season water-hole vigils. Researchers assume that over three days of round-the-clock watches in the dry season, every tiger in the reserve will come to drink at a water hole. At some parks, like Kanha and Ranthambhore, researchers claim to know every tiger on sight by their individual cheek stripes.

But in Sundarbans the enumerators must rely on prints alone. And in the sloppy, slushy silt, most pugmarks look like formless holes punched in the mud.

❖

Sundarbans resists the prying eyes of scientists. Like the guardian of some underworld, a crocodile might lurch from the water and grab you; a tiger could leap at you from land or water; as you wade ashore from a dinghy, sharks may attack. There are six species of shark here, including aggressive tiger sharks that grow to eighteen feet. There are deadly snakes, including those most dreaded by Westerners: the banded krait and Russell's pit viper. But the locals know others that are just as dangerous: the greenish *shutanuli,* which is said to drop from the trees and sting your head with its tongue, and the *kalash,* which crawls into your bed at night. And in the water there are sea snakes with paddle-shaped tails, whose venom is ten to forty times as toxic as the cobra's.

Any time, but especially from August to November, cyclones may rake the shores. The winds have been clocked at 112 miles per hour. Small animals are blown for miles, and for days after a big cyclone the bloated bodies of human victims collect at jetties. They are so numerous that the forest staff has to push the bodies away with bamboo poles so that they float downstream.

In November of 1988 a cyclone struck just as the boats were converging for the tiger census. A large Forest Department launch, the *Rangabilia,* sank, drowning the officers aboard. A team of divers from Madras were hired to look for the sunken ship, but they never found it. The silt of the creek bottom, they said, was as soft and loose as quicksand. Sundarbans swallows its victims whole.

Subtler dangers wreak yet more damage. Rathin told me that an unusually large number of his staff go blind. He has learned from a doctor that a certain fly lives here that is attracted to the human eye. "Thik! It flits in to lay its eggs," he warned me. Fifteen years later the eggs hatch, and by then "there is nothing you can do about it."

The waters here seethe with disease. The Forest Department gets drinking water from tanks near Canning — somewhat muddy and salty but potable. But you can get sick from the river water even if you don't drink it. When we visited the Bangladeshi side of Sundarbans, a French lady with whom we traveled, whose husband was posted in Dacca with the World Bank, dipped her finger into the river water to taste how salty it was; within six hours, while she sat in a car on the ferry to Bagherhat, she was seized with such violent diarrhea that it burst through her dress and covered the back seat. She needed immediate injections of antibiotics; had we not already been on our way out of Sundarbans when she fell ill, she might have died.

In the face of these daily dangers the West Bengal Forest Department has neither the money nor the technology to conduct Western-style science. This is one of India's poorest states, and the department's resources are almost unbelievably meager. Though this is one of the most snake-infested areas on earth, the department has only one polyvenom antivenin syringe. And the serum in it has probably gone bad. Antivenin must be kept refrigerated, so it cannot be carried on Forest Department boats; only the police station at Gosaba has a kerosene-powered refrigerator. If that refrigerator should run out of kerosene for even one day, the antivenin in it would become useless.

Understandably, the gadgetry available to Western researchers — computers, radio collars, satellite telemetry — seems dazzling to the few Bengali researchers who have tried to study the tigers of Sundarbans. What if Western-style technology could be used to explore the lives of the Sundarbans tigers? Kalyan, who has a Ph.D. in ecology and a master's degree in statistics, has been considering this question ever since he visited Bristol, England, on a fellowship in 1986.

"In the U.K. they are telling me that even mental processes can be found out by computer!" he told Dianne and me when he visited us at the Tollygunge Club. "A person who is a criminal, and a person who is good, you can find out by their brain signals who is really a criminal! And if this is possible for man, it is possible for animals. I am quite sure. I am quite sure."

We listened, amazed, as Kalyan proceeded to outline what he believed could be done if the wonders of computers and telemetry could be brought to Sundarbans' forests:

"I think what should be done is, there should be a radio monitoring system, some kind of a collar put on, that gives a signal of the tiger's thought processes," he said, quite excited and very serious. "And also, the person who is going into the forest, their thought processes should also be monitored through a computer. A kind of monitoring system could be developed, and by comparing the thoughts of a person and the tiger, we could come to a very good conclusion in reducing human casualties: we could find what a tiger thinks before he goes to kill a human being, and what that person is thinking. Either could be thinking in some particular manner — and if we got that particular signal, the person could be saved."

Of course this is science-fiction fantasy. No one has developed a machine that can monitor thoughts. Not even conventional telemetry can be used in Sundarbans because the trees would block the signal; the monsoon humidity would fritz any computer; and even if they could work under such conditions, the Forest Department could never afford them.

But Kalyan's view is informative. What he is saying is that he would not use these machines as Westerners might, to map the ranges and movements of the study subjects — but instead to discover what lies in the heart and mind of the tiger.

❖

"Superstition and supernatural qualities attributed to the tigers, however fictitious they may appear, have their basis in fact," A. B. Chaudhuri and Kalyan wrote in the paper they delivered at the 1979 International Symposium on Tiger.

In the paper they reported aspects of their studies that have never been published in Western peer-reviewed journals. After interviewing local people, they wrote that frequently the Sundarbans tiger was able to solve the problem of entering boats by "getting airborne, raising its body in mid-air and effecting a smooth landing." They reported as "a strange fact" — but a fact nonetheless — that in the tiger's jaws "the human body, with less of life, contracts to about half its size, enabling the man-eater to carry it away with ease."

The world of Sundarbans, as even these educated men see it, is held together by a web of enchantment. Sometimes the face of the sea glows with the fluorescence of marine microorganisms called dinoflagellates, and the forest flashes with fireflies. The two researchers asked, "Do the man-eaters derive extra energy or impetus to prowl at night and search for human prey . . . due to this incredible bioluminescence?"

On several of the nights I would spend on *Monorama* over the coming months, Rathin and I often stayed up on deck to look for fireflies and bioluminescent waves. We were never sure whether the silvery shine on the water was the moon's reflection or the glowing spirits of little creatures in the water. Sometimes in the forest we saw points of light, but we were never sure if they were fireflies or eyeshine or moonlight glinting off the dew. Or perhaps something else entirely.

"So many people have died in Sundarbans," Rathin said to

me one night, "that people say the forest is full of their spirits."

But Rathin, who wears the Christian cross his parents gave him on a leather thong around his neck, says he doesn't believe such things. He is, he insists, a modern man and does not believe in spirits. Instead he consults a Dell paperback for his horoscope to see whether the day will be favorable or unfavorable. He is careful to subtract ten hours for each forecast, he told me, to make up for the time difference between India and America, where the book was printed. The idea that stars affect our fates is both logical and scientific, Rathin explains, for the planets and stars physically pull upon the bodily fluids of all human beings. "From the moment of birth these forces are pulling, and the effect is as real as the moon on the tides," he says.

Rathin's staff, however, consults forces closer to earth. Each evening aboard *Monorama* one of the lungi-clad boatmen wedges sticks of incense between the boards at the head of the boat and inside the wheelhouse and utters his prayers. Each time I slept in the cabin I was moved to find that someone had kindly placed incense there for me as well. Its sweet scent smoldered a prayer to the gods, a plea for the well-being of the next day's expedition.

And when the enumerators gather for the tiger census in Sundarbans, the research officer will often kneel to gently touch the first print he finds. Before setting the Tiger Tracer upon a pugmark, he brings his right hand from the print to his forehead and then to his heart, silently honoring the tiger god.

Bonobibi Puja

❖ ❖ ❖ ❖ ❖ ❖ ❖ ❖ ❖ ❖ ❖ ❖ ❖

FROM FIFTY SUNDARBANS VILLAGES, people streamed toward the shrine at Sajnekhali. Every few minutes, it seemed, another large motorboat pulled up to the jetty at the Mangrove Interpretation Center and poured forth more passengers: fishermen and farmers, woodcutters and merchants, wives and children, all dressed in their crispest pajama suits, their finest saris, their best Western slacks and shirts or their cleanest lungis.

The shrine was a simple wood and tin building open at the front, like a lidless shoebox on its side; but it, too, was elaborately dressed this day. Tissue-paper cutouts latticed the walls: auspicious lotus and datura flowers, geese, conch shells, peacocks, Bengali script spelling out MA BONOBIBI. A thick rope of yellow marigolds draped the roof's tin eaves like bunting. Festive foil mobiles hung from the ceiling. Fresh banana leaves carpeted the floor.

But what was most striking about the shrine this day was that all the images inside were new: a plumper, shorter Bonobibi wore a dress of fresh crimson satin and a crown encrusted with gold paper and plastic jewels. Bare-chested Daksin Ray rode a different tiger, this one with glass eyes and long white claws.

Sha Jungli wore a new gold tunic, and his long club was now wrapped in gold ribbon. All twelve human figures boasted freshly painted skin the color of the double yellow line on American highways.

At their feet offerings piled high. On platters of freshly washed banana leaves, artfully arranged mounds of cooked rice overflowed with sliced bananas, fat yellow raisins, the red blossoms of hibiscus, cut apples and oranges, and the sweet white flesh of coconut. Newspaper bags brimmed with sweets. A dish heaped with coins. Along with these offerings, some people brought a household item — often a bolt of cloth — to leave in the shrine during the puja, sharing the company of the gods. Later they would retrieve it and take it home, drenched in blessings.

Incense smoked. Candles glowed. Cloth wicks burned in brass bowls of mustard oil. A twisted newspaper wick flamed in a plastic Wesson oil bottle. Over it all presided the gap-toothed, gray-haired priest, Phoni Guyan, clad in his white shawl. A scar shaped like a fishhook split his upper lip. Nine years ago Daksin Ray sent a tiger for him; the tiger leaped at him from the forest and raked his face with its claws. But Phoni Guyan survived. So it was particularly appropriate that he should officiate at the puja on this day.

Each January, on the day the Bengali calendar calls Makara Sankranti, the story of Bonobibi and Daksin Ray is celebrated in pujas held in villages throughout Sundarbans. This one, hosted by the Forest Department, is the most elaborate. Thanks in part to hefty donations from visitors at the tourist lodge next door, this puja offers fanfare that others cannot: the Forest Department even provides a sound system to broadcast incantations to the crowd. The system is powered by a car battery, itself so valued that someone has honored it with its own covering of banana leaves. The Forest Department's staff prepares for the puja for weeks.

Everyone was exceptionally anxious to please the gods on this day, for Daksin Ray was angry. "Yesterday, four man, tiger accident," Girindra told me. In this case I knew that "yesterday" could stretch back in time only three weeks, for it was only that long that I had been away. When the violence over Ayodhya had finally subsided, Rathin had come to fetch Dianne and me in *Monorama* so that we could return to the States for Christmas. Now, less than a month later, I had returned, this time with my friend Eleanor Briggs, a photographer with the freedom to travel wherever interesting images beckon.

"Tiger, village tour," Girindra joked. None of the attacks occurred in a village; all had happened in the forest, while the victims were fishing or cutting wood. But Daksin Ray, Girindra was saying, had selected each victim from a different village: Dayapur, Lahripur, Ampur, Shomshenagur. One of the men, a woodcutter from Dayapur, the village next to Girindra's, had been attacked only five days before. He'd been cutting wood from the forest with a party of others at ten in the morning when the tiger came and carried him away.

Later I spoke with the area range officer, Kanchan Muhkerjee, whose English is better than Girindra's. He was hesitant to talk because none of the deaths were official: none of the victims held legal permits to be in the area where they were killed, so the Forest Department isn't expected to know anything about such cases. But of course Kanchan knows, and because his office has a two-way radio, his sources are better informed than Girindra's. The actual number of tiger victims, he told me, was fifteen. And they had all been killed in the last eight days.

The puja, he said, was desperately needed.

❖

Eleanor and I had caught up with Girindra near the jetty early on the morning of the puja. Forest Department staff, the clay artists, the priest, and the reader were still making the final preparations, garlanding the appropriate idols with lei-like *pou-ler malas* and moving the images around on the shrine's stage. It was odd to see deities carted around like furniture — valuable furniture, but furniture nonetheless. (Later, back in Calcutta, on the night before the puja for the goddess of learning, we would see whole trucks crowded with identical Sarasvatis, all facing the cars in back of them, their faces in newspaper purdah to protect the delicate clay features during the trip.) But of course the images were not yet deities. Only when the priest blew the holy conch shell would the gods — if they chose — accept the invitation and come to inhabit the clay bodies the artists had so carefully prepared.

While Eleanor photographed, I asked Girindra to introduce me to some of the lesser-known gods.

I pointed to the four-foot-tall image of an old man, to whose chin the artist was still gluing the last ash-blond ringlets of a beard. "Tini ke?" ("Who is he?") I asked.

For a moment, Girindra looked at me as if I had fallen out of a tree. He pointed to the white cardboard label attached by a straight pin to the idol's blue satin pants, where the name was clearly printed in Bengali script.

Then he remembered that I am illiterate.

"Gazi Saheb ache." Girindra spoke very clearly and slowly, as if talking to a child.

"Mussulman nam?" I asked. In Bangladesh I had heard "Gazi" applied to Muslim holy men, teachers, and saints.

"Mussulman, Hindu," Girindra replied, bobbling his head both yes and no. Gazi Saheb, he was saying, may be Mussulman, but he is worshiped by both Hindus and Muslims. To try to clarify, he said in English, "Gazi Saheb *Sundarbans* man."

Next I pointed to a small figure of a woman. Leaning against a clay tree, she was weeping flat white tears. "Tini ke?" I asked.

"Gulalbibi ache," he answered. "Mother, Bonobibi."

Bonobibi's mother! But why was she crying? Was she herself a goddess? I tried to ask, but my question only brought forth an incomprehensible stream of Bengali. It began to hurt me almost physically to see how frustrated Girindra became when I could not be made to understand. So I asked him only for the names. A few days later, when we were scheduled to meet up again with Rathin, I would ask him to explain in English.

What about the figure of the woman standing near Gulalbibi? "Fulbibi," Girindra answered. Some sources list "Bibi" as a suffix derived from Urdu, but others say it is derived from Persian. And in primarily Islamic villages, the goddess of smallpox and cholera is often called Ola Bibi. In primarily Hindu villages she is called Ola Candi or Sitala, and she is often worshiped along with her male attendant, Jvasura, the three-eyed, blue-skinned fever demon. (There is also a god of boils and carbuncles, named Ghantakarna, and one for itches, named Ghentu.)

Next to Fulbibi stood the figure of a man, his expression dismayed, his palms held facing him as if he were reading a book.

His name?

"Ibrahim."

Yet at the feet of figures bearing Persian names, worshipers were piling objects sacred to every Hindu puja: vessels filled with milk and the clarified butter called ghee, celebrating the goddess Cow; pots of rice, coconut, and bananas, symbolizing bounty; hibiscus, showing the purity of the devotees' hearts. Burning candles evoked the power of the ancient sun god, Surya, the day-maker and king of the planets, who is asked to witness all important ceremonies. Jars of fertile, healing Ganges water cradled the living goddess Gonga. Each item speaks deeply to the Hindu heart.

"That which is good and dear to us we offer to our gods," Amarendra Nath Mondal, a schoolteacher from Dayapur, later explained to me in lilting, singsong English. "Suppose you are my guest. I do everything for your enjoyment. The gods and goddesses are similarly our guests, so we must see to their comfort."

Indeed, he said, for certain types of gods, Hindus consider the temple or domestic shrine the deity's literal house. The figure who dwells there may be treated to devotions throughout the day to provide for its well-being. The god must be awakened in the morning, bathed, fed, amused with songs or poems or dance and put to bed at night. The image is often offered the hypnotic betel nut to chew, tobacco to smoke, pillows on which to recline. Priests tend to the comfort of the idols in temples, but for household gods the homeowner must perform these duties.

Eleanor was familiar with these devotions. She explores her spirituality at both a church and a Hindu ashram, and she brought with her to India a two-by-four-inch card bearing the four-armed image of Laxmi, the goddess of success and wealth. Periodically during our trip, Eleanor would take Laxmi out of her purse, set her upon a blue brocade pillow, and offer her songs and sweets. We had done a Laxmi puja on our way to India. Next to a koi pool at the Singapore airport we offered the goddess Gummi Bears in an effort to recoup a missed flight connection — which, to my surprise, succeeded. Once we got to India, though, we had a problem; Eleanor explained that Laxmi likes a clean place, and once we left the Tolly Club, clean places were scarce, so Eleanor didn't often take Laxmi out.

The whole thing reminded me of playing dolls — which of course is playing mother, which of course is playing God. How moving that the gods and goddesses want us to sing to them and feed them, dress and bathe them — the way a child tends to her baby doll, the way a mother cares for her child. Are we not acting out what we ask our gods to do, in turn, for us?

❖

As the Bonobibi puja begins, in front of the forest gods stretches a thick carpet of flowers and food, a feast of scent and sound, a luxurious stage upon which the gods can play, seduced and intoxicated with comfort and delight.

The priest, kneeling and bowing to the images, tweaks his own ears, then his nostrils. This is a way of purifying himself and apologizing for any errors he might commit in the puja, a young Calcutta college student later told me; with his own hands the priest mimics the tweaking a Bengali mother might use to gently reprimand a naughty son.

Finally he folds his hands. A shimmering, shivering "Ulu-oooooooooooooo" goes up from the assembled crowd; someone blows the sacred conch shell. The people are welcoming the gods, who have now arrived and dwell among us.

A reader wearing a white shirt and a pink lungi begins chanting from a hymnal. "Bonobibi his-story," Girindra whispers: this is the Bonobibi story, an epic poem of how the goddess came to dwell in the mangrove tigerland ruled by Daksin Ray.

As the reader finishes a page, he folds it back from left to right. The book begins where an English or Bengali book would end — but where an Arabic text would begin. Yet the words are written not in the long scimitar strokes of Arabic script, but in the shorter, ornamental tendrils of the Bengali alphabet.

I recognize only a few words. One of them is "Allah."

The notion seems at first impossible. Hinduism and Islam are basically antithetical: contrary to Hinduism's colorful, crowded pantheon, Islam's fundamental concept is one omnipotent god: "There is no God but Allah, and Mohammed is his prophet." Throughout the rest of the Indian subcontinent, and even into Europe, Hindus and Muslims had only weeks ago been murdering one another by the hundreds over the irreconcilable differences in their beliefs.

But the people of Sundarbans remained at peace.

Islam came to Bengal in a form vastly different from the Islam of Arabia. It was brought by the Sufi mystics, the spiritual gift of saints who performed miracles, received revelations from the dead and, in some cases, reveled in an eroticism through which, by losing oneself in orgasmic union with the lover, the devotee achieved union with God.

A scholar at the University of Dacca, Razia Akter Banu, recently published a study of these mystics and their effect on the religion of the region. The Sufi interpretation of the Koran, she explained, "is vastly different from the dogmatic creeds of Islam." Bengal's Sufis preached the imminent unity of a god who may manifest in many ways: in trees, in water, in the bodies of birds or tigers, in the guise of a many-armed goddess or a Jew named Jesus. Instead of the orthodox Islamic view of the soul — an individual entity created by Allah, subject to his punishment but destined never to merge with him — the Sufis preached that each human soul is part of the divine soul. From the Koranic verse "We [Allah and his prophet] are nearer to him [man] than his jugular vein," the Sufis conclude that all people may join God in a state like the Hindu mystic's nirvana.

"Islam, in Sufi garb," Banu wrote in her 1992 study, "was intelligible and psychologically acceptable to the people of Bengal." Sufi saints, or pirs, were and are beloved by Hindus and Muslims alike. One of them, Pir Kabir, was also a renowned poet. His disciples included the devout of both religions. When he died, it is said, the Hindus wanted to cremate his body, while the Muslims wanted to bury it. The dead saint himself had to intervene to prevent strife between the two sets of believers. Kabir caused his own body to vanish, and in its place mourners found instead a bouquet of flowers.

In the cities Bengalis of both religions have become more orthodox than they were in the centuries following the Sufis' arrival. But Banu's surveys in Bangladesh, at least, show that in rural areas nearly half of the Muslims attend Hindu pujas, consult dead pirs, and believe in the influence of five kinds of Hindu ghosts, as well as the even more fearful Muslim ghosts called *mamdos*. All these practices are strictly forbidden in orthodox Islam.

Traveling in the Bangladeshi Sundarbans, Dianne and I had seen evidence of the melding of the two religions. The fishermen all wore red cloth bracelets on the right hand and flew small red flags at the bows of their boats. Red, we were told, attracts the attention of a particular pir, sometimes called Barkan Gazi, sometimes called Shagazi, who will protect his supplicants from the tiger. Later I learned that in the myths and legends of Sundarbans, Barkan Gazi, Shagazi, and Gazi Saheb are one and the same. Although he is an Islamic saint, the Bangladeshi Muslims assured us, the Gazi would aid his supplicants, whether Hindu or Muslim, as long as they flew his color.

Red is the most sacred and beloved color of the Hindus. On the Indian side of Sundarbans the bowsprit of almost every boat is painted red or tied with red cloth. And red, the color of our blood, as Girindra told me, is the favorite color of Daksin Ray, the ancient tiger god, whose wrath binds Hindu and Muslim together and under whose transforming spell alien worlds converge.

❖

Seventy-year-old Bakher Gazi, wrapped in a red and silver embroidered shawl, looked uncomfortable sitting on the bench below the deck of *Monorama*. He was probably wishing that Rathin had never summoned him from his home in Dhusnikhali on my behalf. Bakher Gazi had a fever, for which Eleanor and I gave him medicine. He was so thin that the veins on his nearly black arms stood out like ropes on a flagpole. He seemed frail and vulnerable. Only two of his upper teeth were intact. The right lens of his black plastic-rimmed glasses was cracked. But

Bakher Gazi, Rathin told me, is considered one of the most powerful men in Sundarbans.

"He claims to have prevented between fifty and seventy incidents of tiger attack," Rathin said. "Never has a man been killed by a tiger in this man's presence." In some cases he was not present at the actual moment of attack, "but even in these cases, he has always managed to bring back the body of the victim, preventing the tiger from eating it, so that the body could be returned to the relatives and give them some peace. He has rescued seventy bodies from the jaws of the tiger, and he himself has always remained unscathed."

Crocodiles, the shaman claimed, flee from his presence; tigers obey his commands.

Now, as he unwrapped his shawl, he showed us why.

Lodged in his left shin, inside a layer of skin formed like a pouch, lies a matchstick-sized sliver of wood taken from the sundari tree. Between the second and third fingers of his right hand rests another sliver of sundari. And the skin on the palm of his left hand holds a third piece of wood. These charms, he explained, have been blessed by Allah himself. By their power he is immune to attack from crocodiles, to the dangers of snakes and pirates in the night, and especially, because of the wood embedded in his leg, he is protected from the jaws of the tiger.

Bakher Gazi is a *fakir,* a Muslim shaman. His powers are believed to be so effective that they can clear an entire section of forest of danger, allowing the fishermen, woodcutters, or honey collectors in his company to work there safely. He is in great demand in Sundarbans. His powers work equally well for Hindus and Muslims, he claims.

Rathin interpreted while I asked Bakher Gazi how he engaged his shamanic power and why it worked.

The magic wood is called *ascan,* Rathin translated. When Bakher Gazi leaves the forest, though, he must remove the piece from his leg. He keeps it in a matchbox.

To protect large groups of workers, he uses a much larger piece of wood, which he calls *asabari*. First he gathers a branch of sundari and cuts a piece three feet long, then trims it to a few inches in diameter. With a hand drill he bores a small hole in the top. The shaman chants the names of all the workers with him, one by one, and as each is spoken, another small piece of sundari is dropped into the hole at the top. Then the hole is sealed with mud, and a new handkerchief is tied at the top. Finally the asabari is planted on the bank — much as the sliver of wood is planted in his flesh. Now it will protect the people who are working in the forest.

How did he learn the sacred powers of the asabari and the ascan? His father was a great fakir, as was his grandfather before him. His grandfather was also a renowned herbalist, who learned the powers of Sundarbans' roots and leaves and flowers to cure disease. It was he who discovered that wood of the sundari tree would, when enhanced with holy words, repel the tiger. "Just as different plants are used for different types of diseases, but one plant cannot cure another disease, so sundari timber is used for this purpose, to protect against the tiger, and no other plant will do," Rathin translated. "But it will not work without the magic words," he stressed — and the words must be uttered by a man of pure heart. Now, with his father and grandfather dead, Bakher Gazi is the only man living who knows them.

Each shaman in Sundarbans uses his own kind of holy process. Rathin introduced me to a Hindu *gunin*, the spiritual equivalent of a fakir. His name was Ksab Chandra Kayal; he was about fifty-five years old. "There are many wizards who possess these powers, to combat tigers by magic," he explained to me through Rathin. "There are different strains of these powers coming down." His own methods combine chants invoking Gazi Saheb and hymns to Bonobibi to enchant trees, water, and mud, which in turn protect his men.

First, he explained, each man in the work party must wash his hands and face in the river. Then, speaking the name of Bonobibi, Ksab Kayal sprinkles blessed water on the mud banks. He looks for a tree to stand as the workmen's guardian. The first tree they encounter on their right side will be chosen. Everyone places their hands on that tree, and while Ksab Kayal utters the *Bonobibi Hukkum* — the command of Bonobibi — the tree absorbs the spell. Mud from the base of the tree is touched to its trunk, then to their own foreheads; now they may start their work, safe.

How does the water confer blessing? Why is the tree holy? How does the mud protect them?

If they sprinkled a bucket of water from their village on the mud banks, that would not work, Ksab Kayal answered; neither would part of a tree taken from a courtyard, or mud from the marketplace. "It was his guru's command that only the water and mud and trees from the forest be used," Rathin interprets.

And his guru was a very wise and powerful man indeed. Ksab Kayal himself saw him bind a tiger motionless with blades of grass. While the men were working in the forest, the tiger approached. The guru chanted, touched the grass, and threw some at the tiger; the tiger became statue-still and did not move until the men had finished their work. Then it simply turned and walked away.

Mud charged with magic powers, river water conferring blessing, a holy man who merges his flesh with wood to make himself one with the powers of trees. We did not meet these shamans until weeks after the puja at Sajnekhali; but unbeknown to me at the time, their knowledge was at the core of the story that the puja was playing out.

"Gazi Saheb, *Sundarbans* man," Girindra stressed to me that day at Sajnekhali. Whether a saint or a god or a supplicant is Hindu or Muslim is not of crucial importance; in Sundarbans, it is the land itself that gives its saints and its people their wisdom, their power, and their peace.

❖

"Gul-al-bi-bi, Ful-al-bi-bi, Ib-ra-him sha-mi . . ." The reader at the puja chanted on and on, the tale of Bonobibi and Daksin Ray spreading like ripples over a pond. The song sounded like a cross between a Gregorian chant and a nursery rhyme, a repetitive drone with the hypnotic effect of a mantra.

To the villagers sitting in the hot sun, to the supplicants who streamed past the shrine to remove their shoes and kneel before the gods to make their offerings, the words spoke of miracle after miracle. I could not understand the meaning of the words, but I listened with an older ear, feeling the sound and cadence of the story being sung, the way a snake might hear. *"Bon-o-bi-bi, Bon-o-bi-bi, cho-to bhai ac-he . . ."* Instead of a chronicle of events, I heard the same sounds surface again and again, like a heartbeat, a repetitive, mesmerizing promise: so it was then, so it is now, so it will ever be.

The miracles of Bonobibi, the exploits of Daksin Ray happen over and over again, the song's cadence assured. For in cultures older than our own, the concept of time is not linear but circular, a truth learned from watching the rising and falling tides, the waxing and waning moon. This circular concept of time was recognized in Western culture before we turned our attentions away from the cycles of the earth to the idea of a forward-marching progress composed of individual human histories. In the days of Plato and Aristotle the Greeks asserted that every art and science had been established before, had perished, and awaited rediscovery.

There are, according to Hindu knowledge, no single epoch-making historical events in the eternity of time; rather, each age is marked by mythological events that recur in cycles in the great, affirming wheel of life, death, and rebirth.

"Bon-o-bi-bi, Bon-o-bi-bi, Sun-dar-ban ja-be . . ." It is this understanding of time, perhaps, that bestows the serenity you see on the faces of the gods portrayed in the art of so many Asian cultures. Heinrich Zimmer describes Durga, the tiger-riding goddess who saves the world by annihilating a demon buffalo, as she is portrayed in an eighth-century Javanese stone sculpture: even in the moment of dealing the death blow to the enemy, the goddess's face shows "no trace of wrathful emotion; she is steeped in the serenity of eternal calm. Though [her] deed is bound to be accomplished . . . for her, the whole course of this universe, including her own apparition in the role of its rescuer, is but part of a cosmic dream."

For three hours the song of Bonobibi continued like the voice of the hypnotist, like the breath of the hatha yogi, and its sound and rhythm worked their transforming magic. When the chant finally concluded — Gulalbibi's mysterious tears dried, Sha Jungli's club stilled — the great wheel of time had spun again, and calm and peace were again restored. The recent spate of tiger attacks, it seemed, was no longer terrifyingly random: it had its place as part of the circle of time, in the cosmic dream of God-play we mortals see only as Maya.

A pot of stew called *khicheree,* made from the vegetable bounty blessed at the gods' feet, was now served to the worshipers, lovingly ladled out by park staff onto clean banana leaves. As we sat on the Forest Department's folding chairs, eating our warm food in the golden, late-afternoon sunshine, villagers visited with their neighbors, children played on the green grass, and a handful of fat-bottomed gray and white geese, the wards of one of the forest officers, waddled about with outstretched necks, honking fearlessly.

Later we visited with Girindra at his cool, smooth mud home. Girindra's five daughters, aged eight through sixteen, welcomed us with an intimate grooming. Assisted by their beautiful mother, Namita, the girls combed our hair, slicking it with coconut oil until the comb slid like a fish through water. They pinned our hair flat with giant bobby pins, to which they later affixed big red bows and bright hibiscus. They adorned our brows with bindis. Our feet they painted vermilion. And because I am married, they covered the part in my hair with a thin, knife-edged stripe of vermilion powder like Namita's, applied with the back of a comb. Rathin later told me that this, the traditional Hindu mark of a married woman, originated with the Mogul invasion: each day the husband would cut himself and apply his blood to the head of his wife, his visible vow that he would protect her honor from the invaders with his very life. But months afterward, when I mentioned this to Girindra through a translator, he told me Rathin was wrong. "We do this," he told me, "because the goddess has willed it."

The goddess, of course, has willed it all. This was the message of the poem at the puja; this was the chant honked by the waddling goose and gander; this was the mantra spoken by the comb smoothing through our hair: "all is as the goddess has willed it." Surely, it seemed, nothing bad could really happen here.

Aboard the little wooden boat Rathin had arranged for us, Eleanor and I slept deeply that night, floating on the waters where Vishnu slumbers upon the coils of his cosmic snake, secure and serene as the dreamy, graceful Durga riding on her tiger.

Lost

❖ ❖ ❖ ❖ ❖ ❖

"MONORAMA KOTHAI?"

We were looking for the hunched bulk and bright searchlight of *Monorama* in the night. The big launch was supposed to be anchored here at Gazikhali, the crossroads of three rivers in the core area, as Rathin had arranged. "*Monorama* where?" I asked Girindra.

"No idea," he replied.

Half an hour later, as we waited with *Mabisaka*'s motor stilled, he would ask me the same question. "Jani na," I replied — "I don't know." I was finding this an increasingly useful Bengali phrase.

Eleanor, Girindra, and I had left Sajnekhali four hours earlier, before the waning moon slipped beneath a smudge of clouds. In the dissolving mist of evening, only the low yellow wink of a few boats' lanterns had distinguished water from sky. But now there were no boats and no lanterns, and instead of rice and dahl and wood smoke, the wet air carried the scent of the sea.

We were cold as well as tired. In February, although the noon sun still stings like a whip on your back, nights can drop to 40 degrees Fahrenheit. And we were anxious. We were near the big river Matla, which flows directly to the Bay of Bengal. Girindra considered this a dangerous place to be alone.

Girindra held his back very straight. We listened but heard only the slap of waves. No motor. The nearest village was hours away. Only animals and spirits lived here — many tigers, and the ghosts of those they had killed.

Bengalis fear lonely places, because spirits gather there. One woman later told me, you must be sure to braid your hair and cover your head with your sari if you walk outside at night: otherwise tree-dwelling spirits may pull you up by your hair. But I did not know this then.

Where I saw empty night, Girindra could see ghosts, demons, spirits, gods. What did he see now? He was looking upriver at a tiny point of light, which at first, even with our binoculars, Eleanor and I couldn't see. It was not the big searchlight of *Monorama*. It was a single, gleaming lantern aboard a smaller boat. This made Girindra even more nervous. No one was supposed to go into this core area; whoever was here didn't care about breaking the law.

Rathin and Kushal had told us that sea pirates often attack fishermen's boats to take hostages, sending one of the party back to the home village for ransom money. Sometimes they simply take their victims' money and valuables. Sometimes they deem it wiser to murder everyone aboard and cast the bodies into the sea; the sharks and the crocodiles eat the evidence of the crime. All that is left is a ghost ship, rocking voicelessly on the concealing waves.

Girindra asked us to hide in the cramped space below deck. Our foreignness and wealth would stand out even in silhouette, even in the darkness. To a dacoit, Eleanor in particular would seem a gift from Dakate Kali, the goddess Kali in the form pirates worship to bring them successful plunders. They wouldn't even have to bother with her five cameras and their expensive lenses. Three decades earlier, when Eleanor visited India on her first honeymoon, she had heard the Indian proverb "A woman without jewelry is like a ghost." She took it to heart. Every day, no matter where we went, along with her sea-scented face creams and blue eyeliner and orange lipstick, with studied elegance Eleanor wore her diamond pinkie ring, two gold and ruby finger rings, and either gold or amber earrings. She was a pirate's dream.

The boat came closer. Girindra called out. Men called back — a volley of Bangla. They were fishermen and may have been taking this route as a shortcut, since the hour was so late. No, they had not seen *Monorama,* and they were glad of it; had Rathin found them, he could have fined them the equivalent of a week's wages. They had not seen or heard any big launch.

I was beginning to believe that I had somehow acquired a force that physically repelled *Monorama,* like those ultrasonic devices that are supposed to repel moles from your garden. Shortly after the Bonobibi puja, Rathin had informed us that for various reasons he could not keep the promise he had made to me before I'd left India in December — that he would guide and translate for Eleanor and me when I returned. But he would, he assured, be able to provide all the help we needed and would meet us at intervals during our stay. "At any moment," he had promised, "the *Monorama* will be pulling up beside you . . ." But it had not happened that way.

The first time we were supposed to meet up with *Monorama,* Eleanor and I left Canning aboard a filthy, sputtering boat with a hold full of water in which mosquitoes had been breeding for generations. Rathin had arranged for its captain, a Burmese Muslim named Alum, who spoke some English, to take us that night to Jayapur, where *Monorama* would anchor to wait for us. Only a few hours into the journey, after the sun had set, Alum announced he needed to go ashore for an extra lantern. He docked the boat at the town of Basanti. Men's voices growled from crowded tin shacks, and deep laughter rumbled from the dark. We could not hear or see women or children anywhere. Alum got out. The crew got out. They left us alone at the dark dock, with no assurance that they would return.

Hours later, while I guarded our gear, Eleanor ventured into the unlit town for help. She returned with an English-speaking Catholic priest who smelled strongly of country liquor. We persuaded him to help us get a ride on a passing boat to the police station across the river. News of our efforts drew Alum and his crew back to our boat, earnestly promising to resume the journey immediately. But as soon as the priest left, Alum again debarked, and the crew anchored the boat in the middle of the river so we could not reach the dock to escape. They informed us that they were not going to take us to meet *Monorama* that night at all; we would have to sleep on this boat.

At this point I picked up a machete that was lying on deck. Holding it firmly, I reiterated our original plan. Alum had his crew hurriedly weigh anchor. We finally reached *Monorama* around three A.M.

Another time when we were scheduled to meet *Monorama*, Rathin had installed on *Mabisaka* a sometime member of his own crew, a doe-eyed young man named Nicteau, whom Kanchan Muhkerjee later described as "a fool, but a good boy." Nicteau's presence was supposed to ensure that our meeting would take place as planned. But again, hours passed and the light died before our two boats rejoined. It turned out that Nicteau had misunderstood. *Mabisaka* was waiting in the middle of one channel while *Monorama* waited for us, just out of sight, at a bend in the river.

Possibly *Monorama* was now just around a bend. Girindra cranked *Mabisaka*'s motor to search another channel. Eleanor and I emerged from below, where Girindra had hidden us, and covered our heads with our shawls, smoothing the jagged outlines of our Western hair. We sat with Girindra on the boat's roof, nervously peering into the mangrove-lined darkness. No *Monorama*. What to do?

Suddenly I remembered an appropriate phrase from my Bengali language tapes:

"Tumi ki Robindronather gan gaibe?"

("Would you like to sing a song by Rabindranath Tagore?")

Girindra was wearing a maroon balaclava that he had pulled up over his thin mustache, but I could see his smile stretch across his face in the wrinkles that spread out like fans at the corners of his eyes.

No, he would not sing a song by Rabindranath Tagore. Instead he offered a song I knew, the song he had sung into the darkness for Dianne and me on those nights when, dazed with mute frustration, we would make our way back to the tourist lodge under diamond skies. Its melody had accompanied my strange, muttering dreams. Pleading, calling, searching, its notes etched the ebb and flow of all our separate, unnamed longings.

Each syllable seemed to float straight to heaven, as smoke rises in calm air. Many months later, from a tape I had translated in England, I learned the words to the song:

> Dear God, dear Lord, where are you?
> Reveal yourself to me.
> You have brought me to this earth.
> I work all day long
> as you have wished.
> I work all day long.
> I do not know why you have brought me to this earth,
> but I cannot live without you.
> You have brought me to this earth.
> I have sinned one hundred thousand times
> yet I plead of you,
> come and reveal yourself to me
> and forgive me.
> Dear God, dear Lord, where are you?

❖

We finally joined *Monorama* long past midnight. I never understood why we hadn't been able to find each other. Girindra and

Rathin had discussed the meeting location extensively in Bengali before we had left. Now they were discussing it again, speaking softly and pointing to various areas on the big plastic-covered map mounted on the wall below *Monorama*'s deck. It was possible that we had approached the appointed site from different rivers. The *Mabisaka* could navigate much shallower creeks than the big launch. It was also possible the confusion stemmed from a nuance of Dokhno, the dialect of Bengali spoken in Sundarbans. Rathin explained that the dialect is a mixture of Midnapuri, Santal, and other tribal languages; pure Bengali; and relics of the ancient Dravidian language. Any Bengali can understand it, he said; then again, directions seem particularly vulnerable to misinterpretation in any language.

These meetings with Rathin on *Monorama* were sometimes difficult and always exhausting. Eleanor and I would be tired at the start, frustrated at all the time we had spent lost, looking for the boat. Lost! The condition named my dilemma in all its multiple, many-headed aspects, like some hideous demon. Lost: unable to find one's way. Lost: unable to function or make progress. Lost: unable to understand.

Girindra understood my frustration. He took us up and down the rivers at all times of day. He showed us more poles marking the sites of tiger accidents and tried to tell us the stories. He took us to the site where his youngest uncle was killed and showed us the very tree his uncle was about to cut — illegally — when the tiger leaped out of the forest; the tree, a *jad baen*, is now as tall as a barn roof. Eleanor took beautiful photographs. But I was ravenous for information.

On *Monorama*, I hardly ate and almost never slept. All my appetites had converged into a single desperate want: words I understood.

On the nights we met up with *Monorama*, after the formal interviews with shamans were concluded, after Rathin ate his mountainous dinner of spicy fish and dahl and chapatis, when Eleanor had gone to bed, and Girindra and Rathin's staff were playing cards by lamp light, Rathin and I would stay up and he would translate from the Bengali books on Sundarbans folklore he had checked out of the library in Calcutta for me.

The work was painfully slow. The sentences did not always make sense. I later discovered that Rathin left out the parts he considered boring or unimportant. Slowly the outlines of the stories began to take shape, but the shapes felt out of context. I understood them only as a blindfolded person comes to know a room: everything seemed larger than it really was and all arranged at jagged angles. And then, just when it seemed the picture was about to come clear, Rathin would announce that his eyes were too tired to read.

Still, we would stay up. Rathin suffers from insomnia; my eager ears released him from the torture of lying awake, chasing helplessly after sleep. So as if in gratitude he set before me gifts of the strange and glittering facts of Sundarbans, of West Bengal, of his own life. He told me how he had outdistanced a charging elephant on a motorbike; he told how his grandfather had risked death to elope with a Rajput lady. Rathin had married a fiery and beautiful Christian schoolteacher named Manjusree when he was twenty-three. His parents and hers had arranged the wedding. He set eyes on her for the first time after the church ceremony. "I did not even look up at her when the priest was saying the words," he confessed. "I just kept looking at the ring."

With the dramatic flair of a gifted storyteller, Rathin would tell me of Sundarbans intrigue and savagery, of strange winds and high waves, of pirates and tigers and crocodiles. The crocodiles! Oh, they are so vicious, he said, that once, as he helped a captive baby estuarine crocodile hatch out of its shell, "the residual yolk was still hanging from its belly, and immediately it bit into my hand! Its teeth, like small needles!"

"Sundarbans is such treacherous and inhospitable terrain, only daring and desperate people would venture here and survive," he said, prefacing a new story. "I am sure you would like to know how I came across sighting my first human tiger victim." I listened, mouth watering, pupils big as an owl's:

It had happened on an afternoon shortly after he was first posted in Sundarbans. In his launch, docked at the jetty at Patlaptoma Forest Station, Rathin was filling out paperwork. One of his orderlies came to him with news: nearby was the body of a man who had just been attacked and killed by a tiger.

"I was just too excited!" Rathin said — then added, seeing the alarm on my face, "I was very, very concerned." He grabbed his camera and followed his orderly down the jetty. There: the orderly pointed to a small paddleboat on high ground — the boat had obviously approached the jetty earlier, when the tide was higher. Now the boat was grounded on the mud.

In the shade of the little boat's curved, thatched roof, Rathin found the body of a man wearing a worn loincloth and a red gamcha, a cloth Bengalis often use as a sash and handkerchief, around his waist. He seemed to be staring blankly at the thatched roof of the boat, said Rathin; he did not appear to be dead. Rathin saw no wounds on his neck. Three villagers then approached Rathin, and he asked them, "How do you know this man has been killed by a tiger? I don't see anything." At this the men untied the red gamcha. Rathin was adjusting the lens of his camera; when he looked up, to his horror he saw the man's intestines spilling out through a gaping wound in his belly. Only the gamcha had been keeping the intestines inside, he realized; the cloth's red color had come from the victim's blood.

"Who is this man?" Rathin asked, fighting nausea. One of the men spoke up: "He was a shaman, and all three of us were in his party when the tiger attacked him and killed him."

How did it happen? They had permits to cut hental leaves, the thorny palm used to thatch roofs, in the forest at Adjubalmari. Upon arriving, the shaman uttered his prayers. Finally he felt it was safe for his companions to swing their axes.

The shaman's job was to clean and trim the cut hental to prepare it for stacking in the boat. He was hunched over this task when the tiger attacked. It leaped out of nowhere, the men told Rathin, and everything occurred in one moment: "The tiger approached and jumped up on this man and ripped open his belly. And now he is dead." Throwing sticks, they finally chased the tiger away. But it was too late.

The story didn't sound right to Rathin. Even though he had just been posted to Sundarbans, he had worked at the tiger reserve at Buxa, and he knew tigers do not usually attack in this way. Almost invariably they seize human prey by the back of the neck, killing with one bite. A tiger rips open the belly after killing the prey and carrying the carcass some distance, when it has finally settled down to feed upon the flesh.

If the men were not telling the truth, Rathin felt, they must have something to hide.

"And so I used some tactics," Rathin told me, his voice soft, conspiratorial, his mongoose eyes flashing. "I had come to know that this shaman's wife was very young. I mentioned this to them, and then I asked them, 'Was this why you murdered this man? Shall I go to the police?'

"At the word 'police,'" Rathin announced, triumphant, "they fell at my feet. They said, 'Sir, we will tell you everything. But we tell you, sir, it was an accident!'" And so they told Rathin the story.

They had indeed been collecting hental when the tiger had approached. The creature had exploded from the forest and pushed the shaman to the ground. As the tiger's monstrous body was covering the screaming man, before the tiger had found the back of the neck with its teeth, the shaman's companions rushed to his aid. One of the men raised his axe high above his head to bring it down upon the tiger.

But the tiger dodged. The shaman tried to roll away. The axe landed full force on the shaman's belly. They had killed the man they were trying to save.

"We tried to take him to the hospital," the men told Rathin, "but, sir, owing to the long time it takes to reach any habitation in our paddleboat, he died from hemorrhage."

Rathin then took all three men with him aboard his government launch and sailed to the forest at Adjubalmari, a five-and-a-half-hour journey. Only if he saw the place himself could he believe their story was true.

The men led Rathin to the scene. "On reaching the spot," said Rathin, "I found one rubber slipper, and the entire place had the look of hectic activity. Hental sticks had been left in a hurry. I also found pugmarks, fresh pugmarks, and blood stains. I was sure that yes, it was the case of an accident."

Was the shaman a tiger accident victim? A tiger had attacked him, yes, and as a result he had died; but the tiger had not killed him. Because the government pays the victim's family when a permit holder is killed by a tiger, many times people try to blame a tiger whenever a man is killed, Rathin said; this is why he must investigate such cases.

What did Rathin write in his report? "I would not at this point say," he answered slyly, remembering that my tape recorder was on. "But I feel that a man would not do wrong to certify that this case is a tiger accident case." He paused. "Thank you," he said into the tape.

Although he had gone to the trouble to pick two shamans for me to interview and had fetched them for me, Rathin was not much interested in the beliefs of the local people. When Ksab Kayal, the Hindu gunin from Lahripur, was telling a story, at one point Rathin announced to me in English, with a look of disgust, "I am becoming thoroughly bored." When I asked

Ksab Kayal to tell me about Bonobibi and Daksin Ray, Rathin began to translate the gunin's words, but then broke off. "He is telling it all wrong," he said. "I have this in a much better way, in a book. What he is telling you, there are many defects, because he has not gone through the book, he has just heard it, so what he is saying is not exactly authentic." When I persisted, Rathin got annoyed. "I am telling you, it's useless. Do you want to hear the story of Bonobibi from *him?*"

The inhabitants of Sundarbans are nearly all low-caste Hindus and poor Muslims; Rathin, the Christian grandson of three Brahmins and a Rajput, is a well-paid, high-status official in a branch of government almost military in its pride in rank.

Rathin was born to leadership: the eldest of four children, his name means "Head Charioteer." With an intense, sometimes imperial stare and a barrel-shaped chest, he easily dominates his underlings. I was amazed to discover that he is slightly shorter than my fine-boned five-foot, five-inch frame, and that his hands and feet are as small as my own. Throughout Sundarbans, people are afraid of him. He has exchanged gunfire with pirates and led raids on illegal timbering operations, and he is not at all timid about imposing fines on fishermen or relieving them of some of their catch. When Girindra spoke with Rathin, he called him "Sir," and his slight stutter worsened.

So, desperately though I wanted to, I never asked Rathin to interpret so that Girindra and I could talk.

There was hardly enough time, anyway. Rathin's job was demanding and changeable. We never knew when we might be summoned to meet him; when he found time, *Monorama* was usually en route to some assignment where Eleanor and I would not be welcome. After a night's travel we either would be sent back to Sajnekhali or Jamespur aboard *Mabisaka* or would have to wait all day on *Monorama* for Rathin to finish his work, feeling like prisoners.

Eleanor and I tried three times to engage a more reliable

translator. First we arranged to hire a professional from Calcutta. Then we planned to hook up with a young Bengali from Calcutta who was to vacation in Sundarbans. We pleaded with Kushal to come out. None of them showed up. Eleanor joked that our plans seemed subject to a force her first husband had dubbed "Chinese come-apart syndrome" after shoes he bought in Chinatown disintegrated in the rain. But in Sundarbans, it seemed, plans did not merely dissolve; they flew to pieces, leaving us helpless and lost again.

My attempts to communicate with people grew more desperate and surreal. In an effort to interview Phoni Guyan, the gray-haired gunin who officiated at the Bonobibi puja, I'd asked my questions in very simple English — translated haltingly by the manager of the tourist lodge, whose English was only slightly better than Girindra's — and the priest had replied in Bangla. I recorded his answers, hoping to get them translated later. Of course this kind of discourse offered no opportunity for follow-up questions or clarification. In fact, all of my questions had been predicated on the information that he was a Brahmin priest — which, though I did not discover this until months later, turned out to be utterly false.

Girindra and I grew increasingly exasperated. Once he so desperately wanted me to understand a story he was trying to tell that finally — after I had again failed to understand, even though he'd told it in English-studded Bangla twice, complete with drawings — he agreed to tell it a third time, word by word, so I could write it down phonetically. We hoped that back in Calcutta or in the States, I could read it to someone who could then reconstruct the story for me. (Rathin translated it for me at a Calcutta restaurant. But more than a full year later, after Girindra wrote the story out in Bangla and another interpreter translated it, I discovered that Rathin had left out the entire middle portion of the story and omitted the fate of the main character! He had been eating a pizza at the time and had grown bored with chewing and translating at the same time.)

After days like these, I would lie in bed at the tourist lodge listening to the scratch of the rat in the ceiling and the chirp of the gecko lizards — the sound of a coin tapping glass — and wait for sleep to drown me. One night I dreamed that Girindra walked into the room and informed me, "I can understand you. I can speak with you now. I understand what you want to know. Quickly, let me tell you, while we have time." And then I woke up. I had lost my chance.

I tried to piece together words from my phrase book to tell Girindra about the dream. I wanted him to know how frustrated I was when I awoke without learning what he had to say. I'd wanted to cry. But again my Bangla was unintelligible. Due to a typo in my phrase book, the verb "to weep" (*kadi*) was misspelled *kada*. I didn't realize at the time that I was telling Girindra, with great urgency and emotion, "I want mud." At this Girindra stared at me and shook his head. With an obvious sense of loss and frustration — he knew that whatever I was trying to say to him was important — again uttered those words that summed up the void at the center of my heart: "Jani na" — "I don't know."

In the watery maze of Sundarbans, every channel offered another kind of lost.

❖

One morning, after a night half wasted looking for the launch in the dark, Eleanor and I woke aboard *Monorama* to a day flooded with pale yellow light. We saw something big floating beside us in the water.

It was a dead chital doe, blood still oozing from the wounds at her neck.

Rathin's staff fished her out with bamboo poles. We examined her on deck. She was young — perhaps one or two years old, Rathin estimated. Part of her belly had been opened, from her anus to her breasts. Bright red blood gathered at her mouth and nose. We saw four deep holes in the back of her neck. Two teeth had punctured her windpipe; two teeth had crushed the spinal cord near the base of the skull. Rathin announced she had been killed three or four hours earlier. The cool, salty water had preserved some of the grace she had possessed in life: her blood had not clotted and her limbs were still supple.

Again Rathin was on a mission that day, and he left both us and the dead doe at Pakhiralaya. Eleanor and I peered at her wet body on the lawn at the range station. Already she was so different from the creature we had seen floating in the water. The first thing we had noticed then were her eyes. The pupils and irises had rolled back in her head, and only the whites stared out from her open lids. But her sclerotics were not pure white; they seemed to reflect the blue sky and white clouds above. It was as if her eyes were full of heaven, the sight of which had stolen her soul.

But now all traces of that sight had vanished. One of the forest officers knelt beside her and gently closed her eyelids.

❖

It had been half-tide, Rathin later told me, when the tiger found her. The tiger may well have been hunting for a very long time, walking and swimming for perhaps more than a dozen miles before he caught the scent of the chital herd upwind or saw their graceful forms bending to nibble leaves. The tiger would have followed invisibly. George Schaller once watched a tigress surprise a chital buck after stalking him through grass only six inches high to within fifty feet; in the twine and tangle of Sundarbans' root forests, shading the glow of the quarter-moon, the tiger could ooze toward the deer as imperceptibly as a serpent, without making a sound. "The tiger walks so quietly," a

Bangladeshi fisherman had told Hasna Moudud, on the other side of Sundarbans, "that if he makes a sound, he bites his own foot in anger."

Or the tiger might have secreted himself at a place where he knew the chital would come. He may even have lured her. Hunters say that tigers sometimes call their prey. In areas where they hunt the big deer called sambar, tigers call *tonk!* like belling stags. Others say tigers lure deer with a low yawning moan emitted through vibrating lips, bouncing the sound off the ground so no one can tell precisely where it comes from. Rathin said that in Sundarbans he has heard tigers emulate the voice of the chital doe calling her young: a shrill, short burst of syllables like *tik-tik-tik*. Few fawns would confuse this voice with that of its own mother; but deer are surprisingly curious — some in the herd might well approach the sound of a foreign female.

So perhaps the young doe had approached the waiting tiger. Perhaps she had hesitated for only a moment — one moment too long. We imagined her standing stock-still, her ears swiveled behind her, her muscles a quiver away from flight. We imagined the tiger, head low, mouth closed, ears raised. Perhaps, in the last moments, the chital had raised her tail, stamped the ground, yipped an alarm.

But probably the doe saw nothing. Hunters concealed in tree-top blinds, waiting for a tiger to take tethered bait, have nearly missed the arrival of their quarry: one described its appearance as "a puff of smoke or shadow of a cloud passing across the moon." Another as "a ghostly silent figure . . . and but for his shadow, appearing at times as if he were almost transparent."

Oh so carefully did the tiger approach that doe. He had come so far and hunted so cautiously and waited so long for this moment. He was almost certainly very hungry. Schaller estimated that perhaps only one out of twenty stalks was successful for his tigers at Kanha. Tigers may go hungry for many days. Some hunters have written of seeing saliva running from a tiger's mouth as he prepared for the final stages of the stalk. But even well-fed human hunters know the flavor of this desire. It is so strong, and so basic, and so consuming that often it is described as like love. Looking through the sights of his rifle at the deer he was about to kill, one hunter wrote later of feeling that the deer was the most beautiful thing he had seen other than his own babies — his own issue — his own self. So as the tiger held that doe in his sight, surely his eyes blazed with desire, burning bright, as in Blake's poem, as if alight with the power to draw his prey, mesmerized, into the insistence of this all-consuming want.

But the tiger at such a moment is not just wanting; he is thinking. "There is no animal who seems to weigh conditions before making an attack as does the tiger," wrote the American missionary H. R. Caldwell of the animals he observed in south China. Our tiger had to decide how he would grab the doe, how he would take her down, and how he would kill her with his mouth.

Tigers know many ways to kill. If it attacks a very large animal from the front or side, it may seize the prey by the throat and bring it down with the aid of a forepaw. If the prey is very large, the tiger may have to hold it by the throat; both animals, predator and prey, stand nearly motionless, locked in that endless moment when life cedes to death, until the prey collapses from lack of oxygen.

If the tiger attacks from the rear, it may leap on the animal's back and, as the prey is falling, release its grip, reach over the fallen animal's neck, seize it by the throat, and pull the neck up and twist. Or it may grab with a forepaw and pull the hindquarters down. Or it may simply land on the animal's back and bite it on the back of the neck.

That was what this tiger had decided to do. Launching himself toward that moment of union, the tiger had leaped. Because the prey was so small, he had chosen to kill it with almost surgical precision by inserting his canine teeth between the vertebrae "like a wedge," as the German cat expert Paul Leyhausen has observed — or, as Mel Sunquist and John Seidensticker have written, "like a key in a lock." The tiger's teeth and the bones of the deer's neck seem made for each other, like a lock and key.

He had not even unsheathed his claws; the doe's body was unscarred. Only the tiny holes in her neck had killed her. Giant tigers have been described with teeth as fat and long as railroad spikes, but these punctures were only as wide as a bee's head. This could well have been a young tiger. We imagined the joy with which that bite was delivered: in this way, but gently, a tiger seizes a tigress before making love to her; in this way a playful house cat pounces upon a toy.

Joyously the tiger had carried his prey in his mouth. Folding his stiff whiskers forward, he enveloped her with a sense of touch so far beyond human sensitivity we cannot even dream of what it must feel like. Each whisker sits upright in a tiny sac full of nerve endings, like a straw in a bottle. The whiskers, in the words of author and naturalist Fiona Sunquist, who worked at Chitawan with her husband, Mel, act as "a tactile third eye." This is why you can blindfold a house cat and it will not blunder into obstacles. A blindfolded cat can move deftly, sensing silhouettes by the air currents surrounding objects. High-speed photographs of house cats show that in the final split second before it pounces, the whiskers move forward to sense the prey's last movements.

The people of Sundarbans know the tiger's whiskers are capable of great powers: this is why, a man told Hasna in Bangladesh, the tiger only drinks with the water moving downstream from his head; otherwise, the potency of his own whiskers would poison him. So powerful are the whiskers that when a tiger dies, the shaman Bakher Gazi told me, Allah takes three of them away to keep for his own.

Whiskers wrapped around the warm doe, the tiger probably carried her for a time. Finally, at a spot he deemed appropriate, he would have unfolded his whiskers and laid the doe down. He had opened her between her legs. As he began to eat in the cool night, her hot meat would have steamed his face. And he would have been so glad. Even grateful.

"A committed meateater may express affection and even gratitude toward his or her prey — a touching and thoroughly appropriate emotion in a creature for whom captured animal protein is the only source of food," Elizabeth Marshall Thomas writes in her astonishing book *The Tribe of Tiger: Cats and Their Culture*. The author had watched a lion family rending the carcass of a kudu they had caught on an African savannah: "The lion took the intact but severed head of the kudu between his paws and, holding it upright, so that she faced him, he slowly licked her cheeks and eyes intimately and tenderly, as if he were grooming her, as if she were another, beloved lion. . . . Under his tongue her eyelids opened and shut in a lifelike manner. An infant lion pushed up under his father's elbow and helped to wash the kudu's face."

Eating and loving: in the mind of the tiger the two are twined tight. In the human brain the control centers for sex and anger nestle close to one another; they are not opposites, as we would like to believe, but twins.

So here, at this rapturous juncture of tenderness and savagery, the tiger began to consume the body of the chital doe, joining flesh to flesh. But — just as the tiger began to eat, something happened.

What could have driven him from his beloved, from his meat? What could have caused such a grievous loss? That he had permitted such an outrage reinforced the idea that this was a young tiger, easily frightened. Had another tiger scared him away? Had he fled from the sound of our boat? Neither possibility seemed likely. If another tiger had come, it would have eaten the doe. And the tigers here are not frightened by boats,

Rathin assured us; they are not even frightened of guns, for since the hunting of tigers was banned a generation of tigers ago, they have lost the knowledge of what a gun can mean.

What would drive a tiger from his kill? For whatever reason, the corpse had lain abandoned, and the sea had risen to take her away. And now the sea had carried her to us. The tiger's loss had made him visible, his story glimpsed in the holes left by teeth in this slender, spotted neck.

When Eleanor first saw the doe floating in the water, she sucked in her breath. "How beautiful!" she gasped, and grabbed for her camera. I asked Eleanor later what she had seen in this sad little corpse that she found beautiful. Eleanor thinks with her eyes, through her cameras; she understands with images rather than with stories made of words. Once she told me she had nearly been blinded by the beauty of blood at a butcher's stall in Vietnam: the color! so red!

It was not the corpse itself that was so beautiful, Eleanor explained; in fact, she had been angry when Rathin's staff fished the deer out. It was the corpse *floating in the water* that was beautiful to her — floating on the skin of life and death, in the watery blue heaven of Vishnu's ocean.

❖

When I was trying to interview Phoni Guyan — I speaking English, he answering in Bangla — a strange thing happened.

I had written out questions in very simple English. These I read, and then showed them to the curly-headed manager of the tourist lodge. I would watch his face carefully to see if he understood; sometimes I would rephrase a question. Then the manager would ask the question in Bangla, and Phoni Guyan would seem to repeat it. Back and forth it would go, the way cedar waxwings pass a berry back and forth over and over until one swallows the berry and both know they can begin building a nest. Finally the question being asked would be mutually agreed upon, and Phoni Guyan would speak for a long time.

A less promising interview could hardly be imagined. Setting it up had been ridiculously complicated. I'd told Girindra what I wanted to do, and since he is good friends with both the manager and Phoni Guyan, he'd relayed the request. After speaking with the manager for half an hour, Girindra returned to our room to confess: "Your purpose, manager, no idea."

I dug out of my backpack a copy of the first book I had written. "Amar boi" ("my book"), I said, showing it to the manager. "Amar nam" ("my name"), I said, pointing to my name on the cover — the same name he had seen me write repeatedly on the guest register. "Ecta boi Sundarbans subject," I said, employing a miserable mixture of ungrammatical Bangla and ungrammatical English, "you helping book, my purpose."

None of this information was news to the manager. Back in December I had introduced myself as an author ("Ami lekika" was a phrase I had carefully rehearsed). By now half of Sundarbans knew about me; everywhere Girindra took me in *Mabisaka,* I heard him explaining in Bangla, "She is a writer. She is from America. She eats only eggs!" But as the manager thumbed my book and passed it to his staff — they looked at the pictures, they looked for words they might recognize — it took on a meaning it had never had before. The words possessed no poetry, its ideas no force; these values were invisible. Yet the book was important in a different way. Its value was as a physical object, like a bin full of rice or a stack of firewood. The book was a diploma written in Latin, tangible evidence of status and authority.

And so the manager had consented to help.

As Phoni Guyan answered each question, I held up my tape recorder to catch his words. But because no one was there to translate for me — unlike the interviews in which Rathin had acted as interpreter, and the men had answered *him* — now Phoni Guyan was answering *me*. He was handing me words as mute as my book, yet here was a conversation. As he spoke, his sharp brown eyes met mine, widened and narrowed, flew about the room like birds. His slender hands flitted, his voice growled and then softened. And I would nod sometimes or cock my head, and my eyes would follow his, and my mouth would water; in this way I listened. How much listening is done not with the mind or the ear but the muscles of the face! And on my face he could see — I know, for it was reflected in his eyes — how much I valued his skills and his knowledge, how grateful I was for this gift.

It would be months before I learned what Phoni Guyan had told me. But in our mute but meaningful exchange, trading jewellike words bereft of language, he had shown me wizardry as enchanting as his mantras.

❖

Lost: true, it describes the condition of being unable to find one's way, understand, or make progress; true, it describes a thing forfeited, dispossessed. But there is another definition as well: "completely involved or absorbed. Rapt."

Lost: as with everything in Sundarbans, it has another, unexpected meaning, disguised as an opposite, revealed as a twin.

One night as we sat in the wheelhouse of *Monorama*, Rathin told me about the tiger who lived near Gazikhali. He was very old, and his fur was matted. Garlands of fur, Rathin said, hung from his body "like the hair of a sadhu," one of the holy men who live in the forest and smear their bodies with ash and don't comb or wash. The tiger had only three canines — the one on the lower right had broken off. Rathin had never seen him, though he had heard about him. The sadhu tiger was like a legend in the area. Rathin did not know whether he was real.

Until, that is, the day he met a man who had survived an encounter with this tiger. Rathin went to the hospital where, he had heard, a tiger accident victim was recovering. He asked to see the patient. Because Rathin was a high government official, the doctor not only permitted the interview but actually unwrapped the dressing from the man's wounds to show the three large holes at the neck. The tiger's missing tooth had saved the man's life, Rathin said; otherwise there would have been no escape from his viselike grip. Because the tiger was old and had a missing tooth, his first bite had not killed the man. His brave son had driven the tiger away by hitting him with an oar.

Rathin told his staff to keep watch for the sadhu tiger. He wanted very much to see him. There is a watchtower at Gazikhali Forest Station from which tigers are often seen. But no one ever spotted the tiger after that, although the forest staff looked for him daily.

Oddly, though, Rathin did get a look at the sadhu tiger. But at the time Rathin was in Calcutta, and the tiger was young and lithe.

A few days after Rathin spoke with the tiger victim, he visited a fellow forest officer who had spent much time in Sundarbans at his home in Calcutta. They discussed the fine points of wildlife photography. The fellow pointed to the wall where a photo of a tiger he had seen years earlier was hanging. "Now, what do you think of this picture?" he asked Rathin.

"I looked at the photo and I was really surprised," said Rathin. He immediately recognized the tiger, whom he had never seen. "It was snarling. His left lower canine was missing."

As Rathin finished this story, the moon reached its zenith. The boat stood completely still. Mist rose from the river. Rathin said it was ozone and it would cure tuberculosis.

The call of a nightjar burst like a bubble from the forest, to be echoed from the opposite bank. And then we felt the boat swivel beneath us as the tide reversed.

Tiger God of the Jungle

❖ ❖ ❖ ❖ ❖ ❖ ❖ ❖ ❖ ❖ ❖ ❖ ❖ ❖ ❖ ❖ ❖ ❖ ❖ ❖

IT ALL BEGAN, one story goes, when the powerful god Shiva, whose symbol is the life-giving phallus, first set eyes on the fairy Ambika. So overcome was he by the sight of her irresistible beauty that he "shot from his body sperm the color of the moon." From his desire Daksin Ray was born — the miraculous child of a god's helpless lust for a fairy.

Other stories say that Daksin Ray was the son of a goddess, a Brahmin, a human warrior, a hunter, a sage. Certain scholars claim that Daksin Ray was a historical figure, possibly a zamindar, a landlord of precolonial times, or the general of a great army. By all accounts Daksin Ray, whose name means "Lord of the South," was rich, brave, and powerful. His clay image is always handsome, his garments encrusted with jewels, his headdress shining with gold.

Of course he could not be otherwise. Daksin Ray owns the wealth of Sundarbans, the trees and the tides, the silvery little fishes and the giant sharks and the fat bees' combs dripping with honey and laden with wax. His wealth is exceeded only by his power. Daksin Ray embodies the powers of Sundarbans' tigers, beauty and terror incarnate. For this reason he is often shown riding on the back of a tiger, but his abilities far surpass this feat. All the tigers of Sundarbans obey his commands, people say, and everyone knows he can enter the body of a tiger at will.

The stories of Daksin Ray's origin, like the birth story of Jesus, were surely composed long after the hero had come to be venerated. The stories have grown longer, the characters in them have multiplied, incorporating the history of Sundarbans itself. Later the narratives were richly ornamented, like Daksin Ray's garments, with the finest jewels of language that Bengal's poets could offer. And the epic poems, once composed and read, again became the property of memory.

Daksin Ray's story changes — remembered, augmented, confused, transformed. He takes different names: sometimes he is called Daksindar, sometimes Bara Thakur. He takes different forms: sometimes his face is painted white like the moon, signifying a pure, sacrificed life; sometimes it is a deep yellow. The Anthropological Survey of India reports that he is sometimes worshiped as a piece of stone or a fanciful head. But underlying the names and the images, the stories and the poems, like the undertow beneath the tides, flows a primal power. At its heart beats an ancient mystery. For Sundarbans' tiger god is older than the zamindars, older than writing, older, even, than Shiva himself.

❖

"*Bara puja* or Daksinrai starts in the afternoon and continues all night," Rathin read, translating from the Bengali. "There is no ploughing, potting, boiling, or threshing allowed.

"Among the worshipers, a spot in the forest is selected and cleared where the altar is raised, encircled by date palm. A red flag is hoisted nearby. Torches are lit, drums beaten, and chickens and goats are sacrificed."

Rathin was translating a chapter called "Daksin Rai Cult"

from a book of articles titled *A Focus on Sundarbans.* He read on:

"The yard of worship overflows with the blood of the sacrificed birds and beasts. Marking their foreheads with the blood of bleeding beasts, the drunken devotees, with torches in hand, dance and make obscene gestures and utterances. Stunning shouts and pealing music are raised."

During the ceremony, he read, the idol is offered the castings of earthworms, unripe pumpkin, the flesh of domestic cats — items quite different from those offered in traditional Hindu pujas. They are not placed at the idol's feet but thrown into a ceremonial fire; the idol is bathed from head to foot in country liquor and given water from the hookah. These practices, said Rathin, reveal that Daksin Ray is more ancient than classical Hinduism and show his roots as a god of the lower castes.

"Here is the chant they speak to the tiger god," Rathin said, and he read:

> Jatale matal kanda
> Khuno khuni sara
> Mad, magi, rakta, mangsha
> Samal, sama bara.

Then he translated:

> At the altar we stand, intoxicated and weeping,
> Taking life, ending life.
> Wine, woman, blood, flesh —
> Image of God, control me!

As Rathin spoke these words, we were en route to Khahtjhuni, where the Forest Department was running a timber-cutting operation, or coupe, across the river Harinbhanga, near the border with Bangladesh. There woodcutters from villages throughout Sundarbans were massing for the very ceremony we were reading about, the yearly puja to Daksin Ray.

Daksin Ray had been worshiped at the Bonobibi puja also; but a Daksin Ray puja is a different affair entirely, Rathin assured me. Far from any village, away from the taming influence of women and children, this puja conjures powers so raw and bloody and savage that they can be controlled only by the god of the tigers himself.

Rathin would not be able to accompany us. In the morning he would depart on another mission on *Monorama* while Eleanor, Girindra, and I continued toward Khahtjhuni on *Mabisaka*. Not trusting Girindra, Rathin was sending his personal orderly, Tarapada, to chaperon us through the drunkenness and obscenity; for whatever else might crop up, Rathin equipped Tarapada with an ancient Russian-made rifle.

Tarapada was delighted to come along. As it turned out, he spent almost all of the puja sleeping soundly inside the shady hold of *Mabisaka*.

❖

Aboard *Mabisaka* we sailed first to the village of Lahripur. This was the home of the clay artist who had fashioned the image of Daksin Ray to be used in the puja. We were to pick up the idol and ferry it to the shrine at Khahtjhuni.

We heard the procession long before we saw it: the clanging of gongs, the pulsing of drums, the clink of brass cymbals. A shivering "Uluoooooooooo" rose like steam from the unseen crowd, announcing that the god was coming closer, closer. Then, like a moon rising over the mud embankment protecting the village from the sea, we saw him: the haloed, radiant face of the god.

His forehead bore the trident of Shiva. His ears were ringed in silver. His neck was garlanded with pearl and ivory, and his breastplate gleamed with gold and diamond. He appeared to be floating toward us through the air. Only after the image crested the spine of the embankment could we see the arms and shoulders and legs of the faithful who were bearing him toward us, carrying him on a blue throne.

Daksin Ray was loaded carefully onto *Mabisaka*'s fore-deck, along with about a dozen of his entourage. Two men in checkered lungis would protect the idol on his journey with the sounds of the sacred drums — the *dhaee,* made from mango wood and cow leather, and the *kanshi,* a cymballike brass instrument beaten with a bamboo stick. A third attendant held the back of the throne to keep its newspaper backing from peeling off in the wind. Well-wishers helped to load some of the numerous items for the puja: milk, ghee, fruits, coconuts, pots, instruments, rice. Someone blew the holy conch shell, a blast as loud and shrill as a train whistle, for now they were loading the flask of Ganges water, the goddess Gonga incarnate. And finally, as the *putt-putt* of *Mabisaka* joined the din of the drums, we sailed off to the puja.

❖

At all of Sundarbans' timber coupes, hundreds of smaller acts of worship of Daksin Ray are performed yearly. The Forest Department, which oversees the yearly extraction of 6,000 metric tons of timber from small, rotating plots between the Jula River and the Buri Ganga, allows no group of workers to cut timber without a shaman in their party. The shaman's presence, Rathin told me, is as compulsory as the plastic face masks. With mantras and prayers, with charmed slivers of wood or enchanted mud, men like Bakher Gazi and Ksab Kayal and Phoni Guyan entreat the gods of the jungle to be merciful to the men entrusted to their care. The woodcutters may swing their axes only after the shamans have honored Daksin Ray. This is only appropriate. For Daksin Ray's divinity, the story goes, was first revealed to a woodcutter.

Rathin had translated the story one night aboard *Monorama:*
A young and wealthy merchant, Puspa Datta, needed timber

to make boats for his fleet. He selected the woodcutter Rothai Baulya to head an expedition to find and cut the wood. Together with his six brothers and his only son, Rothai Baulya set sail for the very heart of Sundarbans, where the finest wood for shipbuilding could be found.

The party ventured deep into the mangrove forest and went to work felling the timber they would need. After they had loaded seven boats full of wood, they were ready to sail home. But then they saw a single majestic tree growing near the water's edge. It was so stately and tall they could not resist cutting it down.

Blinded by greed, Rothai and his party did not realize that they had felled the very abode of Daksin Ray. Infuriated, Daksin Ray ordered six tigers to seize Rothai's brothers and kill them.

His brothers dead, the grief-stricken Rothai decided to commit suicide. He told his son to return home by boat. But just as Rothai was about to kill himself, Daksin Ray spoke in a voice of thunder. "Your brothers were killed for their insolence and greed," he rumbled; they were punished for violating the dwelling place of a god. "But I, Daksin Ray, am benevolent," the voice continued. "I will restore the lives of your six brothers — on one condition: you must sacrifice to me your only son."

Rothai sacrificed the boy on the spot. Daksin Ray, appeased by this act of faith and humility, restored not only the lives of the six brothers but also that of the son. All fell to their knees in worship. And when they returned home, they told everyone about the mercy and power of Daksin Ray, the lord of Sundarbans and god of tigers.

"Even back then, the ecological concept was present," Rathin commented as he translated this passage from the epic *Ray Mangal Kavya*, written in 1686 by the learned Bengali poet Krishnaram Das. "This equates felling a tree to sacrificing a son!"

The theme has echoed through India's centuries, as Rathin

well knows: in another book he showed me drawings of clay panels uncovered at Mohenjo-Daro, relics of the Indus Valley civilization of 3000 B.C. The first panel shows a tiger in the forest; the second shows a person chasing a tiger from the forest. Another depicts a god who dwells among the trees, his arms held out to the tiger, imploring. A subsequent image shows people cutting down the trees. The final panel shows the forest bare, the tiger vanished, the tree-dwelling god gone. The moral, said Rathin, is quite clear: "You can reclaim lands for agriculture," he said, "but your god will abandon you."

❖

We arrive at the coupe five hours later. The sun is so hot it glints off Daksin Ray's golden crown in needles, and the air feels as heavy as the call of the cowhide dhaee. Dozens of trawler-sized wooden boats are anchored in the surrounding channels. During the weeks they are harvesting timber, the woodcutters live aboard these boats, sleeping in grass-thatched wooden shacks built on top of each boat's hold like a roof. Most of the boats fly red flags. Some sport lei-like malas around their bows. One of the headmen shouts to the workers that Daksin Ray has arrived.

Preparations for the puja begin. One man paints a clay pot with the double trident of Shiva, smearing vermilion with the third finger of his left hand. Another prepares a paste from sandalwood, rubbing it in oil against a flat round stone to yield a rich cream-and-coffee color he will dab on the forehead of each person present. Candles are lit. Incense burns. People are cutting fruits and arranging them on banana leaves. Everything is carefully washed in water or milk before it is placed inside the shrine.

The shrine is a large permanent structure, perhaps twenty-five feet long, raised on stilts, walled with hental leaves, and floored with lumber sturdier than that used for most docks. Other idols, including Bonobibi, seem to huddle in a separate room partitioned off with a plaid sari, like actors waiting back-stage. Today Daksin Ray alone is adored.

The idol is carefully positioned and then surrounded with a low fence of red string. I remember the red string from Girindra's mud-ball puja and also from the Bonobibi puja at the Sajnekhali shrine.

The priest, a young man with enormous eyes and a shallow chest, begins the ceremony. He is a Brahmin; the sacred thread drapes across his left shoulder. He invokes three salutations to Vishnu, each echoed by his assistant, almost as if the two were singing a round. Their voices stretch and pull the words like elastic out of their bodies, out of their souls, out of the past. The motion of their voices awakens the words of the prayer to life, the way kneading hands awaken the yeast in bread.

"He is showing the longing of the people, who ask Daksin Ray to come so they may worship him," Amarendra Nath Mondal explains. Mr. Mondal (we never called him by his first name because Girindra didn't, apparently out of respect) is not himself a worshiper of Daksin Ray; a scholar, as his black-rimmed spectacles imply, he does not believe in Daksin Ray at all. He is, he tells me, "more classical": he worships Laxmi, the four-armed goddess of success and wealth. But Mr. Mondal has accompanied us to the puja because he is interested in observing such things, and at Girindra's request he has agreed to translate for us on his day off.

Someone blows the conch shell. "Now the image is aroused," Mr. Mondal announces. It is for this moment that the low fence of red string was erected around the image. "The red string keeps away the demons, who may try instead to enter the image ahead of Daksin Ray."

The music throbs and bangs, the gong summoning, passionate. Daksin Ray takes possession of the image. The priest tosses a flower at his feet, and the ceremony proceeds.

The god is offered every honor, every comfort that his hosts can provide: pleasing words, welcoming notes, sweet incense, good food. For his refreshment in the heat, he is even offered a bath. This presents a logistical problem, since the image is made of clay. The worshipers have solved the problem admirably by including a mirror in the ceremony, so Daksin Ray's reflection can take a bath.

For two hours the puja continues: an intoxicating tumult of prayers, bells, flowers, food, song, incense, drum, and gong. The music swells like the heat, quickening like the pulse at the approach of a lover, then pounding like a heart at the approach of a tiger — finally throbbing, dizzying, unbearable. Daksin Ray's eyes seem to float in their sockets as if he is watching us all. Below his black mustache a slight smile seems to hover on his lips as if he is pleased.

Periodically, sudden sharp sounds crack through the wet weight of the heat. Mr. Mondal asks one of the Forest Department staff what they are. Just outside the clearing, guards are exploding firecrackers to keep tigers from coming to the puja to worship their lord. But wouldn't the people be safe if the tigers were occupied by religious duties? Mr. Mondal smiled. "The problem is, there is no assurance that all the tigers who would come are true believers. They might only be hungry tigers."

The ceremony continues. There is no liquor. There is no obscenity. There is no animal sacrifice. Years ago live animals were killed at Daksin Ray pujas, as Rathin had read. But when Kalyan Chakrabarti became field director, he abolished the practice, which he considered cruel. (The end of animal sacrifice coincided with many of the Forest Department's efforts to reduce tiger attacks, such as electric fencing around villages, dug rain-water ponds, and, later, masks and electric dummies. But when you talk with local people, they don't bring up any of these changes; they attribute the abatement of tiger attacks to a change in the puja.)

After two hours the priest lies almost prostrate, his voice

breaking, like a man about to cry. He rises, wipes his face and chest with a red towel, redrapes his shawl. He returns to the prayer from the beginning. His assistant repeats the words softly. Another worshiper pours coconut water into a brass pot. Now at last the god departs; the red thread is broken. "OM Shakti, OM Shakti, OM Shakti, OM," hums the priest. The puja to the god of tigers closes with the primal sound, the word for peace.

❖

For centuries Daksin Ray ruled Sundarbans' beautiful forests of ocean alone. But one day newcomers arrived among the mangroves, inciting the tiger god's wrath as never before. Daksin Ray commanded an army of tigers, crocodiles, ghosts, and demons to repel them. The warrior Sha Jungli fought the god's army with his club. But it was Sha Jungli's twin sister, from whom he was separated at birth, who won the battle, unarmed. She became the goddess of the forest, and here, in harmony with her former enemy, the god of tigers, she dwells in peace.

As the sky darkened, the heat abated, and our boat slid out of the small channels of Khahtjhuni, back to the mouth of the sea, Mr. Mondal told Eleanor and me the story of Bonobibi.

From the Bonobibi puja, he said, everyone in Sundarbans knows the basics of the tale, as every Christian knows the story of the birth of Christ from having watched endless Christmas pageants. Each January, at pujas throughout Sundarbans, the text of the *Bonobibir Jahuranama,* composed in 1877 by the Muslim poet Munshi Baynuddin Saheb, is sung, narrating the life and miracles of Bonobibi, Daksin Ray, Sha Jungli, and Gazi Saheb.

The story begins with Gulalbibi crying alone in the forest — the small clay figure weeping flat, white tears at the puja at Sajnekhali. The dismayed-looking man standing near her image at the shrine is her husband, Ibrahim, who has abandoned her, pregnant, in the jungle. He is horrified at his own deed but powerless to revoke it.

With his first wife, Fulbibi, Ibrahim was unable to sire a child. Fulbibi allowed her husband to take a second wife only if he promised to grant her one request. So after Ibrahim had married a second time, and after Gulalbibi had conceived, the jealous Fulbibi announced her wish: that when the time of Gulalbibi's labor approached, Ibrahim should take her into the jungle and abandon her while she slept.

When Gulalbibi awoke alone, she cried out to Allah: *Save me!* Allah ordered fairies to assist Gulalbibi as she gave birth to twins. Bonobibi was the first-born; Sha Jungli followed. But even with divine help it is difficult to nurse two babies. Gulalbibi fled the jungle with her son, leaving her infant daughter behind.

The little spotted deer discovered the baby girl and nursed her from their own breasts. Raised by chital, protected by Allah, and infused with the magic of the jungle, Bonobibi grew into a goddess. And so, the poem continues, when her brother came looking for her, Bonobibi already knew that the two of them must not return to the town to rejoin their parents; instead they were destined to travel to Sundarbans to perform miracles and rescue the people suffering there.

Here Mr. Mondal stopped, for it is difficult to speak for long over *Mabisaka*'s motor, especially in a foreign language. Besides, he said, the miracles of Bonobibi and Sha Jungli are plain to see: they are sculpted in clay throughout Sundarbans. At the shrine at Sajnekhali, to the left of Gulalbibi weeping by her tree, another diorama prefaces a different story. Here the clay images of honey collectors are cutting a comb from a branch. This scene is taken from the tale of how Bonobibi rescued the son of a poor widow. I heard this story on my third trip to India, when a college student from Calcutta translated it from the *Bonobibir Jahuranama*, which Girindra keeps in his house like a family Bible:

Once there lived two brothers named Dona and Mona.

Wealthy merchants, they set sail with their fleet of ships for the forests of Sundarbans, planning to collect honey and wax.

When they arrived, Daksin Ray himself appeared to them in a dream. "I will make your boats heavy with riches," he promised. But at a price: they must agree to offer their young cook, Dukhe, the only son of a widow, as a sacrifice. They must abandon Dukhe at the island of Kendokhali, where Daksin Ray would come in the form of a tiger to claim his due.

Daksin Ray honored his part of the agreement. Dona and Mona found the trees bowed down with the weight of the honeycombs. They loaded their seven boats so full the crafts almost sank beneath the weight; finally they had to pour the honey into the sea to make room for the more valuable wax. But in the morning the payment was due.

Dona sent Dukhe into the forest to collect dry wood to cook breakfast. While the boy was busy with the task, one by one, Dona and Mona's boats slipped away from Kendokhali.

When Dukhe returned, he realized he was alone. And just then Daksin Ray, in the form of a tiger, came roaring out of the forest. Dukhe remembered the words his old mother had told him before he left on the trip: if you find yourself in trouble, call upon Ma Bonobibi. So he fell to his knees, calling out the name of the goddess.

With the speed of the wind, both Bonobibi and her brother appeared before the frightened boy. Bonobibi swept Dukhe into her arms and ordered her brother to chase the tiger with his club — the weapon, I now understood, symbolized by the wandlike latu at Girindra's forest puja. Bonobibi sent the boy safely home to his mother on the back of a crocodile. Dukhe was so afraid of the giant reptile that Bonobibi had to blindfold him during his journey — another moment of fear and promise commemorated in clay at the Sajnekhali shrine.

Naturally Daksin Ray resented the intrusion on his territory. He rallied his troops to chase away the newcomers. But despite his army of tigers, ghosts called bhuth, and female spirits called

dakani, despite lightning and thunder, bows and arrows, Bonobibi was never harmed. When Sha Jungli chased Daksin Ray in
the form of a tiger, the tiger god slunk into a river and ordered
sharks and crocodiles to attack his pursuer. Sha Jungli simply
picked them up by their tails and tossed them away.

Finally the warring factions made a truce. Gazi Saheb, a Muslim saint, negotiated between Daksin Ray and Sha Jungli.
Daksin Ray's mother made a pact of friendship with Bonobibi.
And from that day onward the tiger and the goddess have
shared the Sundarbans forests in peace.

So have the various peoples of Sundarbans coexisted through
the centuries. From the Moguls, whose Sufi saints worked their
miracles on Sundarbans' shores beginning in the thirteenth century, to the peoples of the Munda, Oraaon, and Santal tribes
lured from Bihar and Orissa by the zamindars' promises at the
end of the seventeenth century, this land has amicably absorbed
wave after wave of newcomers. The latest immigrants have
come from the Jessore, Bakharganj, and Khulna districts of
Bangladesh. Beginning in 1947 with the partition of India, un-
counted thousands have crossed into the country via Sundarbans, often in small boats in the darkness, in search of a better
life. Girindra's mother and father were among these immigrants, fleeing the violence against Hindus that had erupted in
their homeland.

The people of Sundarbans remain poor. A survey of the Indian side of Sundarbans published in 1981 reports that most of
these 2.2 million live in debt for their rice or their boats. While
most depend on farming, more than half own no land of their
own; those who have land grow their vegetable gardens and
their two yearly crops of paddy rice on an average of less than
two and a half acres. Less than one-third of the people can read.

But the goddess honored in the *Bonobibir Jahuranama* is also
the savior of the poor. In an episode not illustrated in the clay
forms of the Bonobibi puja, after the truce is arranged between

Daksin Ray and the newcomers, all cooperate to build a pala-
tial home for Dukhe and his mother. Gazi Saheb tells Dukhe
where to dig up seven pots of gold coins. Daksin Ray sends him
the finest timber. Bonobibi arranges for a heavenly carpenter to
build the house. Finally the wealthy merchant Dona begs forgiveness of Dukhe and, as an act of friendship, offers his beautiful daughter as Dukhe's bride. In a grand ceremony followed by
a great feast, the young couple is married, and ever after, everyone worships Bonobibi, along with Sha Jungli and Daksin Ray.

❖

On my third trip to India, I tried to trace the origin of Daksin
Ray. Rathin took me to the village of Dhapdhapi, twenty miles
south of Calcutta. It is not within the present boundaries of
Sundarbans: there are no mangroves here, no waterways, no
tides, no crocodiles, no tigers. The place looks like any other
tidy village in West Bengal, with automobiles and bicycles on
dirt streets, and concrete storefronts, and here and there a big
banyan tree with roots flowing down like the tangled tresses of
a sadhu. But as recently as a century ago, Rathin assured me,
Dhapdhapi was part of Sundarbans. Once it was all mangrove
swamp. This was how the village was named: Dhapdhapi
means "to clear up."

Rathin barks Bengali to our driver, directing him to pull over
along a side street. Now it is monsoon season, when the rain is
warm and as continuous as sweat and the whole world takes on
the fuzzy aspect of a dream from which you cannot quite
awaken. You lose your peripheral vision during the rains, for
you are always looking out through the tunnel of a rain cape or
peeking from beneath your umbrella.

As we emerge from the car, our eyes are busy watching our
feet, trying to avoid the shallow rivers of mud coursing down
the street. When we look up, we see in front of us what looks
like a small British palace: three stories of bright yellow painted

wood and marble, faced with a three-part arcade, surmounted by a tiaralike crest encrusted with enough ornament for a much larger building. This is the temple of Daksindar.

Shortly Manas Kumar Pathak, a graying, mustached man with rectangular black-rimmed eyeglasses and the Brahmin's sacred thread, comes to greet us. He has been the priest at the temple for forty years, he tells Rathin in Bangla, since he was fourteen. Mr. Pathak rings a brass bell hanging over the locked doorway and claps his hands four times before inserting his key. Daksindar is asleep, he explains, and in this way the god is alerted to our presence. We remove our shoes and enter the temple.

In front of us, nearly half a story high, with a black mustache, a conical crown, and a face white as the moon, is the image of Daksin Ray.

This is not the original idol, Rathin translates. The original was riding a tiger; this one sits on a jewel-encrusted throne. The original also held a bow and arrow; this one has been updated and holds a model of a shotgun across his lap. The first temple was made of paddy straw and tin, he explains, but it was destroyed. In its place the good citizens of Dhapdhapi raised the money to construct this magnificent temple in 1909. It even has a wall clock, he points out; this helps ensure that the pujas are held on time, at nine and two-thirty on Saturdays and Tuesdays, and on other days at eleven.

Tell us about Daksindar, I ask through Rathin.

Much of the story has been lost over time, says the priest. But this much is known: once there was a king named Mukut Ray, the king of Brahmannagar in Jessore. Commanding his army was a great chief named Daksindar.

Time passed, and many years later, after Daksindar died, the fishermen and honey collectors made an important discovery in the forests of Dhapdhapi. They felt drawn to worship a particular mound of earth here. They did not even know the name of the deity to whom they prayed, yet after praying at the sacred mound, people found they were magically protected from tigers, crocodiles, and the other dangers of the forest.

Then, said the priest, for a long time much of the land was lost to human habitation. When people returned to Dhapdhapi centuries later, the place had grown back to jungle. The land was now under the rule of a zamindar called Madanmohan Raychowdhuri.

The zamindar sent workers through the vast forest to make clearings, erect embankments, plant paddies with rice. Such work is always difficult, but nowhere more so than here. This place was full of poisonous, thorny trees, the priest said. The workers were unable to clear it, no matter how hard they tried. It was as if nature herself was keeping the place sacrosanct.

One day while trying to clear the forest, one of the zamindar's workers found a tree-covered mound. The moment his axe struck the first tree, he fell to the ground, bleeding from the mouth, and died. His companions reported what had happened to the zamindar.

Zamindar Raychowdhuri himself came immediately to Dhapdhapi, where he erected a pavilion. For days he prayed and fasted. Every day he asked to contact the deity presiding over the place. One night in a dream the deity appeared before him wearing a conical crown of gold, red, and green. His face shone like the moon. And he was riding on the back of a tiger. His name, he said, was Daksindar.

The deity commanded the zamindar: make an idol of me here and worship me every day. This he did, and more. He hired a full-time priest to attend the idol and direct the daily pujas. Daksindar himself taught the priest the secrets of Dhapdhapi's magic tree, secrets that have been passed down from generation to generation. That is how Manas Kumar Pathak came to know them, and he is now teaching the secrets to his own son, who at twenty-three is in training for the priesthood. The tree can cure septic wounds, amoebic dysentery, stomach ailments, cancer, and skin disease, but only if its leaves are fried in ghee and eaten with the blessings of the priest inside the temple.

Mr. Pathak took us to see the magic tree, which grows in a courtyard across from the temple. It is a tall, slender creature, with whitish bark and five-inch leathery leaves. At the base of each shiny leaf stem grows a long thorn.

Rathin did not recognize this tree. Mr. Pathak said it is called *chora dacat,* and it was no wonder Rathin had never seen one before: a botanist from the university had once come out to see it, he said, and he could not identify it either. That is because, he explained, the tree grows only here — a gift from Daksindar himself.

❖

In his most ancient form, we had read, Daksin Ray is worshiped not as a full-bodied idol but only as a head. In this form he is known as Bara Thakur. British anthropological surveys from the turn of the century describe the head as possessing large eyes, a black mustache, and a large conical headdress. No one I spoke with in Sundarbans had ever seen such a thing; Rathin had seen nothing of the sort either. But after Eleanor and I returned to the States, Rathin continued his inquiries about the disembodied head, and eventually he was told that such an idol was still worshiped at a village called Nosha. In Mogul times ships would go there, down the Hooghly River from Diamond Harbor to begin their journey into Sundarbans. Today the village lies twenty miles outside Sundarbans' boundaries. One fragrant, rainy September day on my third visit to India, Rathin took me there in search of Bara Thakur.

Rathin procured directions by shouting out of the car window at passers-by. The Bara, they said, could be found beneath a giant fig tree growing in a little mud courtyard. Arrayed among cascading roots, we saw five red earthen pots. Before them lay the soggy remains of wilted flowers and burnt incense.

Because of the monsoon, few people were outdoors. We stopped passers-by as they dashed through the rain and asked if they could tell us about the deity worshiped beneath the tree. Yes, people worshiped there, we were told, but no one seemed able to say what the pots represented or what this god's specific powers might be. Rathin had been given the name of Haladhar Chatterjee, said to be the priest of Daksindar, but no one could find him. Finally we spoke with a wrinkled old man who gave his name as Kele Khachar — "Kele the Wicked," Rathin translated.

Beneath the thatched roof of his porch, the old man spoke with Rathin for what seemed to me a long time, while rain sheeted off the eaves and churned down the dirt street outside. The conversation ended with a nod. We both thanked the man profusely, and Rathin steered me back out into the muddy street.

"Well," I asked breathlessly, "what did he say?"

"It is so ancient, he says that no one can recollect what they are," Rathin said. And he climbed back into the car.

❖

The *Ray Mangal Kavya* mentions the Bara head. In one episode, during a sword fight, Barkan Gazi (Gazi Saheb) beheads Daksin Ray, although the god miraculously recovers:

> Barkan hurled the sword on his neck.
> In this way the mystic head fell to earth.
> Since, the trunkless Bara head is adored,
> in other places, the full human image on a tiger.

Most scholars seem to agree that Bara worship considerably predates the *Ray Mangal Kavya*. Krishnaram Das acknowledges in his text that there was another Daksin Ray epic before his, but that poem has been lost. Das very likely incorporated the Bara head into his story because this link to the past would lend it further veracity.

One source Rathin uncovered, the Bengali anthropologist Tushar Kuma Chattapadhyay, suggests that Bara worship "signifies the primitive custom of human sacrifice and head-hunting." Certainly human sacrifice was once widespread in India, particularly to Kali, the ten-armed goddess of destruction. Human sacrifice survives even today in India, in the outlawed but occasional practice of *sati,* in which a widow hurls her body into her husband's funeral pyre, a final act of offering her flesh before the altar of her spouse.

Worship of the human head and skull is deeply rooted among our kind: Neanderthal man kept the skulls of his ancestors like holy relics. Yet Bara worship seems oddly out of place among these traditions. Why should worship of the tiger god be directed toward a human head? "It is strange," wrote Asutosh Bhattacharyya, a research associate of the Anthropological Survey of India, one of the few scholars to write on Daksin Ray in English, "that instead of full iconographic representation of the deity, only the head of it should be held in worship. . . . Perhaps," he theorized, "in the past a person who was killed by tigers was afterwards deified in this manner."

"Man-eaters always leave untouched those parts of the victim we associate most with personhood: the hands, legs and head," the British hunter Kenneth Anderson observed. Tigers' well-known dislike of the human face is the reason that for a time, at least, the back-of-the-head face masks protected forest workers from tiger attack. So distressing do tigers find the human face that they will abandon a kill rather than look at it. In *The World of the Tiger,* Richard Perry writes of a police inspector who, on his way to examine a man-eater's kill, heard that a second kill had been made, quite near the first. He did not understand the reason for the second kill until he examined the first corpse. It was, reports Perry, "sitting against the steep

bank of a ravine, with staring eyes bulging from their sockets."
The tigress who had killed the man was gone, of course, but
from her footprints the inspector read what had happened: after
the tigress had dragged the corpse up a steep slope, it had become wedged among the trees, sitting up, face forward. The tigress had paced and circled and finally left. She could see no
way to retrieve her kill without staring into the open-eyed face
of the dead man. So she left a hundred pounds of meat untouched and went to hunt again.

The story is all the more striking when weighed against most
man-eaters' dedicated efforts not to lose the body of a person
they have killed. Jim Corbett reported that one tigress returned
to her human kill four times even though she knew the corpse
was guarded. Another climbed eleven feet to reach a corpse authorities had tied up in a tree; a third climbed and fell out of a
tree at least twenty times in an effort to retrieve a body that had
been moved.

Tigers are not wasteful. Yet again and again one reads reports
of tigers who leave behind the heads of their human victims, as
a house cat often leaves behind the heads of mice and voles. Anderson and his son, Don, observed that one tiger, who had
killed a leper, seemed to have purposely positioned his victim on
a hill so that once the tiger gnawed through the person's neck,
the head would roll away.

In Sundarbans, unless you followed a tiger into the forest
with its kill in its jaws, your chances of locating the body of a
human victim would be slim indeed. But if you did chance upon
the remains of a person killed by a tiger, this is what you would
likely find: a disembodied head, eyes open, lying beneath the
trees.

What would be your reaction to the sight of a severed head
among the mangroves? Revulsion? Anger? Flight? No; here in
these swamp-forests, where the creeks flow as slow and thick as
blood, where the leaves change to birds before your eyes and

then evaporate to sky, where horrors and wonders crawl out of the very mud, this is what you would do: in an action of atavistic fear and awe, like Moses before Yahweh, like Rothai and his six resurrected brothers and resurrected son, you would fall to your knees.

But before whom? Who is Daksin Ray?

The Bengali scholar Sankarananda Mukhopadhyay, in *A Profile of Sundarbans Tribes,* holds that Daksin Ray was a historical person killed by a tiger. It is, this scholar claims, this victim's soul that was originally invoked during the Daksin Ray puja, so that his "revengeful spirit" would "counteract any possible attack by tigers" upon the worshipers.

But I suspect Daksin Ray was a tiger first, who, like so many ancient gods, took on human form later, as bards and poets clothed them with human story. For it is the tiger, not the victim, whom we recognize when we encounter the Bara head in the forest. Most of the time we cannot see the tiger in Sundarbans any more than we can see the gods or the wind; but we can see what they have touched.

Why does the tiger leave behind the head of its human prey? Perhaps the roundness of the skull is annoying; although a tiger could easily crunch it open. Perhaps the human head and face do not offer enough flesh to bother with. Or perhaps, in this act of gruesome mystery, the tiger, like God, recognizes us for what we truly are: certainly he sees our meat, which he consumes, but perhaps he sees, as well, our soul.

Possession

❖ ❖ ❖ ❖ ❖ ❖ ❖ ❖ ❖ ❖

IN THE MONSOON, even when it is not raining, wet surrounds you. The air hangs so heavy it forms a shroud, a sheath, a suffocating cocoon. No longer a temperature, the heat is an obstacle, a viscous weight through which it seems you cannot move. Breathing the air is like drowning. The humidity often reaches one hundred percent.

Most of the time it *is* raining. The rain hisses down. Or it drums, swishes, foams down the muddy streets, hangs flapping in the air like a loose sail.

In Sundarbans there is no joyous "breaking" of the monsoon as there is elsewhere on the subcontinent. Instead the world only becomes progressively more sodden. From late March to late May, a season of sudden rainstorms and occasional hail precedes the monsoon. Then, for well over a third of the year the weather consists of various kinds of rain. The Bengali language accommodates them all. There is *guri guri bristi,* rain like small beads. There is *halka bristi,* a mild rainfall with drops larger than *guri guri bristi.* There is *jhum jhum bristi,* named for the sound the fat, dense raindrops make on the roof; *prabol bristi,* a downpour; *mushal dhare bristi,* rain so thick you cannot see through it. And so on.

Between May and September more than fifty inches of rain may fall. Paper and photos bloom with fungus. Cloth rots, ink bleeds, books fall apart. If kept in a suitcase, a leather belt will grow a coat of mold as thick and long as fur. Fungus grows in the ears and around the eyes and makes feet itch and burn. Sickness is common at this time. Dug rain-water ponds overflow and become contaminated, resulting in outbreaks of diarrhea and other illnesses. In the damp, people develop colds, sore throats, and chills.

This is the worst season for ghost attacks and for snakebites: ghosts and reptiles are made restless by all the water. The ghosts stay outside, but during the rains the snakes, flooded from their holes, come into people's homes and even crawl into beds. Especially the snake called kalash, which is moderately poisonous. The snake only wants to be warm and dry, which is what the person wants too. Often the two sleep together soundly, but if you roll over on this unseen bed partner, the snake may bite you in self-defense.

Many days no one steps outside the hut except to use the latrine, because the neat dirt paths have all melted into greasy mud. When it rains, no one can work in the fields; no one goes fishing; the markets close. Many days there is little to do besides visit your neighbors, drink tea, smoke bidis, and tell stories. When the air hangs heavy with rain, it is through these stories rather than the muddy, sinuous creeks, that one journeys.

That is one reason I chose to make my final trip to Sundarbans during the monsoon.

❖

When I arrived in Calcutta in August, rain congealed out of the skies like grease. It rained not water but heat, in dirty, slippery waves, like someone else's sweat. Nothing, not even a month of field work in Borneo, had prepared me for heat like this.

Rathin met me at the airport. I felt dizzy as he squired me

through the Writer's Building for yet another permit. I could hardly stand. He had arranged for a graceful young man to serve as my translator: Shankar Prasad Mukherjee, twenty-three, a student at the University at Calcutta. When we met, I could barely mumble hello.

During the interminable, bumpy drive from Calcutta to the dock where both *Monorama* and *Mabisaka* awaited us, I was so overcome with nausea I could not sit up. My nose bled. Rathin held my head in his lap. I must have worried him terribly. Later he looked up my symptoms in a medical book, and announced that I had heat stroke, from which, he said, seventy percent of its victims die.

While we sailed to Jamespur, my dreams and consciousness melted one into the other; in the darkness of the cabin the minutes and hours crawled over me like ants. The next morning Girindra carried me off *Monorama* slung over his shoulder like a sack of flour, my head pointing down toward the sticky gray mud into which, with my added weight, he sunk almost to his knees with each step.

Through the mud, up and over the mud embankment, Girindra carried me to his house. A crowd of perhaps forty people pressed around me as I was set down by the small table on his mud and bamboo porch. To welcome me, Girindra's family had bought a blue plastic tablecloth, gathered a bunch of fresh white flowers, and erected a brand-new mirror mounted in a green plastic frame that was supposed to look like the petals and stem of a giant flower. Dear Namita pulled a garland of red hibiscus over my head. I realized that I was expected to sit in this position for a while, to allow the crowd to admire the tableau my presence completed.

But soon I had to lie down. The crowd followed me to the bed — one of three beds for a household of thirteen; the second bed was reserved for Shankar. The third was for the three to five girls who slept in the room with me each night, so I would not be lonely. (To sleep alone is unimaginable for most Bengalis.) Everyone else slept on mats on the floor.

The adults stood around me, a wall of eyes. All the air was used up by other people's breath, and all that was left was their hot exhalations. The children played on the rice-stalk-stuffed mattress, touched me gently with sticky fingers, sneezed into my face. "Gorom," I said — "hot" — and one of the girls came with a huge yellow canister of talcum powder and dumped a quarter of its contents down my shirt. Girindra's eldest, pretty sixteen-year-old Kuku, fanned me with a bamboo fan. Someone lit incense by my head. I looked up through a haze of smoke and a blizzard of talcum powder.

I felt as if I were traveling in a little space capsule, surrounded by the rain, enveloped in the heat, caught between enchantment and illness in dreamlike torpor.

On mythic, mystic voyages, heroes and gods travel atop a mount or vahana. I would have preferred a tiger, like the one the goddess Durga rides. But since I am neither hero nor deity, my vehicle was my illness. I traveled in a space capsule of nausea, hoping to perceive the invisible through the clouded lens of rain.

The voices of Girindra and his family, friends and elders, neighbors and shopkeepers, women who had been possessed by spirits and the shamans who exorcised them washed over me like waves; first Shankar's Bengali, then the speaker's Bengali, then the English echo of Shankar's words — a flow of words with the mesmerizing cadence of a mantra. Like the Brahmin priest's elastic prayer to Daksin Ray at Khahtjhuni, the stories seemed to gather power by passing through the minds and bodies of so many people.

Here, inside the mud womb of the hut, I would finally begin to perceive the hidden tigers, submerged crocodiles, ghosts and gods, fairies and spirits; now, with Shankar to translate, words would make them visible.

In those weeks, as rain and heat and illness ebbed and flowed, my consciousness floated on stories. And finally, like a river leading to the sea, the stories would lead me away from this world of illusion into the spell of the tiger.

❖

"The color of the skin of the tiger is quite dazzling," a heavy-browed fisherman told me as a group of us sipped French Vanilla Café Parisian Style instant coffee I'd brought from the States from the Mridhas' four brown, chipped demitasse cups. "When you see a tiger walking, it is as if he has no bones. He walks as if he is swimming."

"When the tiger is about to attack you," another said, "it is very different from seeing a tiger at rest. You are stunned by its appearance. Your blood goes cold out of fear. The teeth and the red portion of the eyes are mesmerizing. You cannot even utter the words 'help me.'"

Sometimes you feel the tiger's presence before you see it. "You can test to see if your fear is justified," a young man with a pointed face and buck teeth was saying. "If you call out — AHHHHH!!!! — normally you will get an echo. But if a tiger is there, he will eat the echo up."

These last words Shankar translated were spoken by Nironjan Mandal. Although a young man — thirty-seven — he is considered a very powerful gunin. Girindra told me Nironjan's services are revered as far away as Calcutta. With mostly Arabic mantras he learned from the Bangladeshi guru who taught his own father, Nironjan can close down the jaws of the tiger. The process, he explains, is known as *khilan:* "You clench your jaws, you fold your hands, you cross your fingers and recite the mantras," he explained. Using the khilan, Nironjan's father once made a tiger lie so still for so long that he was able to cover its body with leaves. Only when all the men had finished their work in the forest did the great gunin finally release the tiger from the grip of the khilan.

Another mantra Nironjan knows keeps crocodiles away. He says the mantra works so well that crocodiles turn away to swim in the opposite direction. Shankar translated the Bengali mantra for me:

> Dust from heaven!
> Male and female sharks,
> Male and female crocodiles, dangerous ones with
>   sharp teeth,
> If you come to bite or attack, I charge you:
> Stay away for day and night,
> This mantra, like thunder, is a weapon in my hand,
> So I charge you in your mouth, in your teeth,
> To stay away for day and night.

Nironjan often speaks with his eyes closed, perhaps to see more clearly. For Nironjan, like all gunins, is a specialist in dealing with powers unseen: tigers, crocodiles, ghosts, illnesses, and gods. Not only are these powers invisible, they are mutable. A ghost may enter your body in the form of an illness, a god may take the form of a tiger, a being who seems to be a tiger may really be a ghost. Once Nironjan heard ghost tigers roaring in the night: *AA-o-ungh! Ooo-oo-ongh!* Like thunder they roared, their voices echoing up and down the slick dark riverbanks, shaking the mangroves till their stilt roots quivered like treetops in the wind. Nironjan finally silenced them with a mantra.

Sundarbans is alive with such forces. There are *pori* — fairies — beautiful female spirits who seize the souls of men and try to carry them off to the Land of the Fairies, Poristan, where everything is made of pure gold. There are jinn, violent, extremely strong male spirits. If a dying person is not given holy water from the Ganges, if he does not hear the holy names of the gods of the Gita, he may be possessed by jinn at the point of death. There are many other kinds of spirits in Sundarbans. The

nineteenth-century anthropologist Lal Behari Day classified five
kinds of Hindu Bengali ghosts alone — from the murderous,
headless *skandakatas,* who never spare humans, to the filthy,
lascivious *pentis,* who sexually assault passers-by. But the most
common ghosts are bhuth — the departed souls of non-
Brahmins (Brahmin ghosts are inoffensive) who died violently
or alone and so were not able to make peace with this world
and be reborn.

These are the ghosts, Phoni Guyan told me, who make the
small fishing boats sink. "You can't see them," he said, "but
you can see what they do": often they cause strange winds, like
the one my friend saw from his government launch.

Bhuth are very powerful. Because of them Nironjan never
dips his head underwater: a ghost might take the opportunity to
drown him. A ghost drowned his father's second wife (the wife
who replaced Nironjan's mother, who died of diarrhea). Ghosts
also killed one of his brothers and a sister. "If you are possessed
by a bhuth, and no gunin comes to help you," he told me, "you
will definitely die."

All during my illness, which never completely abated until
I returned to the States, I tried hard to keep the Mridhas
and their neighbors from seeing how sick I really felt, for I
was afraid they might think I was possessed by bhuth or
had brought evil spirits to their home. Indeed, I did feel
possessed —all illness is possession of a sort. We are trapped inside the disease that has caught us; we report not that we have a
pain or feel a pain but are *in pain,* trapped inside it, consumed.

My discomfort did not escape the notice of my gracious
hosts. In preparation for my arrival Girindra had constructed a
small motorized fan. Standing about seven inches tall, it sat on
a round base made from a discarded boom-box speaker, and
its blades, cut from tin cans, whirred courtesy of a motor sal-
vaged from a junked tape recorder. Dead radio parts supplied
the rest of its body. Whenever Girindra or the others saw me

suffering particularly badly from the heat, two of them would come running — one carrying the little fan, the other, usually Sonaton, bent over with the weight of the enormous car battery that ran it, connected by two veinlike wires.

But no one mistook my illness for a ghost attack. Possession is something with which everyone here is familiar.

✤

Duli Bala Mondol is a slender, sixtyish widow with thin lips and an aristocratic bearing. Her husband worked in the jungle as a gunin, and that was how she came to be attacked by a ghost twenty-five years ago. She came to Girindra's house to tell me her story.

Accompanying a crab-fishing party, her husband had gone to Gazikhali to clear the place of its numerous evils: tigers, crocodiles, restless spirits. As usual he succeeded. In the face of his powerful mantras, all these beings fled, and his men worked in peace. But one spirit, as it fled, became angry and went all the way to Jamespur to catch Duli.

As she drove the cows home that evening, Duli passed beneath a large tree. Foolishly she had left her hair unbraided, and that was how the spirit caught her, although she didn't realize it at the time. All she knew was that she was seized with a fit of shaking, which stopped just as suddenly as it started.

She returned home, secured the cows in their shed, and stopped at the pond to catch fish for supper. When she cleaned the fish, a terrible smell came from them. And after that she started cooking in a very curious way: instead of frying the fish in mustard oil and spices, she simply put them in a pot to boil.

She knows these things happened because the neighbors told her; she doesn't remember any of it. By this time she could not recognize her own six daughters and two sons, and she began to beat them! Then her face started swelling, and her teeth began to get bigger — and that was when one of her daughters fetched a neighbor to help.

Girindra's mother, Mabisaka, was one of the neighbors who came. She remembers it all well: Duli was throwing stones at people, shouting at them; then she would retreat to a corner and moan. Then she would throw stones and curse again. Neighbors took the children in to keep them safe.

People possessed by ghosts often become violent. Just three months before, Girindra recalled, a fifteen-year-old girl from Dayapur was possessed. She became so strong that she was ripping woven mats in half with fingernails as strong as claws and teeth she used like an animal. "You almost can't stand in front of the ghost, it is so frightening," Girindra said. His mother nodded agreement — and just then a gecko called. "You see," said Mabisaka, "now the lizard has sounded, which proves what we are speaking is true."

Duli continued her story. Two days passed before her husband came home. The spirit saw him coming and forced her to pretend she was merely sick with an ordinary fever. But Duli's husband wasn't fooled. He realized precisely what had to be done and began to prepare for the ceremony.

❖

Exorcism is usually performed at night, for the ghost, Nironjan explained, can flee more peacefully at that time. Though ghosts who are about to be evicted are usually anything but peaceful.

When the ghost inside Duli Bala Mondol saw her husband scratch a circle in the mud floor of the bedroom around the legs of a small stool, it began to fight. It tried to smother the flames of the two lighted torches. It hit. It bit. Two strong men struggled to subdue the possessed body of Duli, to force her to sit on the stool in the center of the circle. The spirit cried out for help: "Mathar Gazi, come and save me! This man is exorcising me!" But once the spirit was brought to the center of the circle, it had no choice but to submit to the interrogation.

"Where are you from?" demanded Duli's husband.

"Gazikhali," answered the spirit.

"Why are you here?"

"The gunin has driven me away from my home."

"How did you possess this woman?"

"I was coming from Gazikhali and saw the wife of the gunin passing under the tree with her hair unbraided, and I took my revenge . . ."

At this point in the ceremony the gunin often tries to reason with the spirit, which often has good cause to be upset. The spirit who possessed Girindra's fifteen-year-old neighbor, for instance, was the ghost of a woman whose husband had poisoned her. (That ghost, in fact, even gave the name of the murderer, a man named Jamni, who lived across the river. And, the assembled crowd realized, he had remarried quite soon after his wife's death. Who wouldn't be angry?)

Few spirits are willing to leave the body of the person they have possessed. They are here, after all, because they have not had enough of this life. But if the ghost doesn't depart voluntarily, it is subjected to the next steps of the exorcism, which may be intensely uncomfortable.

Nironjan evicts spirits by fashioning an image from straw. With a leather thong he squeezes the image, thus squeezing the ghost out of the body. Other gunins progress to a procedure known as *jalan* — "to burn" — which will set the spirit on fire. But it also makes the ghost very angry, and the patient may even try to kill the gunin at this point.

If the spirit still remains, the *agni ban,* or fire arrow, may evict it. The gunin lights a torch soaked in mustard oil. Into the flames he tosses a powder called *dhuno,* made from the dried sap of a tree. The patient will fall senseless, which means that the spirit has left the body but is still hovering nearby. Chanting mantras and stroking the patient's body with branches of the neem tree will accomplish the next step, the *chalan* — transference, or deliverance, meaning the ghost has left that body for good. To ensure that the spirit never returns to the person, the gunin sprinkles water over his patient and the rooms of the house. It must be water drawn from a newly dug well, one gunin explained, because such is the condition of the exorcised person: newly dug out.

Frequently the gunin will ask the spirit to show that it is leaving — by breaking a branch or a clay vessel — to prove the exorcism has worked. Or he will ask the spirit to carry a leather sandal, a full water pot, and a broom in its teeth. Girindra explained that it takes superhuman power to carry a full pot of water in the teeth, and to hold a sandal and a broom in the mouth is so insulting that only an evil spirit would do it.

When Duli regained consciousness, she remembered nothing. The first thing she saw was the broken branch on the tree in the yard.

❖

Ghosts and man-eaters are not the only unseen forces a gunin may be asked to drive away. The gunin may also be called upon to heal illness.

Because I was a foreigner, to cure my foreign illness Girindra called a high-tech modern doctor. He summoned a *hakim,* a homeopathic healer. Shankar's first duties as my translator arose when the doctor addressed me with the single question he would ask before coming to a diagnosis:

"When did you shit?"

I told him, and the hakim solemnly dispensed some tiny, sodden globules for me to swallow.

The same hakim prescribed medicine when members of Girindra's own family were ill. But when their illnesses became severe — when five of the children were nearly paralyzed with diarrhea and vomiting, when Namita developed a high fever — Girindra also called for a gunin.

The children's illness was like a tidal wave of gastric distress: curly-tailed dogs gathered expectantly along the path from the house to the latrine. Finally the kids grew so weak they couldn't make it outside at all. They lay inside, vomiting on the mud floors. The hakim proffered globules. I doled out tablets of Pepto-Bismol. Nironjan prescribed enchanted mud balls.

He performed the ceremony at night. First he purified himself by washing out his mouth with water. Then he touched to his forehead, his mouth, and his heart a ball of mud the size of a pebble. He explained that the mud balls must always come from an altar — in this case the mud was pinched from the altar that stands in the center of Girindra's house — or from mud that has been dug up by rats. For the mud to hold the magic, it must never have been touched by human feet, the lowliest part of the human body.

Nironjan blew upon the mud ball, infusing it with the breath of God. Softly, in a low hum like the drone of bees, he chanted an Arabic mantra. He then divided the mud into five smaller balls, one for each sick child. Each mud ball was now an amulet, to be tied in white cloth and worn around the arm — the left arm for the four sick girls, the right arm for the boy.

The next morning when the children awoke, all of them felt better. By noon they were playing and cheerful.

A different gunin performed the healing rites when Namita got sick. Her illness was more dramatic and called for dramatic measures. At first she seemed to be suffering from a cold. Wiping her running nose with her sari, she still went about her routine, preparing the food, sweeping the house, tending the children, stopping to sit beside me and tenderly wipe my sweat-soaked face with the snot-soaked portion of her sari. Soon, of course, most of us had cold symptoms of varying degrees — except Girindra, who seemed immune to everything. But Namita's symptoms worsened. The skin blistered beneath her nose; her throat stung; she grew weak. Finally she became so ill she had to lie down on the cool mud floor, her forehead ablaze.

In the room where the couple sleeps with their youngest, Nantu, between them, they keep locked in a metal box their most prized possessions: insurance papers, photos, my letters — and, I was surprised to find, a thermometer. Girindra took it out of its case carefully and shook the mercury down. He held it up to the daylight, then inserted it in Namita's mouth.

Her temperature was 104.

For four days her fever remained high. None of my Western medicines — aspirin, Actifed, high-dose vitamin C — had any effect. Neither did the globules prescribed by the hakim. Her symptoms multiplied: her left ear hurt terribly, as did her jaw. Finally, on a night lashed with rain, Girindra summoned a gunin.

Profulla Kumar Mridha specializes in this sort of ailment, as well as cow diseases, skin ailments, and snakebite. The ritual he prescribed for Namita was called *shamnik bhath*. It is aimed at the left side of the head, where her pain resided, but it also acts on the tonsils, he explained.

Namita, roused from the bedroom, sat cross-legged on the floor of the central room of the house, near the altar. The gunin directed her to face east and to cover her head with her sari. He stood behind her uttering mantras. He placed a banana leaf on her head and, with the other hand, touched the leaf with a lighted stick tipped with cotton soaked in mustard oil. Again and again he touched this lighted wand to the banana leaf, until the fire sputtered out.

While the rain outside beat like a thousand drums, Profulla Mridha placed a second banana leaf on the first. Again he touched the blazing wand to its surface. But now, with each touch, the wand produced a loud *pop*. Systematically the gunin touched the fire to the front of the leaf, the left side, the back, the front again. Finally all the popping sounds stopped. He removed the leaves from Namita's head and stroked each leaf three times with flame; he extinguished the fiery stick and rolled it up in the two banana leaves. Namita rose and went off to rest on my bed.

Later Profulla Mridha explained to me through Debasish Nandy (Shankar's best friend, who had replaced him as my translator), how the ceremony worked. First he extracts the disease by the power of the mantra, drawing it onto the surface of the leaves. The popping sounds, he explained, are caused by the disease being burned away by the fire. Did I notice how there was no popping sound at first? That was before the mantra began to work. Now the disease is held in the leaves, he said, and as the leaves dry, the disease will be healed. He said he would continue to perform the ritual for two more nights, and after that Namita would definitely get better. The mantra is foolproof, he explained: it summons the powers of Durga, the tiger-riding goddess, and Shiva, the father of Daksin Ray.

A few days later Namita began to feel better.

Girindra led a puja to celebrate the recovery one evening. Draped in the white ceremonial cloth he wears for such occasions, he gathered his family around the altar like boats at a dock. He set out clean banana leaves on the mud floor. Carefully he spread out the offerings: sweet batasha, uncooked paddy rice, mustard seed, ghee. Over it all he sprinkled Ganges water from an old whisky bottle. Mabisaka lit incense; Kuku applied ground sandalwood to our foreheads from the red petals of a hibiscus.

The only light was from the hurricane lamp and the single wick burning in a saucer of mustard oil. As we sat on woven bamboo mats before the altar, Girindra sang a hymn to Vishnu from a cardboard book in which he had copied the words by hand.

For an hour he recounted the miraculous powers of the Lord Vishnu: how he came from heaven to earth in the form of a common man and sent wealth to the poor, freed the innocent from prison, sank the boat of the evil man. First he met an old and poor Brahmin. Moved by the man's plight, Vishnu revealed to him his godhood, showing his four arms. The Brahmin then performed this very puja, the hymn explained, and went on to describe some of the miraculous results: the dead brought back to life, the sick healed.

When the puja concluded, we ate some of the blessed batasha, ingesting its blessings. Mabisaka then wiped the room's floor with mud and cow dung, which is holy.

❖

Do the mantras really work?

The standard Western answer, of course, is that they do not. More than half of common human illnesses resolve themselves without any intervention: you either get better or you die, no matter what you do. The children likely were suffering from a twenty-four-hour intestinal infection. Namita may have had a virus that had run most of its course before the gunin was even summoned. The tiger's jaws shut down, the crocodile turned away? These creatures do not obey our words any more than do viruses and bacteria. Spirit possession? Mere psychosomatic illness.

"Modern science has not yet arrived in Sundarbans," Nironjan admitted to me one wet afternoon. Here, he explained, it is not like in Calcutta, where science is so sophisticated that people use machines to conduct their seances.

Science was a difficult topic to discuss. At first I thought that my young interpreters were making translation mistakes: I would ask about science, and people would offer answers about astrology or palmistry. When I asked about Project Tiger's scientific work, villagers replied that they thought the Forest Department researchers were altering the tigers' bodies to make them have more cubs more often — an intervention of which they heartily disapproved.

Scientific concepts, even basic medical information, are unfamiliar or grossly misunderstood in Sundarbans. Germ theory is virtually unknown. Although Girindra handles his thermometer carefully, shaking down the mercury and timing the temperature, he routinely withdraws the instrument from one sick person's mouth and, without so much as wiping it with a rag, inserts it into the mouth of the next patient. It is not that these people are unintelligent. When I was not conducting interviews, Girindra and I, through our translators, enjoyed discussions about liberty, equality, work, and fate. He understood immediately why I was writing this book, beyond the usual idea that books are written to inform or entertain.

"Books," Girindra said to me through Shankar one day, "reveal the histories of people who did many charming things years ago. Those people may no longer be living, yet we can read about them today, because books are written. Human beings are mortal. We won't exist for eternity in this world. But your book will stay, and because of it, people will think about me and my family and my work.

"God has sent us to this world to do our duty, our *dharma*," he continued. "My work, moving about in my boat, fishing, is my duty, ordered by God for me to do, and so I am happy, happier than a rich person.

"I am of the opinion that what you are doing, writing your book, is your dharma, what you have been ordered by God to do. What is your opinion?"

It was exactly my opinion. Yet, I told him, often my fellow Americans, even those educated at universities, did not understand the concept of dharma and instead spent their lives in quest of personal happiness.

"Perhaps," he offered, "this is why they may be unhappy."

In villages where people dress in rags, men educated in grade schools made of mud discuss philosophy, poetry, literature with great enthusiasm. Two students from Dayapur, the village next to Girindra's, asked Girindra's family to arrange a meeting with me. They asked me to recite from Shakespeare. In exchange for this favor one of them read for me a three-page Bengali poem he had composed. Its title translated as "O Earth, If Only You Could Stand Still for a Moment."

Some villagers understand science simply as a different system of belief. "If you did not believe in science, how would you fly in an airplane?" one elderly fisherman asked me thoughtfully. "Without belief in science, the airplane would fall down." (Which would destroy the tennis courts Girindra had suspected were on planes, until I set him straight.)

Science certainly has its applications, most people I talked with agreed. Nobody wanted the airplanes to fall from the sky. But it is foolish, they told me, to believe that science is infallible or that its explanations of the workings of the universe are the only truths.

Even the doctors who tried to save the famous Bengali filmmaker, Satyajit Ray, acknowledged this fact. "Even the best doctors of India, in the most modern hospitals of Calcutta, light the incense sticks at their altars," another gunin, Adhir Krishna Mridha, told me. "Satyajit Ray, it is said, asked his doctor, 'You being a man of science, why do you believe in God?' And the doctor replied, 'The more I see the complexity of the human body, the more I believe in God.'"

"There are many incidents when a doctor's medicines have failed and a gunin's chants have worked," Nironjan said. "In front of a doctor I have worked, and within forty-five minutes cured the patient." One of them, an eighteen-year-old woman, was cursing and acting violent. "The doctor gave her an injection in the arm. But I, standing ten or twenty paces away from her, and without touching her, drew a circle on the ground, put a stool inside the circle, and drew a rope tight around the straw image of the ghost, and cured her."

A Western doctor would say it was obviously the injection

that cured the patient, not the rope around a straw doll. But this is Sundarbans, where miracles are as common as the tides. In the jungle a man's life may hang on a hair. But a hair may well be strong enough to hold it.

Profulla Mridha, the gunin who healed Namita, told me this story:

"Once there was a great gunin, whose house was crowded daily by the patients seeking his services. So many people came that he had no rest, and he was annoyed by the crowd. What he did was, he gave one patient an amulet. But there was nothing inside it but a hair. A hair! He sealed the side of the amulet with wax and sent the patient home. He did not tell the patient there was nothing but a hair inside.

"After a few days he was astonished to discover that the patient was completely healed. So you see," he said, "only if you believe in your heart, only then will the gunin's art work."

This was also the scientific conclusion of Anwarul Karim. An anthropologist, Dr. Karim conducted a field study of three villages in Kustia, one of the western districts of Bangladesh, bordering West Bengal. He noted — as did every gunin with whom I spoke in Sundarbans — that most patients treated by shamans were women. As were most of the patients who consulted Sigmund Freud.

(Why should this be so? Gunins with whom I spoke suggested that women are weaker than men, more faint-hearted, less able to defend their own spirits from possession by a ghost. Menstruation makes women ritually impure for several days each month, and therefore vulnerable. I suggested that perhaps ghosts choose to possess women because they are the vehicle through which the human spirit enters the world; the gunins allowed that this might well be true.)

In Karim's field study he found that the women treated for possession were usually wives whose marriages were exceptionally lonely or troubled. In many cases their husbands, like

Duli's, were often away on extended trips. Some wives were treated badly by a husband or abused by a mother-in-law. The traditional female role in family life afforded such women little recourse.

"Although shamanism is rooted in animistic culture, it is extended for correcting disturbances in the individual's social order," Karim wrote in his 1988 book, *The Myths of Bangladesh*. "The shamans perform the same role in a traditional society as psychotherapists in modern society."

True, no doubt.

And yet . . . when you deal with the unseen, there is always more to the story than meets the scientific eye. "Nevertheless," Karim concluded his chapter on shamanism, "I believe that spirit possession is a reality."

Karim reported many things he could not explain. Among the more astonishing cases was the following. One of his colleagues, a professor of geography in a government college, told him he had personally witnessed a ghost along with other members of his family. Neighbors had reported the same apparition. Later the same ghost appeared to the professor in a dream, telling him that he had been murdered secretly long ago at the dilapidated house next door, and no funeral ceremony had been held. The professor excavated the site, and to his astonishment he found a human skeleton buried in a sitting position. The neighbors gathered for funeral rites for the dead man. After that no one ever saw the ghost again.

How can science explain such an event? How can mantras work when Western medicine fails?

One gunin I spoke with quoted no less an authority than a famous Bengali astrologer: "Science can make a mistake, but God cannot."

Between Heaven and Earth

❖ ❖

"IT HAPPENED MANY YEARS ago," Phoni Guyan was telling me, as we sat on the Mridhas' porch with Girindra and Shankar and our small crowd of spectators. Yes — more than twenty years ago, he remembered — before his hair turned gray, when he had all his teeth, before he began to feel the stiffness in his limbs. One morning while he was walking in the forest, he spotted something shining in a tree. He went over to investigate. It was an amulet, and when he picked it up, he saw it was brand-new.

He wondered who could have lost it and how it had landed in the bark of the tree. Because the amulet was very beautiful, he took it with him. But he certainly had no inkling that day that he was witnessing a miracle. He didn't think much about the amulet; in the jungle there were so many other things to worry about. In those days, the old gunin told me, he used to be very frightened whenever he walked in the forest.

I tried to picture a young, frightened Phoni Guyan. I could not. Indelibly he remained in my mind the dignified yet humble elder, presiding over the incense and prayers at the Bonobibi puja, tossing hibiscus at the clay feet of the gods. Surely there had always been a power about him, a magic strong enough to call gods, repel tigers, a magic that had allowed him, even without shared language, to communicate his holy art to me during our interview back at the tourist lodge.

I'd had that tape translated in England. On it Phoni Guyan had reverently recited the mantras he uses to keep tigers at bay. He'd told me he calls on Bonobibi as the Mother: "Ma," he asks, "protect me the way I was protected in my mother's womb." He had explained how he addresses Daksin Ray respectfully as the Father: "We are entering into your domain, Father, to earn our living," he begs in one prayer. "Spare us your wrath." In calling on the gods and infusing his mantras with magic, he said, some of his spells were strong enough to protect an area from tiger attack for as long as three months. Once he had shut the jaws of the tiger so completely that he was able to actually touch the giant cat as it lay peacefully in the grass. That mantra was so powerful that he wrote it down for me rather than speak it.

During that interview he had told me so much; but, I had more to ask. How had he come to possess his powers? This was the question I had just asked him through Shankar. He answered, as wise men often do, with a story: the tale of how a dream and a miraculous amulet transformed a frightened young man into a powerful gunin.

The night he found the amulet, Phoni Guyan slept with his companions aboard the little country boat they had moored among the mangroves. As he slept upon the rolling waters, he had a dream unlike any other. Bonobibi herself appeared before him, soft-edged, almost blurred, as if through a glowing mist. Her brother, Sha Jungli, was with her. What he remembers most was Bonobibi's appearance. She was very beautiful. She wore a dazzling white sari bordered in red. Her pale complexion shone like the moon.

Phoni Guyan fell on his knees before her. To his astonishment, the goddess spoke to him. "Your finding the amulet was no accident," she said. "It was I who placed that amulet there, and I placed it there for you. Wear it on your left arm," she advised, "and keep it always with you. Now you will face no harm in the jungle."

Never since, Phoni Guyan told me, has he been afraid.

Shortly after the dream he sought out a guru to teach him the mantras and manners of a gunin; other mantras were revealed to him in later dreams. Now he prays each day to Bonobibi so earnestly that he breaks down in tears before leaving his house. "I call on Mother's grace every day," he said, "and it is with thanks for her grace that I begin and end each day."

So, with words that could have been taken from a fairy tale, Phoni Guyan concluded our talk. We parted with the same Hindu gesture we had used in greeting: sandwiching his right hand between my palms, I brought his hand to my forehead, and then he did the same to me. Despite the heat and humidity, his tough hands were dry as moth wings.

"By the grace of Bonobibi," he said softly, a sort of benediction.

But where, I wondered, was Bonobibi on the day a tiger's claws carved the fish-hook scar upon this gentle gunin's face?

❖

Nironjan Mandal well remembers the day the tiger attacked Phoni Guyan. It was June 23, 1984. On that day his own brother had been killed, and he, Nironjan, had watched helplessly.

A small crowd gathered to hear Nironjan tell the story again. As we sat on Girindra's porch in the steaming dark, the lamplight flickered on their faces.

Nironjan was one of a party of five woodcutters who had gone to the forest that day. Their problems began almost the minute they arrived. And yes, Nironjan agreed, it is certainly re-

markable that such a tragedy could occur with two gunins in
the party; but everything had happened so fast.

The men had only just left the boat — Nironjan was still
tying it to the stilt root of a tree — when one of their party
slipped in the mud and fell, wrenching his leg. Two of the others
began massaging his hurt leg.

Phoni Guyan, Nironjan remembered, had already reached
higher ground. In front of him was dense bush. The old gunin
turned to look at the injured man, and in a flash a tiger
bounded out of the bush!

One man called out a warning. Phoni Guyan ducked — and
the tiger's teeth missed their mark. At the same moment Nironjan's brave older brother, brandishing his machete, rushed forward to defend his elder. In an instant the tiger turned and
grabbed the younger man instead. Carrying him by the neck,
the tiger slunk away into the forest.

Meanwhile Phoni Guyan was unconscious. The tiger's teeth
had missed, but the claws had left the gunin a mass of blood.
Everyone listening knew this part of the story, and each added
his own bit of horror to the scene: "Flesh gone from the
shoulder, the chest, the cheeks!" said Nironjan. "The face was
all blood!" another man cried. "It was such a horrible sight!"
added Girindra, who wasn't in the party but who had heard
the story so many times. "His face was in so many shreds, it was
like the whiskers of the tiger!" Nironjan exclaimed. "So we said,
he must be the tiger, so let's kill him!"

To my astonishment, the men were doubling over with
laughter.

"Why is everyone laughing?" I whispered to Shankar. He
didn't know either. So he asked, and everyone quieted down. Silence. Then Girindra explained, a little sheepishly, "It was so
horrible that out of bewilderment we are laughing."

And so, Nironjan continued soberly, the party ignored the
fact that one of their men had been carried away. He tried to

run into the forest to retrieve the body of his brother, but the others stopped him. Already one of the five was dead and two were injured. They could not afford to risk losing another man in an attempt to retrieve the corpse.

They tied gamchas over Phoni Guyan's wounds and loaded him into the boat to return to the village and the doctor. But before they left, one of them found a stick and tied another gamcha to it, marking the tragedy so that those who followed would be warned: "Daksin Ray was angry, and there was nothing we could do."

❖

"You are much stronger than me. I cannot match you for strength. I have to protect my men. So if you do appear before us in the forest, please keep your distance, I beg of you."

Phoni Guyan squatted by the small baen tree, where he had carefully laid out three of the mangrove's rounded, waxy leaves side by side, their stems pointing east. Four other men stood or squatted nearby, some leaning on their rusty axes, one holding a hoe. With this mantra the gunin was making the area safe for work:

> You dwell in the forest,
> You deity of the forest,
> I am your humble son.
> Leave me, I pray, and leave my men in this area,
> and go to some other place.

Back in February Eleanor and I had watched this small ceremony in back of the tourist lodge, just outside of the chain-link fence that separates the lodge grounds from the forest and the tigers.

The fence is supposed to be firmly anchored in the mud embankment. But when rain washes some of the mud away, the fence develops gaps, and tigers occasionally come into the lodge compound. In July 1990 a tiger and tigress together entered the compound, the manager told me, and broke into the chicken pen below his quarters, where he kept seven hens. ("The tiger is a selfish species," he had said in Bangla on the tape. "During feeding they disregard each other as husband and wife." But in fact, when he ran to see the tigers, he found one of them eating a chicken and the other sitting politely beside its consort, as if honoring some tigrine code of etiquette.) Ignoring the noisy firecrackers that the lodge staff were setting off in an effort to drive the tigers away, the couple stayed in the compound and roared all night, the manager said. But at dawn they melted back into the forest. They could well be nearby right now, for all we knew.

Phoni Guyan chanted,

> O Mother
> Thou who lives in the forest,
> Thou, the very incarnation of the forest,
> I am the meanest son of yours.
> I am totally ignorant.
> Mother, do not leave.
> Mother, you kept me safe inside your womb
> for ten months and ten days.
> Mother, replace me there again,
> O Mother, pay heed to my words.

As the gunin finished his prayer, the men began their work. With a grunt, one man swung his hoe to cleave a thick shingle of mud from the earth and hefted it onto his companion's bare shoulder. Holding the mud in place with his hands and his head, he carried it to the embankment. The process continued all day, as if this were any ordinary job, until the men were greased head to toe with mud, and the fence once again was firmly anchored.

"It's strange that people can even *live* there," Kushal Mookherjee had said to me back in Calcutta, "much less work in the forest. I mean, in Sundarbans everything is against you. It's a saline environment: virtually nothing will grow. If you want something from nature, you have to go into such dangerous areas. It is almost suicide to go inside the forest.

"Really, it is almost madness. These people," he had said, "they don't have any guns, nothing. All they have is the gunin and his mantras."

For these men, working near a lodge where tigers knew meat would congregate, that was enough. No tiger would come today, they seemed sure, for the gods themselves — Sha Jungli, Bonobibi, and Daksin Ray — had come to inhabit the baen leaves that the gunin had touched.

Yet the gunin in whom the men placed their trust had himself been attacked by a tiger. While under his protection a man had been carried off and eaten! Everyone in the working party knew the story, if not everyone in all of Sundarbans.

One sodden day at Girindra's house, as the rain flowed around us like tears, I asked Phoni Guyan: With such powerful mantras to protect you, how was it possible that a tiger dared attack?

"Hae," Phoni Guyan replied, nodding. He understood why this might seem puzzling to an outsider.

Actually, he had sensed the danger before they went into the jungle that day. But the party already had permits to collect dry firewood in Pirkhali Block. They needed the wood badly. Phoni Guyan's companions had forced him to go. He left in such a rush he didn't even have time to say the proper prayers to Bonobibi; he never had time to try to appease Daksin Ray.

So it was no wonder they were attacked. First, they had ignored a warning. Second, he had failed to chant the proper mantras. And third, the outcome was not nearly as bad as it could have been. By a miracle he, Phoni Guyan, had survived.

"A tigress had killed eight or ten people in that area. The Forest Department investigated it. And it was this tigress who jumped. I heard her roar three times. And I said to myself, 'I have the amulet with me, so the tigress will not be able to eat me.'

"And, see, the tigress did not eat me! She did not even bite with her teeth. The wounds were made only with her claws. And so, although I was bloody from head to foot, and part of my lip was hanging off, I did not die."

Phoni Guyan is quite pleased that his lip is still attached. Had he gone to a hospital after the accident, he said, he is sure the doctors would have just sheared the flesh off. When he regained consciousness, he had insisted on seeing the village doctor, who agreed to sew the lip back up with an ordinary needle and thread.

"But the tigress did not go away that day empty-handed," he admitted. "She took my companion away into the jungle. We could not retrieve the body."

Then Phoni Guyan fell silent for a moment.

"The gunin," he said, "cannot force the gods."

All gunins must remember this at all times. Otherwise Daksin Ray will send a tiger to eat them immediately, he said. No, not even the most powerful gunin or fakir can force the gods to inhabit plucked leaves or balls of mud or even the beautiful idols fashioned by the clay artists. "The gods," he said, "can only be *invited*." And when the gods choose not to come, there is a reason.

"When the gunins fail, it is often because of their own deficiencies," Phoni Guyan explained, "in failing to maintain the code of conduct."

Sometimes a gunin may be sloppy in his ablutions or may fail to prepare a charm properly before going into the forest. Sometimes, unbeknown to him, a spell is broken when holy ground is defiled by the hidden sins of one of his workers. Or sometimes the gunin becomes too proud. This is the greatest danger, of which all gunins are aware, although some ignore it anyway. Their biggest mistake is believing it is *their* power, and not the gods', that keeps the tiger at bay.

Sometimes — even when prayers are uttered and the holiest words employed — sometimes, in spite of it all, the tiger takes a man away in its jaws. There is a saying in Sundarbans: if someone gets a disease, there is a doctor for him. If someone is attacked by a ghost, there is a gunin for him. But if someone is caught by the tiger, there is no resort.

"Even the best gunin cannot protect a guilty man," said Phoni Guyan.

Adhir Krishna Mridha knows this all too well.

✦

"All my life I have been struggling against sadness," said the gray-haired man in the blue checkered lungi. At fifty-two, Adhir Krishna Mridha is a handsome man with regular, open features, but his forehead is deeply lined and the whites of his eyes are a yellowish brown, as if stained with the tragedies he has seen.

His father, his brother, and his favorite son were all killed by tigers. His wife was eaten by a crocodile. His daughter drowned in the river. His house was struck by lightning and burned to the ground.

For twenty-six years Adhir Krishna Mridha has been a gunin. In a dream many years ago, two boys appeared to him and gave him seven holy words. "Whenever you go into the forest, utter these seven words faithfully," the boys had told him. "If you are pure, and those with you are pure, you will be safe. You can forget your fear."

The seven words, the gunin assured me, are absolutely foolproof. But the very year they were given to him, when he entered the forest with five boats to cut goran to make crab traps, a man was taken away by the tiger. It was Girindra's second-oldest uncle, who was himself a gunin — "a greater gunin than I," Adhir Krishna Mridha explained. He paused. "And that is why I did not utter the seven words."

Neither did he utter the seven words to protect his father, his brother, his wife, his daughter, or his house. He was not there to say them. He was away in the forest protecting other people.

He did use the seven words to protect his only son, however. Yet they were not enough. And this, he said, is the source of his deepest sorrow.

It was June 21, 1992. He and his son were part of a woodcutting party. He was saying the seven words, conferring protection on the area in which they worked. He strictly told his companions not to move while they were being uttered.

But someone disobeyed. Someone not only moved but chose that moment — that holy moment while the shaman spoke the holy words — to urinate.

It is considered an abomination to urinate directly on the mud of the forest floor. Men typically break some branches from a tree, put them on the ground, and urinate onto the leaves to avoid fouling the mud, the altar of Bonobibi and Daksin Ray. But to urinate during the speaking of the seven holy words! This was a double abomination.

"The main work of the gunin is to invoke God," he told me. "There are rules with which the gunin needs to comply."

The words, actions, and objects that link the shaman with the gods — the prayers and mantras, the magic wood, the enchanted mud — are themselves sacred. They must be treated with utmost respect; to insult them is to insult the gods they honor. Adhir Krishna Mridha considers his seven words so holy he would not utter them for us. They are also written on a scroll inside an amulet he wears around his neck. He is very careful with the amulet. When he is at home he doesn't wear it but keeps it in the most pure and auspicious place in the house, in front of the altar.

"A lot of lives depend on me," he says, "so before I enter the jungle I am careful. I do not wear the clothes I ate lunch in. I wash my hands and face in the name of God, and say the mantra. If you take food the effect is spoiled."

Other gunins told me about similar proscriptions: some must never eat pork or crab or dip their heads underwater. Observing these rules is an act of respect, and with each act the gunin reiterates the covenant between himself and his gods, between animals and people, between village and forest. The magic he creates is only as strong as the covenant. Like a spider's web, the spell spun by magic is steely gossamer, fragile as a promise.

"You can restore a broken spell," said the gunin, "but the person who broke it must confess."

But as he cut wood that day with his son, he did not even realize the spell had been broken. He didn't know that someone had urinated on the mud until it was too late.

Everyone worked cutting wood for four hours that afternoon, believing they were protected from the anger of Daksin Ray. But then — and the shaman began to cry as he told this — the tiger came and killed and took away his twenty-year-old son.

Only then did he realize what must have happened, why the seven words didn't work and, perhaps most painful of all, that it was his own son who had urinated, his own beloved son who had been at fault.

They never found the body.

"Who will take care of me now?" he wailed. "My oldest son lives in another house, and my youngest is too busy with his own family to care about me. My middle son was my salvation. It was he who loved me best."

❖

Daksin Ray may be a bloodthirsty god, but he keeps his word. He can protect you as tenderly as a mother, said

Phoni Guyan — if he chooses. And he can be an excellent host.

Mabisaka knew a gunin who traveled to the very home of Daksin Ray. One day, as Namita was sweeping the floor with a palm leaf and Girindra was shaving at the table with a naked razor blade and no soap, Mabisaka told me the story.

"Goran Gogan was a great gunin," she told me through Debasish. "He was an illiterate man, but a devout man, and dedicated to Ma Bonobibi and Daksin Ray. On long expeditions in the jungle everyone depended on the powers of Goran Gogan."

One day Goran Gogan reported something alarming to Mabisaka and her husband. "Do you know," he said to them, "that Daksin Ray himself came and took me away in his boat?"

"What do you mean?" Girindra's father asked.

Goran Gogan answered, "Daksin Ray took me away in his boat, invited me to his home, and kept me there with him for a whole night." The gunin described a palace of incredible wealth: gold and silver, silks and satins, pearls and jewels everywhere. He was entertained as an honored guest, treated to platters of exotic foods cooked in pure ghee. And then, after hospitably seeing to his guest's every need, Daksin Ray politely took Goran Gogan back to Jamespur in his boat. Goran Gogan awakened the next morning in his own bed.

"Did he ever see Daksin Ray again?" I asked.

Soon enough, Mabisaka said. The very next time Goran Gogan went into the forest, he was taken away by a tiger.

Girindra at this point had finished shaving and now was submitting to the ministrations of six-year-old Babu, who was locating and yanking out the few gray hairs sprouting from his father's head. Girindra remembered the day, he told us:

About eighteen people were in the party with the great gunin. When he was taken away, they all raced after the tiger into the forest. But they never found the body.

"The day before the funeral rites were to be held, though, we saw a curious sight," he said. At the gunin's house, on the floor of his porch, they found a streak of blood made by the fingers of a hand drawn down. The streak was about fifteen feet long. And inside the prayer room, in front of the altar where the idol of Bonobibi was worshiped, they found a footprint stamped in blood.

Both Girindra and Mabisaka saw it.

"Goran Gogan himself came and sat in front of the altar and prayed that night," Girindra told me. "He himself came, bleeding, after his own death, to worship one last time."

"In older days," Mabisaka said, "these miracles used to happen more often. Nowadays people are impure, and the miracles are less frequent."

The elders often discussed how the good seems to be ebbing from the world. People do not take the time to say the prayers properly, Mabisaka said. Old people are not taken care of by their children, and more people die alone and become ghosts, an older gunin added. Snakes bite more often; tigers attack with greater frequency, they all agreed. The wall between the sexes is falling down, and surely that is evil, Mabisaka said. Things were simpler, clearer, better, in the old days.

But some things have not changed. Daksin Ray still rules the mangroves. He still demands obeisance from the men who enter his domain. He *must* eat those who do not pay him respect, explained Phoni Guyan; otherwise people would lose their respect for the forest, and the relationships between the people and the forest — the rules by which everyone survives — would be destroyed.

Some wish there were fewer tigers here; some — particularly tiger widows, who have never worked in the forest — wish that the Forest Department would shoot known man-eaters rather than attempt to capture and relocate them. But no one who has grown up among the mangroves and worked in the forest calls for the eradication of the tiger. No matter how many men are killed, no matter how deeply the man-eaters are feared, the tiger is not hated. Almost everyone agrees on this point.

In his nine years of fieldwork in Sundarbans Kalyan Chakrabarti found this to be true. He wrote that to his initial surprise, when he would talk with villagers about their feelings about the tiger, "No matter how tragic their encounters with tigers, the references to the tiger are, rarely, if at all, in inimical terms. They have reconciled themselves to co-existence with the man-eaters. . . . Death occurs as decreed by the Tiger God." The lives Daksin Ray takes are considered only his due.

Back in Calcutta, so many months before, I had spoken with Kalyan about how man-eaters choose their victims. How does the tiger god decree who will die and who will live? "I have talked with a number of people in Sundarbans," Kalyan had told me, "and they have said that the tiger always likes a person who is careful, who loves himself, who loves to protect himself. It is a careless person normally executed — a person who feels there is no danger here. The tiger takes this as a sign of disrespect."

As a biologist Kalyan tries to see things from the tiger's point of view:

"Whether you are respectful or not, there is a kind of communication. This is communicated to the brain of the tiger: this is a respectful person, and I should let him go and do him no harm. A watchful, careful, respectful person," the former field director had assured me, "will never be killed in Sundarbans."

Kalyan's belief, too, reiterates the covenant between man and forest: the tiger who guards the forest demands respect. Daksin Ray does not need love, but he commands men's reverence. With prayers and mantras the gunins reiterate the covenant; with his teeth and claws the tiger, upon whom Daksin Ray rides between heaven and earth, enforces it.

❖

At the turn of the century India was still clothed in jungle; trees covered 40 percent of her landmass. Today barely more than a third of the original forest cover remains.

Sundarbans, too, is shrinking, as its geology heaves, its population grows, and its fresh water slows to a trickle. But it is shrinking more slowly than India's other forests. Despite population pressures from two of the world's most crowded nations, despite centuries of ambitious "land reclamation" efforts, the undivided Sundarbans still represents the largest tract of mangrove forest on the face of the earth.

Even with its best efforts, the West Bengal Forest Department cannot claim credit for that. Neither can Bangladeshi forest officials. "Practically, it is the presence of the predator that is checking the loss of forest cover," Rathin told me when we first met in 1992. "Without the tiger's presence, our problems protecting the forest would be increased manyfold."

Many months later I was shocked to hear this same insight voiced by Girindra — a man who had in the past broken the laws the Forest Department tries to enforce.

We had just reviewed another litany of death as we sipped coffee on the porch with Debasish. Girindra had recited yet more tales of friends and relatives who had been eaten by tigers. Why not kill all the tigers? I asked him.

"To save the earth," he replied. "You see," he told me, "inside the forest of Sundarbans is very costly wood. And it is no job of the Indian government to save the forest! And if the forest is destroyed, the water will wash away the land. It is the work of the tiger to save it."

Adhir Krishna Mridha has more reason than most to hate the tiger. Yet, he explained, he cannot bring himself to hate the animal who killed his father and his brother; he cannot hate the animal who killed and ate his son. For the tiger is as integral to Sundarbans as its tides, and its force is as powerful. To illustrate, he told me this story:

Many years ago a timber merchant planned to cut all the trees in the southern portion of the forest. He sent men into the jungle to survey it, but they knew nothing about the forest and did not even offer a puja to Daksin Ray! Immediately one man was taken away by a tiger.

The people of Sundarbans knew what had happened, and they wanted to hold a puja and ask forgiveness of Daksin Ray, Sha Jungli, and Bonobibi. But the rich merchant did not allow the people to hold the puja, for he did not believe in such things. Instead he went into the forest with men and guns. "Where is the tiger? I will kill it!" he vowed.

But no sooner had the group stepped into the forest than thirty tigers appeared and surrounded them. The men laid down their guns helplessly and awaited their death.

That was when Daksin Ray himself spoke. He would let them go, he said, but only if everyone bathed in the Hooghly River and worshiped him, along with Sha Jungli and Bonobibi. And that is what they did.

The rich merchant did not cut the southern portion of the forest. And after that there were no tiger accidents for a long time.

This happened long ago, everyone assured me, before the core area of Sundarbans was declared a tiger reserve in December 1973, certainly before it was declared a national park in May 1984.

But Daksin Ray still demands his due from the authorities who administer the tiger reserve. At the end of June an event had occurred that was so astonishing that Rathin telephoned me in the States to tell me about it the moment he returned to his office in Canning.

Six Forest Department guards had been on routine patrol at the forest station of Haldibari, near the Chotohardi River. At dusk the sareng slid their sixty-foot launch into a creek and anchored for the night. The craft was one of the department's larger and sturdier vessels, not as big as *Monorama* but certainly larger than *Mabisaka* or any of the other boats on which I had slept and felt perfectly safe.

That evening, as the watchman stood on the canopy and the cook was cutting fish for dinner, four of the men were playing cards in one of the boat's cabins.

The watchman saw a green flash on the water. A fish? No — eye shine! Before he could yell a warning, a tiger leaped aboard the boat, burst through the closed wooden door to the cabin, and grabbed Birin Mondal by the back of his neck.

The tiger turned with the man in its jaws. As if awakened from a stupor, one of the guards grabbed the shotgun at his side. As the tiger dragged the man across the deck, the guard fired. The tiger soared into the air toward the water, letting go of the body. But it was dark, and although the men searched, they could not find the body.

Aboard *Monorama* Rathin sped to investigate the scene. In the morning they found Birin Mondal in his khaki uniform, floating among the reeds. Rathin examined the corpse. Crabs had eaten away part of the lips, but otherwise the only wounds on the body were the four puncture wounds at the neck. And on the deck of the vessel Rathin saw a long smear of blood, as uniform as if painted with a brush. It had been left by a playing card, still clutched in the dead man's hand as the tiger dragged him across the deck.

The tiger who had attacked, the men told Rathin, was the incarnation of rage: "It had a black face with low-hanging jowls and horrible white streaks," they reported. But that was not all. "I spoke with the men in the area, Sy," Rathin's voice grew low and dark, as if crouching, about to spring, "and it is strongly believed — *strongly* believed — that the reason this has happened is . . ." and here he paused, his storyteller's voice slowing to a hiss, "an idol of Daksin Ray was left incomplete at the forest station at Haldibari!"

Silence echoed over the line.

"At first I thought it was all shit," Rathin said to me. "Now I am beginning to believe it."

Later, as a gift, Rathin presented me with a poem he had written about the occasion. He titled it "Tiger Magic":

Dusk —
Sighing with relief,
the vessel slides into a creek.
Anchors splash the flowing stream,
its muddy bottom to seek.
Lanterns glow, shadows dance,
men spread out cards,
casting lots?
On the canopy the lonely helmsman
searches the mangroves,
brooding over his weathered past.
Objects gray and inert float past and
fade from memory
like civilizations lost.
Then the arcane depths release a wreath,
a foam of bubbles and a few leaves,
scented with the aroma of meat.
A slight tilt —
strong claws grow out of deadwood
by primitive spell
and clasp the boat in silky stealth.
Blazing eyes and fangs like scimitars etched by magic
spring on black canvas.
Tiger!
In a flash the task is done,
as viselike jaws grip a man.
Dripping blood on the ace of spades
they cross the gate of Hades,
melting into dark void.

As If It Had Fire in It

❖ ❖ ❖ ❖ ❖ ❖ ❖ ❖ ❖ ❖ ❖ ❖ ❖ ❖ ❖ ❖ ❖

IN A DIALOGUE in Hinduism's philosophical scriptures, the Upanishads, a young yogi asks his father to explain God. If the Almighty is everywhere and all-powerful, why can't he be seen?

The father peels a fig and removes one of the tiny seeds. Where, he asks his son, does a fig tree come from?

"From the fig seed," the boy answers.

The father splits the fig seed open. "What do you see inside?" he asks.

The son blinks. "Nothing."

"Yes," agrees the father. "And from that nothing, which is all you can see, a mighty fig tree will grow."

Next the father fills a pitcher with water and adds a handful of salt, which dissolves in the water. The father tells his son to drink.

"What does your drink taste like?" he asks the boy.

"It tastes salty," the young yogi replies.

"Oh? But how can that be," asks the father, "when I cannot see the salt?"

The tiger's power permeates Sundarbans just as salt flavors its rivers. Most often the tiger does not choose to be seen, just as you cannot see the wind. But you can see what the wind and the tiger have touched.

❖

The wind began only minutes after we finished the rice and dahl and curried crab that Namita and Mabisaka had cooked for us. At first it blew the rice that the family had winnowed, which lay in a neat pile in the front yard; then the rain began. We all ran outside the hut to scoop up the rice in our hands and pour it into the round-bellied aluminum pot and move it inside. This was in February, on my second trip to India, when Eleanor was with me; she joked that the rain, the first we'd seen in Sundarbans, was the cleanest water to have touched our bodies since we had left the Tollygunge Club in Calcutta. In Sundarbans even the drinking water is muddy and salty.

We'd been warned that a storm was coming. At dusk, as we returned from a stroll around the village with Girindra, a boy came running to tell us that *Monorama* was here and that Rathin wanted to speak with me on board.

While Girindra and Eleanor waited on the mud embankment, I boarded *Monorama*.

"There is a very severe storm warning," Rathin said to me, "very severe. It is already causing very high waves in Bangladesh. It could become a cyclone! That mud village could be simply washed away. So you must take shelter on *Monorama*. I will make sure that you are safe."

I was doubtful of Rathin's forecast. Unintelligible Bangla crackled on the launch's radio. I couldn't tell what it was saying, but it didn't sound all that urgent to me.

The usual season for cyclones is from August to November, not February — although it is true they can come at any time. If a cyclone had been brewing, Kanchan Muhkerjee would have heard the warning on his radio in Pakhiralaya, just across the river, and dispatched staff to warn the people of Jamespur and the other villages. There would have been other signs too. Girindra, who is named for the rain god, Indra, would surely have known them: a red moon, a purple dawn — the red and purple horses that draw the noisy chariot of Vata, the god of winds. We would have noticed a halo around the sun. And then a final warning: the sea would go flat as glass. "There is an awesome calm before a storm," as John Seidensticker, tiger expert and Smithsonian wildlife ecologist, wrote about Sundarbans' cyclones. "The light changes, and the water and forest, backed by the mottled, steel-grey wall of clouds, take on a vivid texture and contrast which intensifies as the storm closes."

No such storm was closing in, I was sure. The swashbuckling Rathin, I thought, having already fought with pirates and walked among tigers, was merely eager to augment his chivalrous résumé by rescuing memsahibs in distress — even if we were in no distress at all.

It was clear from the gathering gray clouds, though, that we were in for some weather. Even if he was exaggerating the threat of a cyclone, Rathin's concern about our safety was genuine. He had reason to fear high winds. He had lost a good friend, a research officer, who had been aboard the *Rangabilia* in the cyclone of 1988.

Rathin had told me the story earlier aboard *Monorama*. "November 28: two days to D-day," he had narrated theatrically into my tape recorder. November 30 was the scheduled start of the tiger census that year, so the department's boats had begun to converge upon Sundarbans days in advance.

The radio warnings had started at two P.M. on the twenty-ninth. All census vessels were ordered away from the Bay of Bengal as the storm approached. The *Rangabilia* took refuge in a creek about 230 feet wide near Sajnekhali Tourist Lodge, well inland from the sea. The sareng had chosen the location carefully.

At six P.M. it was cold and raining hard, and the cyclone's

wind speed had gathered to about 60 miles per hour. *Rangabilia* swayed from side to side. But the staff were calm. The crew were playing cards behind the wheelhouse; the two officers on board had gone to bed. Even in choppy waters *Rangabilia,* a large launch, gave the impression of stability. It had an unusual design: its freshwater tank was on the foredeck, and its stern rode very low in the water. The last radio transmission before the antenna snapped off reported that all the tiger census boats were safely anchored.

Later that night, slammed by the cyclone-churned waves, *Rangabilia* bucked sickeningly. By eight P.M. the wind speed had reached more than 110 miles per hour. Suddenly the craft lurched, and the water tank slipped to starboard. Weighted down, the *Rangabilia* could not right herself. Water poured into the engine room through the shuttered windows and instantly shorted the batteries powering the lights. Within seconds the darkened launch began to sink.

The boat's sareng and the crew behind the wheelhouse jumped into the swirling water and swam for their lives. The two officers were trapped in their cabins.

At this point in the story, Rathin's words tumbled, rushing upon each other like the water pouring in through the windows:

"And the two officers in the cabin probably couldn't find the latch to the door, and the windows were shut, and the *Rangabilia* is going down, so they had no way to get out of their own cabin. But one staff had the courage to throw a torchlight beam inside the passage between the two cabins, and he started shouting, 'Sir, please come out! The launch is sinking!' But of course they couldn't come because they couldn't find the door in the darkness . . ."

Tarapada, who is now Rathin's orderly, was in the engine room that night, and he had tried to break down the door to the cabin from that side to rescue his officers. "But by that time,"

Rathin narrated, "the things were happening so fast that he had only seconds from being completely drowned, and Tarapada was already underwater, floating on the water, inside the launch. And at the last second, while the launch was going down, he grabbed some object with his hands and pushed himself out the window against the current, and no sooner had he slipped out, the launch had gone down to the bottom, and with the persons — the boatman — oh!"

Rathin's strong face crumpled at the memory.

The brave boatman who had tried to save the officers drowned with them. He tried to dive overboard, but when his body was recovered, his arms and legs were impossibly tangled in *Rangabilia*'s anchor ropes.

Days later Rathin was asked to identify the body of his friend, the research officer. None of the bloated corpses fished out of the rivers after the cyclone were recognizable, he told me. His friend's body was probably forever trapped inside *Rangabilia,* swallowed by Sundarbans' silken creek-bottom silt. The sunken craft was never found. But the government needed a positive ID of each dead man before it would release insurance money to the widow. Rathin dutifully visited the morgue and identified the faceless, purple corpse of a stranger as that of his friend.

After telling me this story, Rathin leaned over the rail of *Monorama* and vomited.

❖

Now Rathin stood before me, asking that I let him rescue us from the storm. But even if Rathin was not overstating the danger, Eleanor and I could not abandon Girindra and his family to the wind.

"We are grateful for your warning," I told Rathin, "but we must stay with our friends in Jamespur. If a cyclone will wash away this village, it will wash us away with it." And even though Rathin and I are both Christian, before I rejoined Eleanor and Girindra I took Rathin's hand between my palms, brought it to my forehead, and for a long moment held it there.

❖

Girindra was glad we had decided to stay with his family. This night was to be our last in Sundarbans before we returned to the States, and everyone at the house was excited to have two Americans as overnight guests. Namita was preparing a special dinner. Girindra had promised to hold a puja. That night we would worship the god Naryan, who he said is the same as Laxmi, the goddess whose image Eleanor kept in her purse.

By lantern light Girindra and his daughters had prepared the puja, painting Shiva's trident in vermilion on the pots, smoothing out banana leaves carefully, as if laying a tablecloth, arranging the sweets and flowers, the offerings of betel nut and rice. Girindra draped his body in the clean white cloth that Mabisaka had earned for healing a sick woman. He sprinkled oil three times in a clockwise direction and shook Ganges water from mango leaves. One of the children blew the holy conch shell, and the women called their shivering welcome to the gods.

Girindra was careful about the proceedings: everything was in perfect order, arranged with the care of a thoughtful host who has plenty of time to prepare for his guests. But what struck me most deeply was how comfortable, how relaxed, he felt, welcoming the gods into his home. As Girindra sang the chants to Naryan — all twenty-seven pages of them, handwritten in his worn cardboard notebook — he sometimes stopped to slap at mosquitoes or yawn or jump when a centipede wriggled out from under the prayer mat, as one would do while entertaining a beloved but familiar elder relative.

The puja continued for an hour. Outside in the dark, men and women were still threshing rice. We could hear fish sizzling in a nearby kitchen. Even as Girindra chanted, some of his older children chatted and some slept. We felt like family gathered around the dinner table — two Anglo American women, eleven Sundarbans Bengalis, and the gods.

When the ceremony concluded, we all bowed our heads to the floor. But I felt less conscious of the god above us than of the feel of the smooth, cool floor against my forehead, as if we were bowing to the earth itself — to the mud from which the floor was made, to the spiders who crawled over it, to the pneumatophores and stilt roots that had stood here before the house, to the forest whose bounty nourished the village, even to the tiger who guarded the forest — to everything for which this family was so endlessly grateful.

The meal we enjoyed afterward was a sort of communion. And shortly thereafter the wind came.

To the poetic authors of the Vedas, the clouds that the winds brought from the ocean were heavy with treasures. These riches were so valuable that the clouds were loathe to give them up; Indra, the god of rain and storm, who rides upon an elephant, must pry open the clouds' fast embrace in order that their riches may shower the earth.

The Vedas say that when Indra was born, the sky and the earth trembled at his appearance. And so it was when Indra came that night: the wind howled and gasped and shrieked. Trees writhed and slapped like a person possessed. The night was as black as a hole, and out of that hole poured rain, lightning, thunder.

Sound and light cracked and rolled through the heavens, through our bodies. We felt the thunder like pain: it seemed to arise both without and within — out of our bones and our organs and our souls — as if the whole world were made of thunder.

We were all shuttering windows, Girindra and the girls and I, when we realized we didn't know where Eleanor was. Girindra and I ran out into the rain, into the blackness, shouting her name: Eleanor! But the storm ate our call, as the tiger in the forest eats the echo of the human voice. We slipped in the mud. Guided by explosions of lightning, we raced in separate directions: Girindra twice to the latrine, in horror that he would find her at the bottom of the filthy ditch, and I to the kitchen, hugging the mud perimeter of the house.

Girindra found Eleanor. She had gone to another portion of the family's complex with Namita and Mabisaka and the two little boys. The women had refused to let her go back outside, even though she could hear us calling. When he brought her back to me, she was visibly shaken — less by the storm than by Girindra. He had been so worried that when he found her safe, he'd flown into a rage and screamed at her furiously, his anger all the more upsetting since he expressed it in a language she didn't understand.

The wind gathered fury, and Girindra was gripped with a new fear: the *Mabisaka!* He had pinned her to the mud in four places at high tide, but still she might be coming loose. With his brother, he rushed to save his hand-hewn boat, his livelihood, from the wind-whipped waves. I tried to follow him, but when he realized what I was doing he yelled at me with such force I was afraid he would hit me; helplessly I returned to the house. Water gushed through the shuttered windows; much of the freshly threshed rice had blown away; lives, it seemed, were literally on the verge of flying apart.

Eleanor later told me that as she huddled in the room with the women, Namita's face had been a sheet of terror. The children were crying. And everyone kept saying, "Cyclone." They were remembering the cyclone of 1988.

❖

It was not until my third trip, with Shankar and Debasish, that Girindra and Mabisaka told me how the family had survived that cyclone.

The wind that night was like a giant who ate everything in its path. The wind ate up sound: when Girindra cried out to members of his family who were staying in another hut a few feet away, they could not hear him; the wind took their voices away. The wind ate up light: even with his flashlight on, Girindra said, he could see nothing in the blackness. The wind ate up matter: to their astonishment, in one of the huts Girindra and Mabisaka watched as an enormous pot of rice — containing enough to feed the family for a month — just flew apart. No one could stand against this wind; it knocked you down and blew you away. This was a wind that brought you to your knees, as if before a god.

Girindra, of course, had known the storm was coming. There had been bulletins on the radio that afternoon. The Forest Department staff had issued warnings. At high tide, Girindra had secured *Mabisaka* firmly to trees. He had fortified the huts — two separate huts had stood where Girindra has now built one big compound — bracing them with bamboo poles. He had planned for the storm. He would stay in the larger of the two huts with Namita and most of the children; his younger brother and Mabisaka would oversee the others in the smaller, newer hut next door.

When night fell, the family huddled in the huts. Outside the wind gathered force. The huts shook. Girindra thought he heard the voice of his brother calling from next door. He managed to push open the door against the wind and crawl out — and found that the other hut had collapsed!

No one was seriously hurt, and quickly Girindra escorted everyone into the larger hut. But by now the rain, as well as the wind, was chewing through the hut. The roof leaked so badly that the smooth, neat floors had become rivers of mud. Soon even the walls began to melt, and the wind swayed the whole structure as if it were a coconut palm. Girindra realized it would not hold for long, so the family fled to his uncle's house. The moment the last one left, their home collapsed behind them.

Five families had already gathered at the uncle's home. There was nowhere dry to sit. Girindra and his uncle dug a ditch to try to channel water away from the house. Then Girindra fetched and laid down wood planks on the hut's veranda and told people to sit there. What he knew but did not tell them was that if they stayed inside the house, the walls would collapse on them.

So, leaving Namita and Mabisaka and his daughters and an infant son shivering under a single sheet of plastic, Girindra went out again into the howling downpour to look for a new place to move.

Outside he could see nothing. His flashlight was useless. He waited for the lightning. In the flickering flash, he saw that all the surrounding huts had already collapsed.

After that he crawled about endlessly in rivers of mud. But at last he came upon a small hut still standing. Two families had already crammed inside. They said they would make room for the Mridhas, but they were all too weak to help Girindra escort the women to safety.

So again Girindra crawled to a crumbling hut to rescue his family. There he found his two youngest daughters unconscious. Wet, cold, and mesmerized with terror, the other members of the family had forgotten about the two girls and were actually sitting on them — they had nearly suffocated. "You cannot know how terrifying it is," he told me, "unless you have experienced it."

One by one, Girindra escorted each member of his family to safety. But even now his job was not done. Next he crawled out again into the storm to see to the cows and the other animals. For hours, in the driving rain, Girindra and four others worked to rescue cows and lambs and sheep from collapsed stables.

When the cyclone was over, the damage was terrible. At sunrise Girindra saw that his brother's motorboat had been smashed to bits. All ten of his uncle's cows were dead. Almost everyone had lost their house. So many villagers had died that for days the rivers were clogged with the corpses. But everyone in Girindra's family had survived without injury. And his beloved boat, *Mabisaka,* although full of water, was still whole.

Girindra told me this story through Shankar, but when he had finished, he spoke directly to me.

"Goddess," he said, touching his right hand to his forehead. "Goddess always, I luke."

Bengali syntax is almost the opposite of English syntax; the position of subject and object are often reversed. At first when Girindra would say this to me, I wondered whether he meant that the goddess was always watching over him or that he always looked to the goddess for her help. Now I realized he meant both at once: even in the storm Girindra could see the goddess clearly.

❖

Across Sundarbans in Bangladesh, Hasna Moudud, too, has faced cyclones. As the wife of the former vice president, as a member of Parliament herself, as a patriot of her country, as a disciple of Mohammed, she has felt it her duty to help the victims of her country's deadly floods and cyclones, and again and again has found herself in the midst of the worst devastation.

In 1974 she worked distributing emergency supplies to flood-stricken villages. "The women were hiding from us," she said, "and I wondered why. Then I saw: everything had been destroyed, and they'd had to divide one sari among three women. Their houses had been washed away. The children had scabies and disease. It was as if they had forgotten about the human body."

The aftermath of a cyclone took her to Nijumbe, a beautiful, peaceful village in central Bangladesh. The wind had blown people out of their houses, off the ground. "Now there were bodies of women and children caught in the trees — like a garden of corpses, like a forest of bodies."

In the nine years between 1960 and 1969, eleven major

storms killed more than 54,000 people in Bangladesh alone — an area the size of Wisconsin. And then, in November 1970, a cyclonic storm coupled with a high tide killed more than 200,000 people in two days. The cyclone of 1988 topped that figure by no one knows how much. "The situation of the Gangetic Delta, at the head of the funnel-shaped Bay of Bengal," wrote the Smithsonian ecologist F. R. Fosberg, "poses perhaps the most serious threat from surges driven by storm waves to be found anywhere in the world." The resulting tidal waves along the Bay of Bengal may rise as high as 250 feet. On both sides of Sundarbans, villagers face four to eight "cyclonic depressions" each year.

Fleeing the flood and cyclone of 1988, villagers from coastal Bangladesh surged into Dacca. Thousands took refuge in the stadium. Hasna remembered women — Muslim women, whose modesty normally demands that they keep even their faces discreetly veiled in public — giving birth there, right out in the open. "You wonder, then, who can help this nation?" Hasna said in her mellifluous voice.

"And then," she said, "you come back, weeks or days later. You will not believe it. It is a mysterious thing: all this tragedy makes it more beautiful than before, as if it was all swept clean and now is greener and more lush. It is a fantastic thing. A mysterious thing. A miracle."

❖

The Lord Vishnu, it is told, brought the world into being this way:

At first, all was water. Vishnu himself was water. He slept on the water, yet the water was also him. The god-water was a fathomless ocean, and within it lay all the fluid powers of the universe: blood, milk, sap, rain. Calm lay over the water as Vishnu slept. But then he awoke and with a finger gently stirred the cosmic ocean.

This subtle action created a subtle change: small ripples

formed. The ripples spread. Between the spreading arcs of the ripples ether — the upper region of the heavens, that which we now call space — came into being.

Ether, like the ripples, began to spread and grow larger, resounding like a joyous hymn. From the sound arising from its growth came another element, wind.

Wind grew, gathered energy, rushing, sweeping, bounding, swirling, full of power and joy. It stroked against the waters of the cosmic ocean. It drove the currents. It aroused the waves. From the powerful friction of the wind on the waves arose the third element, fire.

When a great wind gathers in Sundarbans, it is easy to see that this story is true. When Eleanor and I, with Girindra's family, felt the wind that February night at Jamespur, I recalled the words the man from Chittagong had used in describing the cyclone of 1991: "The wind," he said, "it was as if it had fire in it."

It is said that the burning of wind-created fire created heaven itself. And only then did Vishnu put forth the thousand-petaled lotus from which arose the radiant Brahma, the four-faced creator of the earth.

In wind we face the invisible power that created the world. This is surely the case in Sundarbans. Its mangroved shores are born of wind as well as water. "It is during these periods of high-energy influx that much geological work is done," John Seidensticker wrote, "and the storms guide the long-term development of mangroves and forests." As he was researching the management plan for Bangladesh's tiger reserve in Sundarbans, he was amazed to see that even mild storms sometimes ripped every leaf from the mangroves. But the mangroves recover. All the creatures here depend on change. The bounty of the trees plunges into the waters, which the tides then offer back to the land. The rapid cycling of Sundarbans' nutrients, the great wheel of rebirth, is driven, in large part, by the force of the cyclones.

Through it all the tigers seem unperturbed. Even after the violent cyclone of 1988, forest officers reported seeing surprisingly few tiger corpses among the rivers of storm dead that clogged the channels for weeks. Forest officials believe the tigers survive cyclones by climbing into trees as the water rises. The deer, too, are said to cope well with storms. Rathin told me the deer wedge their heads into tangles of stilt roots so they will not be carried away by the wind and the water; when the tides rise to the tops of the mangroves, the deer anchor themselves among the uppermost branches of the trees. After such storms, he said, you will sometimes find a deer and a tiger clinging to the same tree.

The workings of Sundarbans' cyclones are still poorly understood. Some storms, Seidensticker reported, "appear to be literally sucked up the estuaries" — the power of the wind absorbed, swallowed, dissolved by the mangrove forest. Under certain circumstances "the stable cool air over the water, hemmed [in] by the warm air rising from the land, forms a trough along the axis of the storm path which acts as a funnel." In these cases Sundarbans' forests protect the millions of people inland from the cyclone's fury.

But this does not always happen. In fact, Seidensticker writes, as the forests have shrunk, the devastating storms have grown more frequent. In the sixty-nine years between 1891 and 1960, sixteen severe tropical storms raked Bangladesh; in the sixteen years between 1961 and 1977 there were nineteen.

❖

As Vishnu marshals the wind to create fire, and fire created heaven itself, so too does Vishnu use wind to take back the universe.

It happens at the end of each world cycle, Hindu mythology tells us. Vishnu becomes the sun, and with its devouring rays consumes the moisture of the world. Then he becomes the wind and withdraws the life-breath from all living creatures. The friction of the sucking cyclone then ignites the universe. Everything is consumed in fire.

Finally, when all of creation lies in smoldering ash, Vishnu, clothed in cloud formed by the fire's smoke, again pours forth his delight in the form of rain. The flood creates an ocean so profound that it dissolves the moon, the stars, the sun. And here, upon the fathomless, pure waters, Vishnu slumbers, dreamy and serene, until he is stirred to evoke the universe again.

Dreams of Tigers

❖ ❖ ❖ ❖ ❖ ❖ ❖ ❖ ❖ ❖ ❖ ❖ ❖

THE TIGER MUST ACCOMPLISH its dharma. It must hunt, it must eat, it must raise its young. And if the tiger is the guardian of Sundarbans' forests, it is because it kills and eats people.

This I accept. A tiger swam after my boat. It could have eaten me, which doesn't particularly bother me. But a tiger could kill and eat people whom I love, and I find it difficult to live with this knowledge.

Every few weeks I get a letter from Girindra and his family, translated into recognizable English by the schoolteacher, Mr. Mondal. Every so often I hear from Rathin. I cherish the letters, but they are like light from a star. By the time I get them — especially Girindra's, since he mails them from Jamespur — their words are usually six to eight weeks old. While I read their words, I can't even know for sure that the writers are still alive. And again, as in Sundarbans, I feel lost, bewildered, afraid of what I cannot see.

At these times, to quiet my longing, I try to remember what these dear people taught me by showing me the truths they'd learned about the waters and the sky and the future.

So often Sundarbans' brown rivers look like solid ground,

shining slick like mud; in placid waters covered with leaves dropped from the mangroves, the water looks like a forest floor. Sometimes the water's surface shines like a mirror, and you will see the image of your own face reflected there. (Believing in our own reflection is perhaps our most common mistake.) But you must remember you can see only the water's surface, and the surface is a mirage, Maya, an illusion. This is the central mistake of science, the gunins say: it examines only surfaces and allows our own reflection to obscure the deeper powers.

Occasionally, though, the water's surface opens to reveal a dolphin, a sea turtle, a crocodile. Such openings, the people of Sundarbans believe, are our dreams, our palms, and the stars.

❖

Girindra often dreams of tigers. He wakes covered with sweat. In his dreams the tiger comes after him, but he always manages to escape: the tiger jumps, but he ducks or kicks the tiger or pushes in its eyes so he can get away. Quite often he dreams that he is in a boat with three or four other people, and a tiger comes — sometimes three tigers at once — but only for him.

One night he dreamed about a very odd type of animal — "like a wild boar but very furry, jet black, with two small horns on its head" — that rushes out of the forest to chase him. Other people are standing by and doing their work, but the animal only chases *him*. Nobody comes to his aid; in fact, they just stare as he runs and runs through the forest. Finally he comes to a stack of logs and scurries to the top. The animal can't jump up to get him. But now Girindra is trapped. He wants to get down from the platform and run away. As his agitation mounts, Bonobibi, wearing a white sari with a red border, appears magically before him. The animal disappears.

Bonobibi takes Girindra in her arms, and he begins to weep with relief; he tells her that never again will he go into the jungle.

Unlike the Bonobibi dream Girindra had told me about earlier, in this dream Bonobibi speaks. As she holds him in her arms, she says, "If you go into the jungle, you will be eaten by a tiger. But if you do not go into the jungle, you will still be eaten by a tiger. It's your fate." And then she disappears.

"No! It can't be true!" I heard myself cry at Girindra. I felt the blood drain from my heart. Once before I had felt fear like this, when Rathin told me about the tiger who broke down the cabin door to seize Birin Mondal on the boat at Haldibari. Before that I had felt that Rathin was fairly tiger-proof, with his gun and his staff and his big government launch. But with the Haldibari incident, I had lost that comfort. "What if a tiger attacks you on board *Monorama*?" I asked, stricken.

"I will shoot it," Rathin replied, and his matter-of-fact answer calmed me for the moment. But I rejoiced when, many months later, I learned that Rathin would be transferred from Sundarbans and promoted to field director of another park. His horoscope forecasts great things ahead, he tells me, and I am sure they will come to pass.

But probably Girindra will always live in Sundarbans, among its tangled mangroves and snaking channels and heaving tides, among the sharks and the crocodiles and the tigers. "Your dream can't be true!" I cried at him. "I won't let it happen!" Debasish translated, but Girindra already understood.

"Whether this is true or false, I do not know," he told me gently. He wonders why the Mother would take him in her arms and then pronounce a death sentence.

"I do not fear the tiger, even after those dreams," Girindra said. "Besides, if a tiger attacks me, there is nothing I can do. If I am fated to die by a tiger, I cannot avoid my fate."

In the villages around Bombay, Marathi-speaking people have long told the story of how the fate of every child is inscribed on its forehead by the goddess Satwai, and not even she can alter what she must write. She even writes upon her own daughter's forehead that she is fated to marry her own son. Elsewhere in India many people hold that our fate is written on our palms or in the stars. In the West we consider faith in fate to be a resignation, an excuse for giving up. But for most Indians, fate is nothing of the sort. Fate is the promise that life is not a random string of tragedy and comedy without meaning. Fate proclaims that our lives are in fact so meaningful, so necessary, that our stories are written by the gods and goddesses, by the heavens themselves. We may only glimpse our fate, hinted in the stars or the creases of our hands; but even this glimpse is evidence of our contract with the universe, that we are players in the great wheel of life and death and rebirth.

❖

About fifteen years ago, when Girindra worked mainly as a crab fisherman, he visited a palmist in Canning. "Tell me my future and do not hide anything from me," he asked.

The fortuneteller looked at his callused palm and read it like a book. "No one will be able to inflict harm on you," she said. "There are a few dangers in your life, but you have already passed them. You will live to the age of ninety." He asked her what he should pay. She replied, "I cannot accept any money from you, you have such a fantastic hand."

Girindra then told me the story of a wealthy man who had his palm read but refused to believe it. The man lived in Calcutta, yet the palmist predicted that he would die soon and that he would be killed by a tiger. A tiger in Calcutta! Impossible! The palmist even gave the time and date when he would die. The man went home laughing.

When the date of his predicted death arrived, the man called his friends to his house. Many made merry, others came to see if the prediction would prove true. But as they were all from Calcutta, few had ever seen a tiger. One guest didn't even know what a tiger looked like. "You have not seen a tiger? Then I will draw one for you," offered a companion, and with a pencil he carefully began to create the figure of a tiger: first the outline, then the stripes, then the nose, the whiskers, the claws, the eye . . .

And just as the pupil of the eye was darkened, the tiger in the drawing came alive, leaped from the paper, and killed the host of the evening.

"So even if I lived in America with you, my sister," said Girindra, "if I am fated to die by a tiger, I cannot avoid my fate."

But, he added, with a confidence I still draw upon, "I believe in my lifeline, and it is very long."

Epilogue: The Kali Yuga

❖ ❖ ❖ ❖ ❖ ❖ ❖ ❖ ❖ ❖ ❖ ❖ ❖ ❖ ❖ ❖ ❖ ❖ ❖

ACCORDING TO THE HINDU notion of time, we are now in the last of the four *yugas*, or world ages, that make up the lifetime of each universe.

The first of the four yugas is known as the Krita Yuga, an Edenic age when the world is young and moist and whole, fresh from divine emanation. Saintliness comes naturally, and from the moment of birth everyone knows their dharma, their purpose in the world, and fulfills it with joyful devotion.

But in the following yugas, beauty, peace, and moral order diminish bit by bit. In the Trita Yuga duties are no longer inborn but must be learned. In the Dvapara Yuga, true saintliness is extinct.

Today's era is called the Kali Yuga. The goddess Kali is known as the great destroyer, the black one, who adorns herself with the blood-dripping hands and heads of her victims like jewelry, who dances on the corpse of her husband, who stretches out her tongue in her hunger to devour the world. Both the goddess and the era take their names from the word *kaal,* or time. For time is the great destroyer, and by the end of the Kali Yuga, our time is up. It could be very soon, sages warn.

As Karan Singh, the former chancellor of the University of Jammu and Kashmir points out, Hindu texts claim that each world cycle is 4.3 billion years long. "If you insist on scientific confirmation," he says, "you might note that 4.3 billion years is roughly the age of the earth."

In a passage of the *Vishnu Purana,* a classic text of Hindu myth and tradition, the Kali Yuga is described so clearly that everyone today will surely recognize it as the modern era: in the Kali Yuga, "Property becomes rank, wealth the only source of virtue, passion the sole bond of union, falsehood the source of success."

The Kali Yuga is the final age before this world dissolves. It is the era in which we repudiate our gods. It is the era in which we extinguish rather than revere life. It is the age in which our sins drown our virtues.

Only in an age of blind greed could we accomplish the cataclysmic evil of obliterating from the earth as many as a dozen species a day. Yet this, biologists tell us, we are now doing without fanfare or mourning. Most of the victims are invertebrates, animals like worms or insects, or plants or fungi so little known that scientists have not yet given them Latin names. Most of them are lost as people overrun these creatures' homes, converting wild lands to farms and roads and condos, factories and pipelines and mines. Liverworts and termites, jellyfish and dragonflies, flatworms and orchids: we crowd them out in a ravenous grab for more space, more jobs, more money.

"But does it really matter?" asks an *Asiaweek* editorial accompanying its cover story on the tiger's precarious survival. "Species come and go," writes its author. "Now it is the tiger's turn."

To exterminate any species — each the culmination of millions of years of evolution — for economic reasons, says Harvard sociobiologist E. O. Wilson, is a tradeoff as foolish and wasteful as "burning Renaissance paintings to cook dinner."

But if we eradicate the tiger, our sin is greater still. If we eradicate the tiger, we murder a god.

❖

Everyone in Sundarbans knows that Daksin Ray can enter the body of any tiger at will. Thus all tigers are sacred and holy, expressions of the power of God.

Even the skeptical Rathin sees the sense of the idea. The man-eater, he says, is the most powerful force protecting Sundarbans' forest — and protecting the people who depend upon its bounty. "The tiger is silently doing the work of ecodiscipline," he told me. "In that way the tiger *is* a god — the tiger is looking after the forest, and the forest is looking after it." It is no accident, his words suggest, that the largest population of tigers in the world lives in Sundarbans, and that here survives the largest remaining tract of mangrove forest on earth. Here the tiger still wields its most potent power over people.

With the same ease that Daksin Ray enters the body of a tiger, so do tigers of Asian mythology bridge the gaps between living and dead, village and forest, heaven and earth. Tigers help people understand their past and their future and their relationship with the forces that govern the world. Without the tiger, the human world is incomplete.

This truth is understood in cultures wherever tigers have roamed. These peoples' sacred stories tell us that tigers are our kin, our teachers, and our guardians. In India many tribes claim they are descended from tigers, including the Baghel Rajput, the Bhil, the Santal, the Khond, the Baghani. The Sudanese of Western Java and the Acehnese and Minangkabau of Sumatra also claim that tigers founded their clans.

So strong is the Khond kinship with the tiger that the people claim they can even *become* tigers through a spell. The anthropological scholar Robert Wessing presents the story of one Khond tribesman who routinely changed into a tiger to go

hunting. But when he wanted to change back to a person, someone had to pronounce the right spell. The tiger-man taught the
spell to a friend, but his friend died. So he taught the spell to his
wife. The next day he changed into a tiger to hunt. When he returned, carrying his kill in his mouth, he approached his wife.
But she was so frightened of his tigrine form that she began to
scream and run. By jumping about and roaring, he tried to remind her to pronounce the spell, but she only screamed louder.
He eventually became so irritated that he ate her. He then realized that he had eaten the one person alive who knew the spell
to turn him back into a person. His wife, of course, had been
just as foolish in failing to recognize her own beloved husband
there on her doorstep, bringing home their dinner.

It is important, this story tells us, to remember who we are,
and who the tiger is to us.

Who are we? Never before this age have people been so pre-
occupied with this question. Never before have we been so ob-
sessed with the search for the self. It can be argued that until
relatively recently in our evolution, we did not have the luxury
of time to consider such things; we died too young, before we
could acquire the wisdom to wonder. It can equally be argued
that today, as we stand at the brink of extinguishing the tiger,
we have come closer than ever to destroying the knowledge that
could answer our question.

Thanks to the tiger, the people of Sundarbans still understand
what the rest of us pretend to ignore: that all who share the sacred breath of life — chital and boar, frog and fish, idiot and ge-
nius — are made of meat. And all bodies made of meat bow before the divine, humbled by the spell of the tiger.

❖

Can we believe what the people of Sundarbans say is true?

Can tigers fly through the air? Appear from nowhere? Shrink
a human body to half its size? This I do not know. But of this I

am certain: in this permeable, mutable world, surely God may at any time enter the body of a tiger to remind us who we are.

If, in the height of our hubris, we exterminate the tiger, we risk losing sight of the deepest truth our kind has ever known: that we are not God.

"What will it say about the human race if we let the tiger go extinct?" asks Ashok Kumar, director of World Wildlife Fund's trade monitoring unit in India. "What can we save? Can we save ourselves?"

Selected Bibliography

❖ ❖ ❖ ❖ ❖ ❖ ❖ ❖ ❖ ❖ ❖ ❖ ❖ ❖ ❖ ❖ ❖

Much of the library research for this book was conducted in the Oriental and India Office Collections of the British Library in London and in the National Library of India in Calcutta. Some books were obtained through the interlibrary loan systems at Harvard and at Antioch/New England Graduate School. Books written in Bengali, generously translated for me by Rathin Banerjee, are not listed here. But many excellent books that informed my research are available in bookstores and public libraries, and I list them here.

TIGERS, WILDLIFE

Anderson, Kenneth. *This Is the Jungle: More Tales of Man-Eaters.* London: G. Allen and Unwin, 1964.

Corbett, Jim. *Man-Eaters of Kumaon.* New York: Oxford University Press, 1946.

————. *The Temple Tiger and More Man-Eaters of Kumaon.* New York: Oxford University Press, 1955.

Dunstone, N., and M. L. Gorman, eds. *Mammals as Predators.* Oxford, Eng.: Oxford Science Publications, 1993.

Jackson, Peter. *Endangered Species: Tigers.* London: Apple Press, 1990.

Leyhausen, P. *Cat Behavior: The Predatory and Social Behavior of Domestic and Wild Cats.* New York: Garland STPM Press, 1979.

McDougal, Charles. *The Face of the Tiger*. London: Rivington Books, 1977.

Perry, Richard. *The World of the Tiger*. New York: Atheneum, 1965.

Schaller, George B. *The Deer and the Tiger: A Study of Wildlife in India*. Chicago: University of Chicago Press, 1967.

Singh, Arjan. *Tiger Haven*. New York: Harper and Row, 1973.

Singh, Kesri. *One Man and a Thousand Tigers*. New York: Dodd, Mead, 1959.

Sunquist, Melvin E. *The Social Organization of Tigers in Royal Chitawan National Park, Nepal*. Washington: Smithsonian Institution Press, 1981.

Sunquist, Fiona, and Mel Sunquist. *Tiger Moon*. Chicago: University of Chicago Press, 1988.

Thomas, Elizabeth Marshall. *The Tribe of Tiger: Cats and Their Culture*. New York: Simon and Schuster, 1994.

Tilson, Ronald L., and Ulysses S. Seal, eds. *Tigers of the World*. Park Ridge, N.J.: Noyes Publications, 1987.

Ward, Geoffrey C., with Diane Raines Ward. *Tiger Wallahs*. New York: Harper Collins, 1993.

FOLKLORE AND FOLKTALES

Jasimuddin. *Folktales of Bangladesh*. London: Oxford University Press, 1967.

McNeely, Jeffrey A., and Paul Spencer Wachtel. *Soul of the Tiger: Searching for Nature's Answers in Exotic Southeast Asia*. New York: Doubleday, 1988.

Ramanujan, A. K., *Folktales from India*. New York: Pantheon, 1991.

Wessing, Robert. *The Soul of Ambiguity: The Tiger in Southeast Asia*. Detroit: Northern Illinois University, Center for South East Asian Studies, Monograph Series on South East Asia, 1986.

RELIGION AND PHILOSOPHY

Banu, Razia Akter. *Islam in Bangladesh*. New York: E. J. Brill, 1992.

Coomaraswamy, Ananda K. *The Dance of Shiva*. New York: Farrar, Strauss, 1957.

Kinsley, David. *The Goddesses' Mirror*. Albany: State University of New York Press, 1989.

Ross, Nancy Wilson. *Three Ways of Asian Wisdom*. New York: Simon and Schuster, 1966.

Snead, Stella, with texts by Wendy Doniger and George Michell. *Animals in Four Worlds: Sculptures from India*. Chicago: University of Chicago Press, 1989.

Thomas, Keith. *Religion and the Decline of Magic*. New York: Macmillan, 1975.

Zimmer, Heinrich. *Myths and Symbols in Indian Art and Civilization*. Princeton: Princeton University Press, 1946.

———. *Philosophies of India*. Princeton: Princeton University Press, 1951.

TRAVELS IN INDIA AND BANGLADESH

Blank, Jonah. *Arrow of the Blue-Skinned God: Retracing the Ramayana Through India*. Boston: Houghton Mifflin, 1992.

Frater, Alexander. *Chasing the Monsoon*. New York: Knopf, 1991.

Gardner, Katy. *Songs at the River's Edge*. London: Virago, 1991.

Mehta, Ved. *Portrait of India*. New Haven: Yale University Press, 1967.

Novak, James. *Bangladesh: Reflections on the Water*. Bloomington: Indiana University Press, 1993.

Nugent, Rory. *The Search for the Pink-Headed Duck: A Journey into the Himalayas and down the Brahmaputra*. Boston: Houghton Mifflin, 1991.

Siegel, Lee. *Net of Magic: Wonders and Deceptions in India*. Chicago: University of Chicago Press, 1991.

OTHER BOOKS

These books are difficult to locate in the United States and may be hard to find even in India, but I cannot help but acknowledge here their usefulness to my project. Determined readers may be able to locate some of these through interlibrary loan or order them through an exceptionally helpful bookstore.

Chakrabarti, Kalyan. *Man-Eating Tigers*. Calcutta: Darbari Prokashan, 1992.

——. *Man, Plant and Animal Interaction*. Calcutta: Darbari Prokashan, 1991.

Chaudhuri, A. B., and Kalyan Chakrabarti. *Sundarbans Mangrove Ecology and Wildlife*. Dehra Dun: Jugal Kishore, 1989.

De, Rathindranath. *The Sundarbans*. Calcutta: S. K. Mookerjee, Oxford University Press/India, 1990.

Kakar, Sudhir. *The Analyst and the Mystic: Psychoanalytic Reflections on Religion and Mysticism*. New Delhi: Viking Penguin India, 1991.

Karim, Anwarul. *The Myths of Bangladesh*. Kushtia, Bangladesh: Folklore Research Institute, 1988.

Rathore, Fateh Singh, and Valmik Thapar. *With Tigers in the Wild*. New Delhi: Vikas Publishing House, 1983.

Acknowledgments

❖ ❖ ❖ ❖ ❖ ❖ ❖ ❖ ❖ ❖ ❖ ❖ ❖ ❖ ❖

During my travels in India and Bangladesh, hundreds of kind people shared with me their information, advice, and solace. In particular, I thank Sara Camblin Breault, Kalyan Chakrabarti, Kisor Chaudhuri, Jenny Das, Bonani and Predip Kakkar, Hasna Moudud and her family, Kushal and Diti Mookherjee, P. K. Sen, Pranabesh Sanyal, Anne, Bob, and Belinda Wright, and the management and staff of the Tollygunge Club.

Shankar Mukherjee and Debasish ("Raja") Nandy deserve special thanks for their translation work, scholarship, and friendship. I am also grateful to Amarendra Nath Mondal for interpreting and explaining the Daksin Ray puja and to Kanchan Muhkerjee for his help and advice. I thank the management and staff of the Sajnekhali Tourist Lodge.

Of course this book could never have been written without the generosity of the people of Sundarbans and the West Bengal Forest Department. In particular, I thank Rathin Banerjee. The West Bengal Forest Department could never find a more dedicated officer, nor I a colleague more thoughtful or thorough. I am especially grateful to Girindra Nath Mridha and his family: *amar ma,* Mabisaka; *amar choto bon,* Namita; and Sonaton, Shumitra, Shubadra, Shushitra, Shushoma, Shoroma, Monuds, and Modhusudan. I thank all the Mridhas' friends and neighbors who shared their stories with me, particularly Phoni Guyan. As much as to preserve the tiger who dominates their world, this book is written in honor of the lives and work of these wise, brave people.

❖

In addition I acknowledge the help of the following individuals and institutions:

Al Lambert, Harold Paretchan, Mary Rabb, and the library staffs of Harvard's Museum of Comparative Zoology and Antioch/New England Graduate School for locating obscure articles and out-of-print books.

Richard Estes, Peter Jackson, George Schaller, and David Smith for sharing with me their insights and experiences with tigers.

Jaya Bapa Jhala and Syed Hasnath for reading the manuscript and averting heinous errors.

Elizabeth Marshall Thomas for her example.

Gretchen Vogel for prayers and protection.

The Reverend Graham L. N. Ward for spiritual guidance.

C. M. Jha for bureaucratic guidance.

Peg Anderson, Peter Davison, and Sarah Jane Freymann for literary guidance.

Dianne Taylor-Snow for laughing at inappropriate moments.

Eleanor Briggs for the beautiful photographs in this book.

Finally, I thank my husband, the writer Howard Mansfield, who discovered after my third trip to India that I had no life insurance. Sorry about that.

To Help Save the Tiger

❖ ❖ ❖ ❖ ❖ ❖ ❖ ❖ ❖ ❖ ❖ ❖ ❖ ❖ ❖ ❖ ❖ ❖

World Wide Fund for Nature International finances field projects to study and conserve tigers throughout the world. Donations earmarked for tiger conservation may be sent to

> World Wide Fund for Nature International
> 1196 Gland, Switzerland

The Cat Specialist Group of the World Conservation Union–International Union for the Conservation of Nature includes most of the world's top specialists on wild tigers and advises on conservation measures. Donations to support their scientific work may be sent to

> IUCN Cat Specialist Group
> Attn. Peter Jackson
> 1172 Bougy, Switzerland